GLOBAL TRENDS IN EASTERN EUROPE

T0346628

To my son Nikolai

Global Trends in Eastern Europe

NIKOLAI GENOV
Free University Berlin, Germany

Routledge
Taylor & Francis Group

LONDON AND NEW YORK

First published 2010 by Ashgate Publishing

Published 2016 by Routledge
2 Park Square, Milton Park, Abingdon, Oxfordshire OX14 4RN
711 Third Avenue, New York, NY 10017, USA

First issued in paperback 2016

Routledge is an imprint of the Taylor & Francis Group, an informa business

British Library Cataloguing in Publication Data
Genov, Nikolai.
    Global trends in Eastern Europe.
    1. Europe, Eastern--History--1989- 2. Europe, Eastern--
    Social conditions--1989- 3. Social change--Europe,
    Eastern. 4. Globalization--Social aspects--Europe,
    Eastern.
    I. Title
    303.4'0943-dc22

Library of Congress Cataloging-in-Publication Data
Genov, Nikolai.
    Global trends in Eastern Europe / by Nikolai Genov.
        p. cm.
    Includes bibliographical references and index.
    ISBN 978-1-4094-0965-6 (hardback)
    1. Globalization--Europe, Eastern. 2. Europe, Eastern--Politics and
government--1989- 3. Social change--Europe, Eastern. 4. Europe, Eastern--Social
conditions--1989- 5. Cultural pluralism--Europe, Eastern. 6. Europe, Eastern--Economic
conditions--1989- I. Title.
    JN96.A58G46 2010
    303.48'247--dc22

                                                                    2010017092

ISBN 13: 978-1-138-27874-5 (pbk)
ISBN 13: 978-1-4094-0965-6 (hbk)

Contents

List of Figures

List of Tables

Preface

There was once a world region called Eastern Europe. It was clearly defined by the centralized political and economic organization of the societies in the region. They shared the same official ideology and were members of the same economic, political and military alliances. The region was diplomatically recognized and geo-strategically respected. It was a key international player in the divided world which emerged after the Second World War. On both sides of the polar division many experts believed that this situation would last for long. They assumed that the change could only be the result of war. It was supposed to be a nuclear war.

To the great surprise of millions, the global region Eastern Europe disappeared as quickly as Atlantis. The cataclysm was not due to natural but to historical forces. However, it was no less spectacular, for Eastern Europe disappeared as a global actor in a peaceful manner. It collapsed in an economic, political and cultural implosion. What were the moving forces of this profound change on the world map? How did the historical cataclysm happen? What are its consequences 20 years later? Could we try to reasonably foresee any future developments in the former global region?

The present monograph is an effort to answer these questions in a theoretically coherent and empirically sound way. The guiding assumption of the analysis and argumentation is that at the end of 1980s the integration mechanisms in Eastern Europe could no more resist the overwhelming power of global trends. It was the hasty adaptation to these trends which made up the essence of the societal transformations in the region. Consequently, what we observe today is a large variety of more or less successful societal adaptations to these global trends. The process continues. Many options for change are still open.

The global trends to be analyzed in this book are called "upgrading the rationality of organizations", "individualization", "spread of instrumental activism", and "universalization of value-normative systems." These concepts were initially elaborated and applied in the small monograph *Managing Transformations in Eastern Europe*. It was commissioned by the MOST Program of UNESCO and published in 1999. The monograph was dedicated to the tenth anniversary of the fall of the Berlin Wall and to its consequences for the Eastern European societies. The general assessment of the situation in the region could only be rather critical at that time. After ten years of reforms most Eastern European societies were still far from the level of GDP which they had in 1989. Apart from a small group of central-east European countries, large parts of the former region were politically unstable. Disappointments were strong. Values and norms were in flux.

The situation changed rapidly between 2000 and 2008. This short period was the success story of globalization. The GDP growth of most Eastern European societies reached and exceeded their GDP level before the changes. The economic recovery was accompanied by the stabilization of political institutions. These used to be still characterized as imperfect, defect or show-case democracies. But in the history of most Eastern European countries they were the first democratic political institutions ever. The value-normative re-integration celebrated real achievements. Millions of Eastern Europeans could enjoy the rise in living standards and the practical relevance of universal human rights. The critical stance which marked the monograph of 1999 seemed to be questioned by the social processes.

This experience made the need to re-think the Eastern European transformations an urgent task. The intellectual process was facilitated by my move to the Free University in Berlin. The detailed study of changes in Eastern Europe became my professional obligation. The conclusion of the studies was unmistakable: Eastern Europe had joined the achievements of globalization but also the global accumulation of tensions and conflicts. These intensified as a result of the lost correspondence between the financial markets and the real economy of goods and services, between the globalization of markets and the striking delay in the development of global governance, between the rapidly growing global demands and the fragility of the global environment.

It seemed that the looming economic, political and cultural challenges might initially explode in the weakest parts of the global interconnections. Eastern Europe could be the first region struck by the coming global crisis. Contrary to this assumption, the pattern of 1929 was repeated. The crisis struck the most powerful economy in the world first. The effects irradiated from the centre of the world economy towards the Eastern European periphery. Several national economies went bankrupt there. The consequences of this development will be probably far reaching.

Thus, the work in the laboratory "Eastern Europe" became highly intriguing once more. The conditions for precise analyses are favorable now. Today we possess better elaborated concepts and reliable empirical information. Social scientists are aware of the way in which globalization works and about its consequences. Nevertheless, the cognitive challenges are tremendous: What is the impact of the new regional divisions on the continuing societal transformations? What can be achieved in the social science explanation and prognostication of societal development in the context of global trends? The present monograph is the result of efforts to connect questions and answers concerning two turning points in the European and global development – the crisis and renewal around 1989 and the new challenges 20 years later. The structure of the analysis and argumentation is transparent. In Chapter 1 the problem situation and the suggested theoretical solution are discussed by referring to the four global trends.

Chapters 2–5 are dedicated to the analysis of manifestations, controversies and effects of the above mentioned global trends in the Eastern European societal transformations. Chapter 6 contains conclusions which are relevant to the development of social science knowledge as well as to the study and management of social development.

Nikolai Genov
Berlin, March 2010

List of Abbreviations

AWS	Akcja wyborcza Solidarność [Electoral Action Solidarity]
CEFTA	Central European Free Trade Agreement
CMEA	Council for Mutual Economic Assistance
CPSU	Communist Party of the Soviet Union
EBRD	European Bank for Reconstruction and Development
EU	European Union
FDI	Foreign direct investment
FIDESZ	Magyar Polgári Szövetség [Hungarian Civic Union]
GDP	Gross domestic product
HDR	Human Development Report
KGB	Komitet gossudarstvennoy bezopasnosti [Committee of State Security]
KOR	Komitet Obrony Robotników [Committee for the Defense of Workers]
PHARE	Poland and Hungary: Aid for Restructuring of the Economies
PZPR	Polska Zjednoczona Partia Robotnicza [Polish United Workers' Party]
SME	Small and medium-size enterprises

Chapter 1
Globalization and Regional Development: Social Reality and Social Science Concepts

The fall of the Berlin Wall was largely misunderstood as the end of the profound tensions and conflicts in the world. There were some reasons for this assumption. After the turbulent autumn of 1989 the polar division and the global balance of terror did not exist any more. It seemed that one could return to Max Weber's diagnosis of the times after the First World War. Amidst the turmoil he warned that the small gods of everyday preferences had grasped the opportunity to wage their own wars. Small scale conflicts seemed to have become the norm. (Weber 1992 [1919]: 101)

This diagnosis corresponded to the situation during the nineties. There was the Kuwait Crisis and there was the war in Bosnia, the conflict in Chechnya and the Kosovo War. All these were conflicts of "small gods" although world powers were involved. In the Western advanced societies affluence and monotony dominated the agenda. Substantial parts of the labor force were involved in production and services which required a high level of education and vocational training. The challenging jobs were well paid. Millions of Western Europeans and North Americans could afford high quality housing, goods and services, entertainment and leisure time, travel and well-organized life-long learning. For them the freedom of speech, organization and communication posed no problems. State institutions worked smoothly, guaranteeing the security of mass well-being.

In Eastern Europe the dust from the political rallies settled fast. What followed was the fierce struggle for the benefits of the privatization of public property. Some individuals and groups managed to accumulate wealth, power and prestige fast. Others, and they were the vast majority, became the losers in the re-distribution. Mixed feelings accompanied the new experience. But there was no ideological or political alternative in sight.

The first signals of alarming instabilities came from the Asian financial crisis in 1997, the Russian financial crisis in 1998 and the economic crisis in Argentina between 1999 and 2002. However, the signals were understood as referring to isolated local or regional events. Their destructive effects could be managed quickly. In Eastern Europe some societies were approaching the economic parameters of the advanced parts of the world. Others struggled with economic, political and cultural problems typical for the less developed regions. The situation changed at the turn of the century. The time span between 2000 and 2008 was generally marked in Eastern Europe by high GDP growth and political stabilization. The eastward enlargement of the European Union and developments in the world markets gave reasons for an optimistic assessment of the prospects of the former socialist societies.

The global context changed abruptly in 2008. The worldwide economic crisis provided the evidence that the neo-liberal economic policies had dramatically failed. Markets had focused on the chase for speculative profits at the expense of national and global economic stability. What followed was the global financial and economic crisis of 2008–2009. It made clear that national political efforts cannot be sufficient in order to successfully cope with the challenge. It required global mechanisms of political management which are not available yet. (The Global Economic Crisis 2009: iii–iv) Against the background of this new experience the management of national transformations in Eastern Europe will have to be re-thought and possibly re-directed.

1.1 The Heritage of the Twentieth Century and the Global Challenges

The recent developments question the view that the new institutions and value-normative systems have already been stabilized in the post-socialist societies. Analysts have to continue adjusting their concepts and methodology to a reality in flux. Most societies in the region are still plagued by substantial disparities between aspirations and need satisfaction, between knowledge and practical action, between change and order. A large variety of situations in the region still can be best described by referring to the concept of *risk society.* The situation is particularly difficult since most Eastern European societies do not posses the resources needed to manage the national consequences of the global economic crisis single-handedly.

One may metaphorically describe the situation as "a crisis foretold". Symptoms of the coming global troubles have been identified well ahead. (Hamm 2006: 53f.; Pieterse 2008) But nobody could have foreseen the magnitude of the upcoming turbulences. Even less could one have predicted the magnitude of the organizational and financial efforts needed in order to stabilize production, exchange and consumption. This should not be surprising. Alarming signals came from the inefficient Eastern European economies and from the stagnating political and cultural life in the region before 1989 too. But even the best informed analysts (Brzezinski 1989) could not predict the timing or the amplitude of the changes which shattered Eastern European societies at the end of the 1980s although the processes were deeply rooted in the *longue durée* of the modern history. (Wallerstein 2004)

Two decades after the end of the Cold War, a series of open questions still concern the recent past of Eastern European societies, their present day puzzles and their future prospects in the world system. Another set of open questions concerns the capacity of the social sciences to develop and apply concepts which could effectively guide descriptions and explanations of the ongoing processes in the former global region of Eastern Europe. The questions have their deep roots in controversial global developments during the twentieth century. It was marked by tremendous achievements in creativity and productivity in all action spheres. However, it will also be remembered for terrible human suffering, loss of life and annihilation of productive assets. No other period in human history has heightened the opposition between the constructive and the destructive potentials of humankind more impressively.

On the surface, this is most visible in the development, use and abuse of *science and technology*. Research and technological development became the fastest growing sector within the national economies of advanced societies. The century was marked by scientific achievements and new technologies which changed the world profoundly. One may immediately notice the ensuing changes in organization and quality of life by looking at the tremendous improvements in transportation and communication. These have compressed time and space immensely. Due to the advancement of economic and social sciences, socio-economic systems are much better manageable nowadays than was the case before the Great Depression. In the same time, the First and the Second World Wars marked enormous leaps forward in the rationalization of warfare due to the development of science and technology. The hot wars together with the Cold War consumed resources which could have helped to radically resolve the burning issues of hunger and illiteracy worldwide.

The history of the twentieth century offers impressive examples of both *the use and abuse of nature* by humankind. The involvement of larger and larger quantities of natural resources in the production process and the careless pollution of the natural environment with industrial and household waste has put the planet's environment under existential pressure. To make the complexity of the puzzle even more confusing, the economic and social consequences of genetic engineering are still unclear. In the long run, they will most probably make human life longer, more comfortable and secure. But they also bring about effects which raise deep legal and moral concerns. (Eastham 2009)

Together with the very substantial increase in the intellectual, organizational and technological capacities to manage economic and social processes, the twentieth century has been also marked by *tremendous abuse and destruction of human capital*. Dictatorial regimes, disparities in the distribution of wealth and income, in the access to information and in the participation in decision-making prevented the development of millions of individuals, of societies and regions. Even today more than one billion people suffer from perennial malnutrition despite the decisions on the eradication of extreme poverty. In no way could this be regarded as a life full of choices, accomplishments and dignity. Pandemics show that the capacities of the present day civilization to cope with life threatening diseases are still rather limited. The global progress in education is very encouraging but the number of illiterate people has remained constant for decades.

East Europeans were massively involved in these encouraging and disappointing developments. On the territory of the former global region of Eastern Europe a social-technological attempt was made to develop patterns of economic and political organization as well as patterns of culture and behavior which would make economic crises and wars, inequality and injustice obsolete. This happened in a highly controversial context. The rapid Eastern European industrialization by using outdated technologies contributed to the global environmental pollution. The polar division of the world and the ensuing political and military confrontation consumed tremendous resources. The confrontation undermined the universalism of global culture.

This was the global situation reflected in the famous small book on the system of modern societies published by Talcott Parsons at the beginning of the seventies. Casting a closer look at it from the vantage point of present-day debates on globalization and regional development, one may notice how underdeveloped his conceptual framework was at that time. He hardly made any mention of the relevance of supranational integration schemes or of any global processes. His research interest had a different focus. It was society defined as "the type of social system characterized by the highest level of self-sufficiency relative to its environments, including other social systems". (Parsons 1971: 8) In his interpretation the major integrating and innovating factor in social life was the maintenance of value-based patterns and value generalization in societal systems. (Parsons 1971: 13) This is probably the best elaborated theoretical system based on methodological nationalism, or, more precisely, on *methodological societalism*. This is the key for understanding Parsons' interpretation of the achievements and deficiencies of both parties in the polar confrontation of the Cold War.

Parsons defined the leading position of American society in the system of modern societies through its successful accomplishment of the industrial, democratic and educational revolutions. In his conceptual framework this meant a successful adaptive upgrading achieved by the national economy and effective differentiation of decision-making, implementing and controlling in politics. The success was also characterized by the full inclusion of citizens in the normative societal community and by the efficient value generalization. These achievements had to be regarded as typical for the accomplished modernization of advanced societies or as future tasks of modernizing societies.

Parsons recognized the achievements of the Soviet Union in the rapid industrialization and in the fast increase of the educational level of the population. But he also identified a crucial problem in this variant of modernization since it did not produce or reproduce the cultural legitimacy of the political leadership: "we suggest, then, that the process of the democratic revolution has not yet reached the equilibrium in the Soviet Union and that further developments *may* well run broadly in the direction of Western types of democratic government, with responsibility to an electorate rather than to a self-appointed party". (Parsons 1971: 127) The prognostic implications of Parsons' analysis for the further development of Eastern Europe were strong. Nevertheless, his analysis invites for elaborations.

The modernization strategy of the Soviet Union and of Eastern Europe was not an isolated regional phenomenon. The state socialist modernization had its roots in the common European tradition of class divisions, enlightenment, revolutions, dictatorships and democratic developments. The Russian Revolution of 1917 was intellectually prepared not by the Russian historical experience alone. The Soviet social-technological experiment was prepared by the rationalistic believe of the European Enlightenment that man and society can be purposefully improved. Another inspiration of the Russian revolutionaries was the reaction of the Western European social democrats to the grievances caused by industrialization. The political programs of the Russian social democrats were local adaptations of programs of Western European social democratic parties. Later, the geopolitical shape of the Eastern European region after the Second World War was determined by decisions taken with the active participation of Western powers in Yalta and in Potsdam.

The accelerated industrialization carried out all over the Eastern European region under the guidance of party-states was no local ideological and political invention. During the whole twentieth century industrialization was the core of all programs for modernization in the world. The forced industrialization in the Soviet Union was implemented with very high social costs during the thirties. But without this effort the survival of the Soviet Union during the Second World War would not be possible. Given the large hidden unemployment in the agriculture of the other Eastern European societies, their accelerated industrialization after the war was the only solution of the deep structural problems of their national economies. The over-centralization of the planned economy and the political authoritarianism were not simply due to local Eastern European traditions, utopian thinking or political extremism. Non-communist or anti-communist efforts to catch up on technological, economic, political and cultural modernization (in Singapore, South Korea and in other countries) were also implemented by means of political authoritarianism and by the use of massive state intervention in the economy.

However, the particularly high degree of penetration of states into the economy and culture was a regional specificity of Eastern Europe's "catching-up" modernization. This organizational strategy made possible the concentration of rather limited resources into strategic industrial projects. They shortened the region's technological and economic lag behind the most advanced countries. Due to the policy of centrally imposed rapid industrialization Eastern Europe was regarded as a serious competitor to the West during the fifties and the sixties. This held true not for the military confrontation alone but for all walks of social life – from research to high-tech development and from mass education to sports. However, the strong state intervention in the economy and culture started to reveal its long-term inefficiency as early as the sixties. The over-centralized economy and the hierarchical politics of state socialism became less and less able to meet the organizational needs of the growing complexity of Eastern European societies.

The Prague Spring in 1968 gave the signal for the urgent necessity to introduce mechanisms fostering the individual initiative and responsibility in the Eastern European economy and politics. The crush of this reform movement made obvious the lack of innovation capacities in the Eastern European region. It was already about to lose the global competition of the Cold War. This became particularly visible in the rapidly increasing distance between Western and Eastern Europe in the development and use of information and communication technologies. State socialism was getting less and less innovative and organizationally efficient as compared to the market economy and democratic politics of the West. The implosion of the state socialist system in the late eighties was just the end of the long agony. Was the implosion the only possible outcome of the processes? The developments in China and Vietnam show that other developmental paths "after administrative socialism" were basically possible. But neither the elites nor the people in Eastern Europe were able and willing to move in the direction of new socialist experiments.

The outcome of the Eastern European implosion could be so described in a simplified way: "ours is a world of regions, embedded deeply in an American imperium". (Katzenstein 2005: 1) Another general assumption might read that currently territories matter less than in the times of the predominance of nation states. Although states are still marked by a strong concentration of economic, political and military power, the traditional type of hierarchical domination *in* and *by* nation-states is over. Multiple channels of exchange foster flexible coordination *and* multi-polarity. Thus, regions have changing geographical, economic, political and cultural parameters. They might powerfully appear like the region of Eastern Europe after the Second World War or disappear just as this same region did at the end of the Cold War.

Being the legacy of the turbulent twentieth century, the present day human civilization is far from harmonious and stable. The assumption that the end of the Cold War and the spread of neo-liberal ideology together with market mechanisms would put an end to the conflicts in the history of humankind (Fukuyama 2006) soon turned out to be utterly utopian. It is common knowledge nowadays that the seeds of future disparities, confrontations and conflicts are in-built in the very social and economic organization inherited from the twentieth century. They are due to technological and informational divides, economic and political inequality, and traditions of cultural intolerance. We witness the end of the dreams and the return of history full of conflicts as it has always been. (Kagan 2007)

The controversies of the global development exploded at the very beginning of the new century with the events of 11 September 2001 and the war in Afghanistan thereafter. Currently we are facing the tremendous challenges of the all-embracing global economic crisis. It was caused by the financial speculations of global economic actors whose headquarters are in North America and in Western Europe. However, the worst suffering hits the less developed societies of the global and continental periphery. The Eastern European societies immediately manifested their low capacity to manage the local consequences of the global economic tsunami. (Ehrke 2009)

What should be the theoretical lessons from this development? What should be the practical reactions? Given the controversial legacy of the twentieth century and the current global crisis, the conclusion is evident: the human civilization is facing tremendous challenges. Most of them are continuation of the twentieth century's notorious tensions and conflicts. But there are very substantial new nuances in the global picture. The emerging knowledge-based societies (Castels 1999) need to have their cognitive and technological potential better organized than in the most advanced present day societies. Another implication is the increasing dependence of all activities on technological systems. Industrial disasters signaled their destructive potentials. The worst imaginable scenario continues to be *large-scale high-tech war*. Its implications could be comparable to the collision of large objects in the outer space. This warning remains a deterring factor as it was in the times of the Cold War. Unfortunately, the level of deterrence declined together with the proliferation of nuclear weapons.

Aside from large-scale wars, a major challenge is the need to cope with the *uneven growth of the world population*. The growth comes about only in the poorest countries and regions. After the "green revolution" of the fifties and the sixties, grain production has registered a rather slow increase worldwide. There is a looming global shortage of fresh water needed for agriculture. Large agricultural plots have been made unusable for agriculture due to excessive irrigation and the ensuing salination of the soil. Climate changes and deforestation have resulted in progressing desertification. The issues concerning the *use and protection of environmental resources* are becoming more and more complicated and urgent. Humankind continues to overexploit the natural environment and has turned out to be still unable to introduce effective controls on environmental pollution as the failed summit in Copenhagen 2010 has shown. It seems possible that the human civilization could become increasingly incapable of controlling the destructive processes in physical and biological systems. This is an existential threat since these systems are already part of the social metabolism itself.

The issues of population growth and preservation of the natural environment are becoming additionally complicated in the context of *rising inequalities on the world scale*. (Kreckel 2006) Economists usually argue that inequality in property and income is needed in order to motivate people to work efficiently and to calculate the expenses rationally. The argument is basically valid, but the deepening disparities between haves and have-nots undermine the motivation of the underprivileged for productive work by eroding their trust in public institutions. Humankind has to cope with these implications in a constructive way or suffer the destructive consequences. Deprivation of access to education, health care, housing, clean water, sanitation, political participation and prestige due to poverty have far reaching impacts on the social cohesion in societies, regions and human civilization. (World Development Report 2006) The task of reducing poverty is difficult to accomplish since inequality has deep roots in the global trends which shape structures and processes in the present day human civilization. (*A Fair Globalization* 2004) In the long run, the "digital divide" in the access to information and to means of communication is probably going to become explosive.

There is no doubt that the *contradictions in the global culture* have their roots in the existing and deepening global cleavages in wealth and political power. If combined with powerful geostrategic interests, the cultural divisions, tensions and confrontations might become the very centre of intensive international conflicts as the developments after September 2001 already signaled.

Thus, globalization is the threatening juggernaut that humankind will have to cope with in the decades and centuries to come. (Lane 2008) Globalization is manifesting itself in a variety of patterns of orientation, decision and action in five major action spheres. The first type is undoubtedly the *environmental globalization*. The man made destruction and pollution of the natural environment affects literally everybody by disrespecting nationality, social position or territorial location. The *technological globalization* is manifest in the deepening worldwide technological division of labor and in the rapidly progressing unification of technological standards. In the field of *economic globalization* the global financial markets have expanded much faster than the markets for goods and services. The bulk of transfers consist of speculative movements of financial resources chasing fast profit. The outcome is the fragility of the whole system of markets. The *globalization of politics* is obviously in a dramatic delay in developing the very much needed global political regulation of global economic processes. Instead, regional organizations took the initiative of peace-building and peace-keeping at the global level. These developments and the current economic crisis clearly show the urgent need for innovation in the global political regulation. (Langlois and Soltan 2008; Weiss, Kanninen and Busch 2009) It is a matter of everyday observation to recognize that the *globalization of culture* is increasingly manifest in preferences concerning work, family, leisure time, etc. The powerful entertainment industry and the global communication channels effectively spread unifying views on practical utility, moral ideas and aesthetic norms. At the same time, the global information and communication systems make the local cultural preferences of *their* headquarters global. The channels of cultural globalization serve – intentionally or unintentionally – structures and processes of economic and political hegemony.

Two decades ago nobody possessed the above concepts needed to describe, explain and predict trends in the accelerated globalization and its implications for Eastern Europe. Today we know that many societies are under the double pressure to catch-up in their adaptation to globalization by following established institutional patterns and by searching for innovative adjustments to the new challenges. This double pressure was and is particularly strong on the Eastern European societies. (Széll and Ehlert 2001)

1.2 From "Transition" to "Societal Transformations" in Eastern Europe

The historical events of the autumn of 1989 caught Eastern Europeans by surprise. Many desired changes in the region. But nobody expected them to start so rapidly in a basically peaceful manner. Consequently, the reforms started with strong political slogans but in a conceptual vacuum. A catchy slogan was "Back to Europe". Intuitively, the meaning was clear and persuasive. It was about the desirable movement in the direction of economic wellbeing, political stability and cultural pluralism as exemplified by the advanced societies in Western Europe. But what was the precise meaning of the slogan supposed to be? At what previous time was Europe united? When had Eastern Europe belonged to a united Europe?

Another popular slogan was "Back to normality". It seemed to be fully transparent. After the aberrations of state socialism, restoration was needed. But restoration of what was actually needed? With only a few exceptions, the Eastern European societies had been economically dominated by agriculture before state socialism. Nearly all of them had dictatorial regimes. The level of education was low as a rule. Who actually wanted the return to this 'normality'? No restoration was possible since there was a fundamental discontinuity in the economic, political and cultural development of the region. What one could only expect was an all-encompassing *adaptation to qualitatively new domestic and international circumstances*. Not slogans with the sense of "back to" but concepts focused on "forward to" were needed. Thus, the concept of "transition to" was hastily put in circulation to fill in the conceptual vacuum.

The meaning of the concept seemed to be clear enough. The question "Transition to what?" could be immediately answered: Transition to democratic political institutions and to market economy. But the first discussions about constitutional changes signaled how deceptive the transparency of the transition concept was. Eastern Europeans had to learn fast that there were many versions of democratic political order. It was not the issue of democracy "as such", but the choice between parliamentary or presidential democracy, between a proportional or majoritarian electoral system, between one-chamber or two-chamber parliament which mattered. The aim "transition to a market economy" turned out to be blurred as well. Eastern Europeans learned in due course that there were liberal market arrangements in the world but also tightly regulated "social market economies". Thus, the nebulous slogan "transition to a market economy" had to be replaced by discussions about institutional arrangements which could presumably be best adapted to the local conditions.

The time was already ripe to focus less on slogans than on the explanation and management of the ongoing social processes. In this intellectual context serious attention was paid to the famous "dilemma of simultaneity". (Offe 1991) In its extreme versions it stated the very impossibility to rationally manage simultaneous changes in economy, politics and culture. Casting a glance at the accumulated historical experience one may see that simultaneous changes in economy, politics and culture were possible and practically unavoidable. This experience questions the meaning of the debates on the sequence of political, economic and cultural changes as well. Democratic political institutions had to be established first. Thereafter the green light for economic reforms could be given. The Eastern European governments had to start with economic liberalization followed by the stabilization of the liberalized macro-economic conditions. Then privatization had to come to the top of the agenda of reforms. As for privatization itself, the experts of the World Bank were unanimous: Big-Bang privatization had to have absolute priority. (Sachs 1993: 1–34) The gradualist strategy of privatization was basically rejected since it could only increase the losses due to reforms and thus deepen and prolong human suffering. (Åslund 2007: Ch. 2)

Some analytical reasons and conceptual outcomes of these debates cannot be denied. But the achieved analytical precision was negligible. Decision-makers did not care about the "dilemma of simultaneity". They had to opportunistically react to *simultaneous* burning needs for urgent reforms of economic, political and cultural institutions. Nowhere did reforms follow the normative visions of "liberalization – stabilization – privatization". No financial resources were available for stabilization of enterprises before their privatization. The typical answer of leading Russian reformers to the question of why they started privatization immediately after the liberalization of markets was rather simple: Otherwise there would have been hunger throughout the country.

The weaknesses of the intellectual debates concerning the Eastern European transition to democratic political arrangements and market economy were not due to the immaturity of social sciences alone. The complexity of the transition process itself was immense. If taken in isolation, the transition to democracy in Eastern Europe exhibited nearly identical features to the political change in countries of Southern Europe or in Latin America. (Linz and Stepan 1996) However, there was also a profound difference since nowhere in the world had the means of production been as largely socialized as in Eastern Europe in the course of the socialist transformations. Many other specifics of the Eastern European processes could be identified in terms of conceptual pairs defining rationality. (Genov 1991)

When examining the relationships between *individual and collective rationality*, one could refer to the emerging knowledge based society. It made the state-socialist centralized definition of tasks and top-down hierarchical control less and less adapted to the changing work content. It increasingly required strong work motivation, initiative and responsibility on the part of the individuals. They were increasingly expected to effectively participate in decision-making and in the control of technological, economic and political processes. The trend towards participatory democracy was greatly facilitated by the rising educational level. Better educated young people increasingly challenged the paternalistic economic and political structures in Eastern Europe. Contrary to this trend, Eastern European rulers continued to keep to the centralized system of economy, politics and culture.

The deprivation of large groups of their right to develop initiative and to take responsibility questioned the collective rationality of state socialism based on the state ownership on the means of production. It was intended to eliminate negative effects of capitalist competition driven by greed and causing alienation and economic crises. But the excessive state intervention in economic affairs produced its own irrationalities by suppressing the evolutionary achievement of market competition. This de-differentiation of economy and politics was the major reason for the slow pace of technological innovations in Eastern Europe. The deficit of incentives for responsible work and creativity in innovations could not be efficiently compensated by indoctrination, use of violence or by the mere necessity of earning a living. In the long run the disrespect to individual interests brought about mass dissatisfaction with the conditions of work and the standards of living.

Another part of the organizational problems of state socialism was the clumsy bureaucratic regulation and control. Bureaucracy reinforced the lack of incentives for initiative and responsibility in the work performance. The circle was thus closed: the shortcomings of centralized economic organization caused permanent shortages of goods and services. In turn, the shortages reproduced organizational pathologies in the enterprises and in the national economy, as indicated by diminishing returns on new investments. (Kornai 1992)

This type of economic organization was imposed by political means in order to achieve political ends. The economic monopoly of the state was intrinsically related with the single-party domination of political life. Under the conditions of "partymonialism" administrated politics penetrated every sphere of society. This was a paradoxical kind of politics which prevented the articulation of group interests in a legal way. The artificial over-politicization of social life turned into its opposite by causing a deficit of political initiative and responsibility. No vibrant civil society was possible in such a political framework. The full-scale involvement of politics in economic life and the suppression of civil society became major characteristics of the de-modernization of the Eastern European societal systems.

Given this complexity of the inherited contradictions of state socialism, the transition to democracy required a fundamental reshuffling of the institutional framework of socialist societies. The state monopoly in economic life and politics had to be demolished. However, there were no elaborated and proven mechanisms for transforming state ownership into private ownership on such a large scale. There was no free domestic capital in the Eastern European countries which could be used for private entrepreneurship. To the contrary, most Eastern European societies were overburdened by international indebtedness. All Eastern European countries had extreme difficulties in adapting to competitive foreign markets. In addition, the political culture was dominated by patterns of authoritarianism. The ideal of the non-zero sum political game could not easily take the lead. Political victory was typically understood as the total defeat of the opponent.

Thus, the task was to introduce the modern market exchange in Eastern Europe and to develop political institutions which could regulate it in a democratic way. The democratic institutional reforms implied a temporary dysfunction of state administration. It came about under the conditions of a deep economic and cultural crisis. Unstable situations of this kind tend to nourish political frustration and forces which are inclined to break with the rules of the democratic political game in favor of authoritarianism.

In the transition to democracy a twofold change concerned the *rationality of means and that of ends*. Disenchantment with the proclaimed humanistic ends of state socialism occurred as these ends strongly contradicted realities. Egalitarianism and collectivism lost their power to orient action and to integrate societies. The instrumental ends of survivalism took the lead as ultimate ends in the life of large groups. The transition seemed to support the revitalization of ultimate values expressed in the right to private property, free speech and in the flourishing of diverse beliefs. Over a long period the official Eastern European ideology promoted the dividing idea of class cultures. The transition to democracy introduced a new understanding of the universal values of the individual human rights. However, together with the new social differentiations of income, prestige and power, new polarizations of values took shape and influenced social action.

The dogmatic ideological unanimity in state socialism was succeeded by fierce struggles concerning value priorities.

Intensive cultural and political problems were focused on the relationships between *short-term and long-term rationality*. The background was the striking difference between the slow social time of state socialism and the accelerated social time of the transition. Under state socialism the attention was focused on the grievances and conflicts of everyday life. In a sharp contrast, the official propaganda was future-oriented. At the end of the eighties Eastern Europeans did not want to accept the ideology and politics of permanently postponed gratification any more. They could no longer bear the contradiction between the promised future welfare and the reality of housing shortage, deficits of goods and ecological disasters.

Thus, the reservations against centralized long-term planning were well founded. But the crucial points were neglected that liberal markets are short-sighted and can never perfectly balance themselves. The neglected evolutionary universal of market arrangements was reinstated at the expense of the evolutionary universal of long-term state regulation of economic activity.

These controversial processes occurred in the context of a high density of events characterizing *accelerated social time after the start of the reforms*. Eastern Europeans were experiencing the growing impatience as a reaction to decades of postponed or blocked change. There was a danger that the acceleration of social processes could get out of control. The political mechanism for solving the problem was expected to be the functioning democracy by balancing contradictory interests in a rational way. However, the newcomers in democratic politics had to learn that the competitive democratic politics also tends to focus on short-term political dividends related to the electoral cycle. The situation was even more confusing since the Eastern European politicians could not refer to any experience of long-term oriented democratic decision-making.

The discussions on the moving forces, ends, means and outcomes of the Eastern European transition invigorated intellectual life in the region and worldwide. Some of the discussions had real theoretical meaning and implications for decision-making. But generally the studies in the framework of "transitology" did not develop any clear conceptual core. Their degree of theoretical cohesiveness was low, their capacity to reach systematic descriptions and explanations of the ongoing processes turned out to be rather limited. Their contribution to the development of social science and politics came increasingly under suspicion. Other conceptual frameworks were urgently needed in order to guide research and policy recommendations. The time was ripe for taking stock of the rapid social and intellectual developments.

First, Ralf Dahrendorf timely warned (1990) against over-optimistic time-schedules for the societal restructuring in Eastern Europe. The announcements about finalization of the transition in some countries only several years later turned out to be political speculations. Serious studies used to present a different picture. The newly established institutions of market economy and democratic politics were tension-ridden. Important reforms were still to be implemented. Disillusionment dominated the cultural climate. It became common knowledge that the desired stability of markets, political institutions and values could not be reached in the immediate future. The re-emerging peripheral status of the Eastern European societies became the subject of new debates.

Second, the social space of the historical events became more differentiated and less transparent than it was at the end of the eighties. Eastern Europe was already divided into quite different parts. Each society in the region had shaped its specific profile in the course of its reforms. New boundaries appeared due to the changing relationships of societies in the region with the European Union and NATO. (Bömer and Viëtor 2007)

Third, the new historical experience required new interpretations and conclusions. Why did the optimistic expectations of a brief and smooth transition of Eastern European societies fail in such a dramatic way? Why were the ongoing processes still so difficult to manage in cognitive and in practical terms? Open questions concerned the moving forces of the changes, their major actors and the emerging economic and political structures.

Consequently, the experience of the early nineties drove *the need to change the conception of change* in Eastern Europe. Failures of national adjustments to the global economic environment strengthened the view that the technological and economic lag would continue to be substantial much longer than expected. (Berend 1997: 12f.) The inevitable conclusion followed that the level of material well-being in both parts of the continent would remain rather different in the foreseeable future. Competitive politics brought about turmoil and disappointment even in the Polish society which was praised for its pioneering achievements in the post-socialist economic restructuring. It was already common sense in Eastern Europe that the commercialization of all action spheres had undermined moral and aesthetic values and norms. Unemployment, impoverishment and crime prevented the self-realization and undermined the future prospects of large social groups in the region. The previous hierarchical system of power relationships was replaced by steep inequalities of income and wealth. The social time decelerated for large segments of the Eastern European societies. This casted doubts on the meritocratic effects of the post-socialist reforms and re-vitalized the culture of survivalism.

Therefore, it turned out that the seemingly clear goals of the *transition* as defined in the early nineties became blurred in the course of the complex and uncertain *transformations* of Eastern European societies thereafter. The need to develop and apply a well-defined concept of societal transformation became urgent. The related debates will continue to be topical in the long run like the debates on the concepts and approaches related to the French Revolution of 1789. (Stone 2002; Kates 2006) The Eastern European reforms needed new conceptual developments and systematic empirical tests of the elaborated concepts.

When searching for explanatory models analysts had to be selective. The time was ripe to exclude narratives like those concerning the stages of *cultural trauma.* This conceptual model only allows for sketchy references to structural dynamics. The same holds true for the temptation to explain the tensions in the economic and political development of Eastern Europe by referring to *civilizational deficiencies* in knowledge and in organizational skills. More promising options offered, for instance, the three-dimensional conceptual framework developed and applied by T.I. Zaslavskaya. It makes meaningful operationalizations and multidimensional explanatory variations possible. (Yadov 2007: 19–20)

The major reason for the variety of conceptual models is the diversity in the changes themselves. (Thomas 2008) Each society in Eastern Europe is performing its own *specific* transformation. Nevertheless, comparative analyses of societal changes in the region show that there are identifiable *common features* in their starting points, their course and their preliminary results. These features characterize the historical type of the *post-socialist societal transformation.* It took a variety of specific paths and brought about different results from country to country. How could this large variety of problem situations, changes and their outcomes be conceptualized? The complexity of the task might be partially managed by using *sensitizing concepts* which serve *ad hoc* historical explanations. If the intention is to achieve systematic descriptions and explanations of individual societal transformations and to try to theoretically generalize the cognitive outcomes, then the development and use of sensitizing concepts cannot be a promising strategy. It questions the possibility of developing generalized sociological knowledge with systematic explanatory potential.

Thus, the task could be resolved by developing the explanatory potential around a concept based on stable ontological foundations but allowing constructive freedom. The concept is expected to resolve traditional dilemmas of the relationships between individual and collective action, between economic, political and cultural factors of social development, between stability and change in social life. The differentiated concept of *social interaction* might help to resolve the complicated task. The concept combines the structural and action-oriented theoretical approaches in sociological theory building by referring to five subsystems of the societal system, namely the environmental, technological, economic, political and cultural subsystems of society. This differentiation can be further elaborated concerning typical structural issues which the transformations have to resolve, the ensuing specific tasks and the intended effects of their resolution.

First, in the context of the Eastern European reforms the most urgent task was the change of the distribution and use of political power. In the course of the reforms the political systems in Eastern Europe developed polyarchic structures (Dahl 1998) which were qualitatively different from the hierarchical institutional patterns of state socialism. The most important changes were the establishment of a working division of powers and the differentiated party system. In addition, national politics in Eastern European societies had to be adapted to the controversial dynamics of international politics.

Second, new patterns of economic organization were introduced. The changes primarily concerned the ownership of productive assets, but unavoidably also the patterns of investment, production, distribution and supply. In the historical context, the key issue of economic restructuring was and remains the adjustment of the national economic systems to the open global markets of goods, services, financial exchange and labor.

Third, the change in the value-normative systems of Eastern European societies occurred simultaneously with the change of political and economic institutions. The very core of the new value system came to be the concept of universal human rights together with the concept of sustainability in all its dimensions.

Fourth, in this broad context of simultaneous changes, the productive infrastructure was transformed in order to bring about more efficient technological chains and patterns of participation in the international division of labor.

Fifth, although the environmental limitations of technological and economic growth had been well known since the beginning of the seventies (Meadows, Rander and Meadows 2004), the comprehensive approach to environmental protection only became possible in Eastern Europe in the course of the societal transformations. They opened up access to environmentally friendly technologies, to the market calculations of natural resources and to patterns of democratic control on the impact of technology and economy on the environment.

The so differentiated transformation processes in major action spheres and between action spheres occurred within the impact of regional and global processes:

Global and regional impacts	Issue		Task		Potential effect	Global and regional Impacts
→	Environment-friendly restructuring	→	Ecologization	→	Adjustment to the need for environmental protection	←
	↕					
→	Technological restructuring	→	Informatization	→	Adjustment to the information technologies	←
	↕					
→	Cultural restructuring	→	Universalization	→	Adjustment to the innovations in culture	←
	↕					
→	Economic restructuring	→	Marketization	→	Adjustment to the dynamics of the open markets	←
	↕					
→	Political restructuring	→	Democratization	→	Adjustment to the rationalization of politics	←

Figure 1.1 Structural dimensions of societal transformations in Eastern Europe

The next step of conceptualization concerns the *action dimension* of the Eastern European societal transformations. The major analytical concepts refer to individual and collective *social actors,* their *relations* and the *social processes* in which they are involved. Following this analytical differentiation, the adjustment to more efficient institutional and behavioral patterns requires changes in the major *action characteristics* of society. New types of *actors* are emerging in the course of the transformation. Private entrepreneurs, democratically responsible state officials and associations of civil society are taking the lead as bearers of new forms of social and economic organization and action. The problems in this context are focused in the convergence and divergence of the interests of *individual* and *collective, national* and *transnational* actors. New actors create and sustain new social *relations.* These are marked by the shifting focus from the distribution of political power to the economic reproduction of society and from hierarchical to associational relations. The societal transformations in Eastern Europe engender an immense variety of relations between *coordination* and *conflict* as well as relations between the traditional institutional *hierarchy* and the dynamic institutional *poliarchy.* The emergence of new actors and relations is a *process* which brings about a variety of expectations, desires, decisions, actions and outcomes. *Short-term* goals and their effects characterize some of these processes. Others are bound to exert *long-term* impacts on individuals, groups and societies. Some processes have or will have only *local* relevance by influencing specific groups or communities. Other processes have or will have broader geopolitical and even global relevance. The analytical differentiation of tasks and effects according to the three action dimensions of the societal transformation can be schematically presented together with the impact of the context as follows:

Global and regional impacts	Dimension		Tasks		Effects	Global and regional Impacts
→	Actors	→	Initiative and responsibility	→	Competitiveness	←
	↕					
→	Relations	→	Balancing hierarchy and poliarchy	→	Meritocracy	←
	↕					
→	Processes	→	Effective allocation of resources	→	Innovation	←

Figure 1.2 Action dimensions of the societal transformations

The multidimensional concept of Eastern European societal transformations is intended to theoretically reproduce the complexity of the ongoing processes in the region together with the concomitant uncertainties and risks. The concept is not rooted in any assumption about linearity or the inevitable success of the transformations. To the contrary, the underlying assumption concerns the possibility of both achievements and failures in the transformation of Eastern European societies. (Rüb 2007) Some social groups, some organizations or territories do adapt successfully, while others do not. Some societal transformations bring about evolutionary achievements while others reach only modest and others rather sobering results.

Bearing in mind the level of organizational development of Eastern European societies at the beginning of the nineties, one could have assumed that the post-socialist transformations would be implemented in the form of controlled social innovations. The processes in East Germany, in the Czech Republic or in Slovenia tentatively followed this pattern. In most other Eastern European countries influential neo-liberal visions and policies favored spontaneous market forces. Thus, the societal transformation deviated there from the pattern of organized change. Transformations were additionally influenced by the worldwide recession cycle at the end of the eighties and the beginning of the nineties. Its negative imprint leaves the much deeper recession 20 years later as well.

Another set of circumstances concerns the different path dependence in individual Eastern European societies. It turned out that the cultural and institutional legacy of state socialism has been more influential than could have been assumed at the beginning of the nineties. Now it is a widely shared view that the egalitarian and statist characteristics of the previous social system corresponded to economic and political preferences of large segments of the population in the Eastern European societies. These preferences legitimized state socialism before the changes and give impetus to the nostalgia for it today. This development seemed to be astonishing in Central Europe in the mid-nineties. (Machonin 1997: 28–30) But it is even more telling in most recent times. When 62% of representative samples in Bulgaria and Hungary and 72% of the same sample in the Ukraine state in 2009 that most people in their countries live now worse than under the state socialist regimes (*Two Decades after the Wall's Fall* 2009: 5), this is a serious signal to the social sciences and politics. It should be taken for granted now that values, norms and behavioral patterns inherited from the socialist past will continue to exert their impact on the economy, politics and everyday life in Eastern Europe. This long-term impact is being mostly strengthened by preferences for high social security. However, radical criticism of the state-socialist past provoked emotional reactions since it questioned the biographies of two generations. Negative attitudes to the new structures were fostered by vivid examples of new elites unable to manage the complexity of the ongoing transformations. Some new elites turned out to be even less socially responsible than the elites before the changes.

The turn of the initial euphoria to disappointments and skepticism has still another reason. Eastern Europeans had to learn that the institutions of market economy and political democracy could not be transferred from the West without adaptations. Some adaptations turned painful and time consuming. The countries from the European Union were seen as models for the restructuring of Eastern European societies. Their integration into the Union became the major impetus for their development according to the standards of the information age. (Castels 1999: 336f) However, the European integration is a challenge itself, it raises a series of difficult questions. Will the Eastern European new member states remain in the economic and political periphery in the European Union? What are the prospects of the Eastern European societies which will remain outside of the European integration for the foreseeable future?

Table 1.1 HDI ranking, GDP per capita (PPP, US$) and life expectancy at birth in Eastern European societies

Country	HDI ranking (2009)	GDP per capita (USD, PPP, 2007)	Life expectancy at birth (2007)
Austria	*14*	*37,370*	*79.9*
Slovenia	29	26,753	78.2
Czech Republic	36	24,144	76.4
Estonia	40	20,361	72.9
Poland	41	15,987	75.5
Slovakia	42	20,076	74.6
Hungary	43	18,755	73.3
Croatia	45	16,027	76.0
Lithuania	46	17,575	71.8
Latvia	48	16,377	72.3
Bulgaria	61	11,222	73.1
Romania	63	12,369	72.5
Montenegro	65	11,699	74.0
Serbia	67	10,248	73.9
Belarus	68	10,841	69.0
Albania	70	7,041	76.5
Russian Federation	71	14,690	66.2
Macedonia	72	9,096	74.1
Bosnia and Herzegovina	76	7,764	75.1
Armenia	84	5,693	73.6
Ukraine	85	6,914	68.2
Georgia	89	4,662	71.6
Moldova	117	2,551	68.3
Egypt	*123*	*5,349*	*69.9*

The answers should take into account the fact that the processes in Eastern Europe are full of constructive dynamics but also of high intensity risks. International comparisons highlight the causes for risks mostly in the substantial differences between the Western European core of the modern civilization and the continental periphery or semi-periphery. The data vary substantially, but the overall picture is clear enough. On the average, it tangibly deviates from key parameters of the advanced Austrian society on the one side and of the developing Egyptian society on the other side. (Human Development Report 2009: 171ff) (Table 1.1).

The information provided by the above synchronic comparisons might be complemented by diachronic comparisons. It is striking to notice the deviating ways in which particular societies in the region reacted to similar challenges and managed them. In a simplified way, this might be exemplified by the GDP growth of Eastern European societies in the time spans between 1980 and 1989 and from 1989 to 2008 (UNECE 2004b: 190; EBRD 2009b) (Table 1.2).

Table 1.2 Real GDP growth of the Eastern European countries 1980–2008 (1989 = 100)

Country	1980	1989	2008
Albania	79.4	100.0	159.2
Armenia	73.5	100.0	156.4
Belarus	65.7	100.0	155.2
Bulgaria	76.2	100.0	113.6
Croatia	99.0	100.0	114.6
Czech Republic	-	100.0	141.2
Estonia	74.5	100.0	153.7
Georgia	79.4	100.0	61.6
Hungary	86.3	100.0	136.5
Latvia	68.5	100.0	125.6
Lithuania	64.7	100.0	120.1
Macedonia, FYR of	93.3	100.0	101.2
Moldova	72.1	100.0	56.3
Poland	91.1	100.0	175.2
Romania	88.5	100.0	128.6
Russian Federation	78.1	100.0	109.6
Slovakia	-	100.0	162.1
Slovenia	98.9	100.0	119.9
Ukraine	75.0	100.0	73.5

How can this wide range of synchronic differences and diachronic divergences be explained? It is now taken for granted that the diverse technological, economic, political and value-normative starting conditions of the Eastern European societies did and still do determine the *path dependency* of their specific post-socialist transformations. Just as important is the theoretical focus on the *quality of strategic decisions* of national elites. Still another well tested assumption concerns the relevance of the *external impacts* on the Eastern European societal transformations. In the historical context this conceptual framework refers mostly to the impacts of the International Monetary Fund, the World Bank, the European Union and other international organizations on the development of particular post-socialist European societies.

All these partial explanations are possible, useful and necessary since they emphasize the distinctiveness of the national transformations and their specifics in the first place. One may take the national transformations in Poland and in Bulgaria in order to identify specific commonalities and differences. Poland is a good example for the Central European part of former Eastern Europe. Bulgaria is a typical case of the South Eastern part of the region. The comparison of both societal transformations is particularly intriguing since Poland and Bulgaria had strikingly similar characteristics along the parameters of human development before the start of the rapid changes (Human Development Report 1990: 128ff.). (Table 1.3).

The above similarities were mainly due to the same general pattern of development of both societies after the Second World War. Bulgaria and Poland accomplished their industrialization simultaneously, starting from the background of significant hidden unemployment in the countryside. In both national settings industrialization was implemented by using the organizational scheme of directive

Table 1.3 Parameters of human development of Bulgaria and Poland in the late 1980s

Parameter	Bulgaria	Poland
Urban population	69	62
Percentage of labour force in industry (1985–1987)	37.9	38.9
Women as % of the total labour force (1988)	46.3	45.5
Real GDP per capita (1987, PPP$)	4750	4000
Combined primary and secondary enrolment ratio (1986-1988, North=100)	98	98
Life expectancy at birth (1987, years)	72	72
Infant mortality rate per 1,000 live births (1988)	15	16

planning. Heavy industry was prioritized. It was built at the expense of the production of consumer goods. In the context of the forced industrialization, the decades after the War were marked by the rapid urbanization of both societies. The well-being of large segments of the population increased slowly but tangibly. The educational achievements of Poland and Bulgaria during the post-war period were recognized in international comparisons. Although of a modest quality, healthcare was largely accessible to citizens.

The cultural background of this development was the common statist and egalitarian ideology, which changed over the years. The major reason for the changes was the recognition of permanent and increasing deficiencies in the social and economic organization of Eastern European societies. It was relatively efficient in mobilizing scarce resources for the strategic aims of the first industrialization. However, this type of economic and political organization turned out to be less and less able to cope with the growing complexity in production, distribution, consumption and life styles. The protracted over-centralization of economic and political decision-making was the key factor in the accumulating constraints on societal development. The technological lag of Eastern Europe started to increase in the mid-seventies. Economy, politics and culture in the region did not manage to creatively adapt to the oil shocks of 1973 and 1979. They signaled the need to switch to resource-saving production and the growing importance of information technologies. As a result, contrary to the rising aspirations of the educated population, the economy grew in the region only slowly. Politics remained stagnant after the suppression of the reform movement in Czechoslovakia.

The social explosion caused by these accumulated disparities and tensions came from Poland in 1980 with the *Solidarity* movement. At that point in time, Bulgarian society was totally unprepared for this type of upheaval. Why did similar institutional processes in both countries after 1945 lead to so strikingly different outcomes? Some answers might focus on the differences in national traditions or on the specifics of the national social psychology. In reality, the major issues concern fundamental social structures and institutional arrangements.

Poland only partly followed the institutional model of economic, political and cultural centralization which dominated Eastern Europe after the Second World War. Polish agriculture remained basically private. There was institutional space for private initiative in all other economic spheres in Poland during the entire post-war period. The Roman Catholic Church was an influential institution, which managed to preserve its autonomy under state socialism. The numerous Polonia abroad kept the economic, political and cultural ties with the country of origin intact. Because of geo-strategic reasons the West was very much interested in Poland and was massively involved in activities influencing the processes in the country. On the other hand, there were historical reasons which used to put limitations on the capacity of the Soviet Union to influence processes in Polish society. All these factors together brought about the rise of *Solidarity* movement and the open conflicts of 1980–1981. At the end of the decade the ruling Polish elite did not have legitimacy any more. The Polish Round Table became the standard example of civilized start of the post-socialist transformations (Adamski et al. 1999: 69f.). These processes in Poland influenced the modern Eastern European nearly as strongly as the *perestroyka* in the Soviet Union did.

Nothing like that could have happened in Bulgaria during the years before 1989. Due to historical and geopolitical factors, the forces implementing the transformation of Bulgarian society after 1944 were able to mobilize substantial public support. After the complete socialization of industry and collectivization of agriculture, the space for private economic activity was rather narrow and under tight political control. By the late forties all the institutions in the country could effectively be brought under centralized rule. Influential traditions supported official policies towards a closer linking of Bulgaria with the Soviet Union. Due to the recognition of this fact and to geo-strategic considerations, the efforts of the West to influence the processes in Bulgarian society were much less intensive as compared to the efforts concerning Poland. One of the reasons was the lack of any relevant Bulgarian lobby in the West arguing and acting in this direction. Under these circumstances even a slight semblance of a mass opposition movement like *Solidarity* could not have appeared in Bulgaria before 1989. Because of the weakness of the opposition forces the initiative for change could only come from the party-state.

The substantial differences in the accumulation and manifestation of conflict potential in Polish and Bulgarian societies notwithstanding, at the beginning of the nineties they followed very similar paths of change. The philosophy guiding the liberalization of prices and trade in Poland after January 1990 and in Bulgaria after February 1991 was neo-liberalism. It nurtured optimistic expectations in both countries that the "big bang" would spontaneously arrange the new institutional configurations in a fast and efficient manner. However, due to the resistance of political forces the "big bang" reforms could not be implemented in either Poland or Bulgaria. The privatization of large industrial enterprises lasted a decade or even longer. The expectations for fast economic improvement could only be disappointed. The transformation shock brought about economic, political and value-normative uncertainty. During the first years of change Poland and Bulgaria suffered similar political instabilities, conflicts among state institutions and deepening mistrust in the capability of the elites and institutions to cope with the challenges of the transformation. The economic and political turbulence facilitated the nearly simultaneous election of left-wing governments in both countries in the mid-nineties. In spite of all the differences in the path of economic and political development, mass unemployment took strikingly similar paths in both countries (EBRD 2009b):

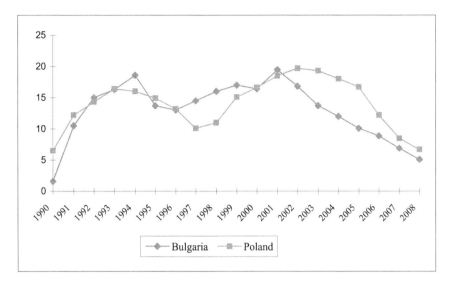

**Figure 1.3 Registered unemployed in Bulgaria and in Poland as % of the
total workforce 1990–2008**

There were also substantial differences in the post-socialist transformation of both societies. In the course of the nineties a value-normative consensus was reached in Poland as to the principles of the new social order. (Domanski and Rychard 1997: 7–29) No relevant differences existed in the country concerning the geo-strategic orientation of its foreign policy. This clarity was rewarded by a very generous reduction of the Polish foreign debt by international money-lenders. The PHARE Program of the European Union started as economic assistance for the transformation in Poland and Hungary first. The support to the Polish economy was the priority. Due to the influence of all these domestic and international factors the Polish economy went through a J-curve of recession and recovered by the mid nineties. Special economic conditions were negotiated for the entrance of Poland to the European Union. These conditions mostly favored the large agricultural sector in the country.

Due to its specific history and traditions, Bulgarian society needed a longer period to develop commonly shared visions about the means and ends of the transformation and the country's geo-strategic orientation. Consequently, the reactions abroad were rather different as compared to the reactions to the Polish transformation. Bulgaria was able to join the PHARE and similar support programs much later than Poland and received a modest help from them. The national economy was beginning to recover slightly in the mid-nineties but the country did not receive any financial support from abroad due to political calculations of the international financial institutions. The specific geostrategic treatment of the country and a series of false local decisions like the early full liberalization of banking brought about a combined devastating effect. The country experienced a second economic recession in the mid-nineties. The gradual stabilization in economic, political and cultural terms could only be achieved after the introduction of the Currency Board in 1997. In the end effect, Bulgarian economy returned back to its GDP level of 1989 as late as in 2006.

The strategy for economic reforms was better elaborated and more efficiently implemented in Poland than in Bulgaria. The quality of decisions on the management of the transformation was generally lower in Bulgaria than in Poland. However, this is a halfway explanation of the different outcomes of reforms in both countries. In all post-socialist countries there were phenomena of civilizational deficits hindering their efforts to cope with the challenges of the transformation. The conditions of this social learning were more favorable in Poland than in Bulgaria.

Because of Poland's liberal migration policy during the decades before 1989 and the good conditions for fellowships and work for Poles in the West, numerous Polish experts and workers had the opportunity to learn about market economy and democratic politics on the spot. Leszek Balcerowicz and many others developed their visions about the future of post-socialist Poland in the West before 1989 and could apply their expertise after the changes in Poland started. Only a small part of the emerging new Bulgarian elite could rely on direct experience from countries with developed market economies and democratic politics. This civilizational deficit was particularly relevant among Bulgarian industrial managers and workers who did posses only superficial knowledge about the modern economic and legal culture at the beginning of the changes.

The detailed explanation of the above mentioned differences should take into account the location of both countries in the geographical, political and cultural space. Poland enjoyed the advantage of being geographically, geo-strategically and historically closer to Western Europe. Bulgarian society differs substantially in all of these respects. In addition, the crisis in former Yugoslavia contributed to the general instability of the South-Eastern part of the continent. This development substantially reduced the attractiveness of the country to foreign investors. Public opinion in Poland is clearly in favor of creating links with the Western part of the continent. The traditional cultural preferences are more complex in Bulgaria. All of these factors, together with the protracted economic reforms, explain the low level of foreign direct investment in Bulgaria during the nineties as compared to the level of investment in the Visegrad countries (Drahokoupil 2009). However, the situation changed later substantially:[1]

---

1   Author's calculation according to (EBRD 2009a).

**Table 1.4 Foreign direct net investments in Bulgaria and in Poland
(1990–2008, thousand USD per capita)**

Year	Bulgaria	Poland	Year	Bulgaria	Poland
1990	0.5	0.0	2000	123.2	241.6
1991	6.5	3.1	2001	101.7	150.4
1992	4.9	7.4	2002	112.3	101.1
1993	4.7	15.1	2003	265.4	112.1
1994	12.5	47.8	2004	369.1	307.9
1995	11.7	93.7	2005	519.8	234.3
1996	16.6	115.2	2006	952.3	281.5
1997	61.0	125.7	2007	1072.8	471.8
1998	65.5	156.3	2008	1068.1	360.5
1999	97.8	187.1			

The comparative analysis leads to general and some more specific conclusions:

First, the experience of Bulgaria and Poland shows that transformation in the region as well as in individual countries was quite complex. Profound changes came about in all action spheres simultaneously.

Second, the differentiation among the Eastern European countries was due to various structural causes (*path dependency*) and situational reasons (*quality of decisions*). Their impacts on the transformation processes exerted also various factors *external* to the societal systems undergoing transformation.

Third, as seen from the point of view of the social sciences, the most fruitful approach to the variety of national transformations consists of paying close attention to all three types of factors determining the societal transformations as well as to the unique combinations of these factors under local circumstances.

The latter point poses the most important challenge to social sciences in the context of transformation research. In the early stages of the transformation system- and structure oriented, actor-focused and culture-biased explanatory strategies were applied and tested on the complexity of the individual Eastern European societal transformations. (Merkel 1999: 77ff.) The explanatory efforts were not futile. As shown above, the focus on structural changes in particular societies was and remains a fruitful theoretical and methodological approach. However, it has its limitations. What remained from the explanatory activities focused on societal systems is mostly a general dissatisfaction. In some cases the effect is the general questioning of the explanatory potential of the conceptual schemes applied in transformation research. By taking the famous "dilemma of simultaneity" as an example of explanatory failure, Wolfgang Merkel goes to the extreme by concluding that the societal transformations in Eastern Europe had succeeded "against all theory". (Merkel 2007) While the critical remarks concerning the focus on the possibility or impossibility of simultaneous reforms in one societal context are correct, the conclusion is not.

Given the large variety of national, regional and global historical circumstances, one should notice both the theoretical strength and the limitations of the concept of societal transformation. It is actually the most sophisticated conceptual model for the study of structure and dynamics of modern societies which has been proposed thus far. The strength of the model consists in its link to the conceptual framework of societies organized by nation-states. However, this is also the limitation of the model since *the major moving forces of societal change are increasingly the moving forces of supranational globalization.* Societies have to adapt to changes which come about due to the global technological division of labor, the fierce global economic competition, global political insecurity and to the global convergence and divergence in culture. Therefore, the limitations of "methodological nationalism" cannot be overcome by interdisciplinary approaches (Bönker, Müller and Pickel 2002). "Methodological nationalism" is in-built in the concept of societal transformation and could be radically overcome only by opening of this society-centered model towards processes of global relevance.

How can this methodological and theoretical shift be implemented? (Albrow 2004) One may start from the re-orientation of production. The turn from the processing of matter and energy towards collection, processing, and use of information is obvious. It is also obvious that the powerful information processes which triggered this change are concentrated in organizations. They need huge amounts of information for the preparation of organizational decisions, for their implementation and control on the implementation. Briefly summarized, omnipresent formal organizations need larger and larger amounts of information of a better and better quality in order to steadily *upgrade their organizational rationality.* The process has far reaching consequences in the development and realization of individuals. In the context of the progressing division of labor and development of knowledge-based society they receive more and more differentiated and broader social spaces for the autonomous orientation, decision and action. This is the global trend of *individualization* as defined by two complimentary processes. The first one concerns the social-structural changes of the conditions for individual action. The second refers to the cognitive quality of the preparation and implementation of action by individuals. The strategic orientation of the actions of individual and collective actors worldwide today is towards increasing the efficiency of the means for conquering and dominating the natural and social world. The rising influence and relevance of this pattern of orientation and action might be conditionally called the *spread of instrumental activism.* This process is closely related to another cultural and institutional trend of the *universalization of value-normative systems.* The trend is developing around the concepts and practices of human rights and sustainability.

The following analysis and argumentation will be guided by the assumption that the transformations of the post-socialist Eastern European societies could be best described and explained as adaptations to these four global trends. (Genov

2007) These concepts will be further elaborated and applied in the analysis of the processes in former Eastern Europe.

1.3 Societal Transformations as Opening to Global Trends

The above presented four global trends penetrate the structure and functioning of all present-day societies, albeit in different ways and with different effects. The major channels of the penetration include the global transfer of technology, worldwide commercial and financial transactions, trans-national political processes and the diffusion of cultural patterns. Individual and collective actors may or may not explicitly refer to these trends. Even unknowingly, actors contribute to their diffusion around the world.

The essence of the global trend *upgrading the rationality of organizations* is the growing attention to *efficiency, calculability, predictability and objectified control of action* in formal organizations (Ritzer 2008: 13f.) accompanied by the rising relevance of the timely and sufficient *differentiation and/or integration* of social structures and functions. By resolving these tasks formal organizations manage to more and more efficiently allocate resources in ways unattainable for traditional societies. However, formal organizations tend to abuse resources for the servicing of their own bureaucratic needs. In this way, they tend to close themselves to changes in the organizational environment, blunt the 'cutting edge' of their creativity and power of innovation, and lose winning positions in the competitive world.

Western Europe was the pioneer in technological innovations and in developing efficient markets, functioning political institutions and creative culture in the early modernity. These achievements became possible due to the development of formal organizations in all sectors of social life. Governed by contractually employed professionals, Western-type bureaucracies reach high organizational efficiency. In order to remain competitive, organizations implement permanent innovations. They rationalize organizational means and ends, structures and functions as well as the relationships between organizations. Their permanent reshuffling is guided by the need to break the vicious circles of pathological over-concentration or excessive dispersion of decision and control.

The controversial path of upgrading organizational rationality is due to two major factors. The first one is the need to quickly resolve difficult tasks in often unfavorable domestic and international environments. The second stems from the controversies of the process itself. Democratic participation is the most promising modality of the upgrading of organizational rationality. But various actors quickly learn to abuse the democratic decision-making process and to avoid the mechanisms of democratic control. The ensuing disappointments in the public mind are strong since organizational reality is evaluated by referring to visions about the desirable efficiency of democratic procedures. These visions produce and maintain illusions and consequently disenchantment. In many cases it is caused by the rationalization trap due to the lack of adequate financing of rationalization procedures. Even the best designed reforms degenerate into organizational pathologies if they would not be adequately funded. (Lane 2002; Alber and Merkel 2005)

The 'learning of democracy' is a permanent and universal issue in present-day democratic societies (Putnam 1993). This holds particularly true for the vast majority of countries which have limited democratic experience. They must undergo intensive learning in order to adapt to regional and global processes of organizational rationalization. In the historical context of the 1990s the proof concerned the neo-liberal vision of the automatic self-regulation of markets. Events swiftly falsified this assumption and prompted the conclusion made by Karl Polanyi decades ago: "To allow the market mechanism to be sole director of the fate of human beings and their natural environment ... would result in the demolition of society". (2001 [1944]: 73) Given the ongoing globalization, one may observe that the imperfection of rationality is particularly strong at the level of supranational processes, where it brings about rather destructive effects. The global economic crisis which started in 2008 provides abundant support for this claim.

Pathological developments in organizations have a lot to do with the rather uneven conditions for taking part in the worldwide technological competition. Three major centers – North America, Western Europe and Japan – account for more than 90% of all investments in research and technological development and for an even higher percentage of all technological patents worldwide. This is one of the major reasons why the technological gap between this core of the modern civilization and the technological periphery is widening. This is a frontline for conflicts determined by technological disparities and by concomitant economic and political inequalities. In the area of technological development, tensions and conflicts are particularly intensive since vested interests and economic survival are at stake. Repeating crises of national, regional and global finances have strengthened beliefs that the conditions of technological competition are unfair, that markets are fragile and the whole system of market arrangements needs substantial improvements in terms of national and supranational regulation. This experience has been reflected in conceptualizations and in practical actions of various analysts and decision-makers. The effect was the turn away from the liberal orthodoxy which had dominated economic and political activities until the mid-1990s. Key international organizations have been already laying stress on the connection between economic growth and the efficiency of state institutions in dealing with burning economic and social issues. (World Development Report 2006)

The practical effects of the institutional learning vary from case to case. The most effective policies for counteracting negative scenarios seem to be the establishment and maintenance of regional and global centers of political decision-making and action. The regional efforts in this respect have already been successfully channeled in the development of the European Union, NAFTA, ASEAN, Mercosur, etc. But the realities at the global level deviate from this pattern and cause deep concerns. Technology transfer, trade and financial exchange are global but there is no corresponding political framework which would be able to manage their complexity. The desirable high level of rationalization of global politics has a long way to go.

Given the many dimensions of upgrading the rationality of organizations worldwide, the discussion on these processes in Eastern Europe will be hereafter focused on the following questions:

- What has or has not been achieved in the differentiation of economy, politics and culture in the region of Eastern Europe and why?
- What has or has not been achieved in the differentiation within specific action spheres and why?
- What has or has not been achieved in the re-integration process in Eastern European societies and why?
- What has or has not been achieved in the management of outstanding social problems in the course of the upgrading of the rationality of organizations in the Eastern European societal transformations and why?

In structural terms, the powerful global trend of *individualization* concerns the differentiation and widening of the social spaces for individual choice, development and realization. In terms of social action the trend includes the rise of personal capacities for efficient orientation, decision and action. Innovations in the division of labor, in market economy, competitive politics and in pluralist culture make individualization one of the major characteristics of modernized societies. In such conditions the trend takes various forms of *institutionalized individualism,* as Talcott Parsons called it. (Parsons 1978: 321)

In its manifestations the trend is rather complex and controversial. Unstable transitional situations in personal biographies are becoming the rule. Dynamics of multiple identities turn into deficiencies in the integration of personality. As seen from this point of view societies offer *risky freedoms* to individuals. Anomic disorientations of individuals are coupled with organizational pathologies if individualization is not effectively linked to the strengthening of the mechanisms of social responsibility and societal integration. (Beck and Beck-Gernsheim 2002) Nevertheless, individualization is conceived of as a blessing by millions of people, even though it encumbers individuals with duties and uncertainty.

Experience from modernization implemented under various conditions suggests that *individualization is an evolutionary achievement.* It may be delayed or interrupted by dictatorships, by nationalistic or religious politics guided by the idea of a 'return to the community'. But individualization cannot be stopped. In the course of only one or two generations, advanced industrial societies have experienced a profound change of their culture and institutions in this direction. The pattern of institutionalized individualism has taken shape in legislation, organizational structures and processes as well as in everyday thinking and behavior. This institutional setting offers a large and broadening pool of options for individual choice of positions, roles and paths of mobility. The options are considered and realized by individuals who are improving their capacities to take well substantiated decisions and to implement them efficiently. This is due to the increase in the general educational level and the increasing material resources at the disposal of individuals.

The trend of individualization is so complex that it is unavoidably conflict-ridden. One of the major reasons for controversies is the growing multiplicity of individual identities due to crosscutting connections with various groups. Another fundamental reason is the clash of individual and communal interests. In addition, rapid technological and economic change is making the traditional certainty about the level of attained education, vocational training and production skills of individuals disappear. Mass unemployment or jobless economic growth is a threat to millions. Individuals all over the world have become dependent on the global fluctuations of technological transfers, commercial and financial exchange and have been exposed to international political instability or terrorist actions. Welfare support for the losers in the competition is getting more and more difficult even in the wealthiest countries. The rapid differentiation and specification of life-styles is making the traditional forms of solidarity less and less attractive and effective.

The key problem does not concern prospects for personal freedom from institutional or community constraints. This is impossible to achieve. Nor does the solution of the problem lie in more and more stringent institutional regulation – this would question the evolutionary achievement of individualization. The crucial issue is the efficient balancing of individualization *and* institutionalization based on communal solidarity. It is not only the individual who is involved in permanent self-shaping. Societies and communities permanently have to adjust to new challenges and opportunities as well. The prospects for successfully handling this task in advanced societies are promising because of their relative stability. Stable institutions incorporate and preserve the common good efficiently. In other parts of the world the institutional instability makes individualization more stressful and its consequences more controversial. *Anomic developments* are omnipresent. Their typical effect is the neglect of the common good.

What is regarded in advanced societies as social and psychological tension and risk facing the individualization is being multiplied by additional stress factors in less developed societies. This is due to the lower level of efficiency, stability and reliability of social institutions. Opening up to the opportunities for individualization clashes with tremendous obstacles on the way to their realization. Thus, it seems that the lowering of aspirations in personal strategies is an effect of basic importance in the economically and socially underdeveloped parts of the world. This is due to insecurity and disorientation and, in many cases, complete helplessness. The theoretical and practical issue is broader, however. In the course of the last two centuries, the world has witnessed the dissolution of the integration patterns of traditional societies – extended kin relationships, tribal bonds, rural communities. Fundamentalist nationalism, which strived to re-establish pre-modern forms of communal life, lost the historical battle at the end of the Second World War. During the 1970s and 1980s the state socialist type of communal organization was gradually losing the technological, economic, political, ideological and military competition and collapsed. What remained after the disintegration of communities were functionally differentiated and integrated social systems. The individual has to adjust to this new situation. Parts of his or her socialized self were lost but there was a gain of efficiency in the adjustment to the social environment.

There is a permanent need to re-establish communal bonds in the production process, in settlements, in religious communities, etc. in order to make social reproduction work properly and to stabilize it in the long run. Behind the seemingly separated and episodic outbreaks of community inspired feelings and activities lurks regularity. Social life cannot be reproduced efficiently in the absence of reference to community. Stable individualization needs autonomy based on the mobilization of personal intelligence, will, emotions and creativity *in the context* of well functioning communal networks. Stable social integration needs the informality, affection and human touch of the community-type interactions of mature autonomous individuals. (Etzioni 2004)

The need to elaborate on concepts covering individualization will continue to be a focal point in theorizing on socio-economic development. One of the reasons for this is the paternalistic tradition of the strong state in many parts of the world. The reliance on state paternalism may foster solidarity but may also hamper individual initiative and responsibility both in institutional and in value-normative terms. Another long-term limitation facing the development and realization of individuals is the economic underdevelopment. Last but not least, in many parts of the world civil society is immature and cannot secure the institutional rights of individuals. That is why social policy has to cope with manifold manifestations of anomie. It is facilitated by extremes of the ongoing individualization or by institutional obstacles in its way. (Howard 2007)

The only remedy against pathological extremes of individualization is the progressing improvement of the organizational framework of individual orientation, decision and action. There is no way of reducing complexity in modern societies other than by developing efficient organizations.

The discussion on issues of individualization in Eastern Europe will be hereafter focused on the following questions:

- What is or is not being achieved through the opening of social space for individualization in Eastern Europe and why?
- What has or has not been achieved in the upgrading of the capacities of individuals to efficiently use broader social spaces for individualization and why?
- What has or has not been achieved in the balancing of individualization and common good in the Eastern European societal transformations and why?

After Max Weber the historical relevance of the inner-worldly orientation of Western European rationalism is taken for granted. The related pro-active attitudes and dynamic action patterns are the crucial precondition for immense practical achievements. Without abandoning the transcendental ends or ascetic meditation, Western rationalism shifted the problem-solving capacities towards the domination of nature and society. Therefore, Parsons had good reason to define the rationalist core of the value-normative system of modern societies as *instrumental activism*. (Parsons 1965: 172)

Instrumental activism is marked by a concentration on instrumental values and behavioral patterns which make up the core of modern industrialism. (McQuaid 2003) This is the ideology and practice of the Western type of *Weltbeherrschung* (domination of the world) as Max Weber understood it. (Weber 1988 [1919]: 1–16) After Weber it is taken for granted that, when *Weltbeherrschung* and not salvation was assumed to be the major goal, the selection, preparation and use of instruments of activity became the major orientation of action. Instrumental value-normative orientations are a vital moving force of modern production and economic exchange. They animate competitive political systems as well as the culture of entrepreneurship and responsibility. They dominate the life-world in advanced societies and make up the core of their 'civic religion'.

As successful as it may be, instrumental activism is the major threat to technological, economic, political, social and environmental sustainability. The global commercialization of social action is evoking disparities between the rich and poor, highly developed and underdeveloped regions, society and nature. These disparities undermine sustainability. The dilemma is profound: How could or should a "win-win" situation be accomplished, which would guarantee preconditions for the full-scale instrumental activism together with wide range of options for sustainable development in the sense of 'fair globalization'? (A Fair Globalization 2004)

Capitalizing on the value-normative orientation and practical arrangements of instrumental activism, the West was able to secure its domination over the rest of the world. That is why the moving forces and effects of instrumental activism are at the centre of processes which invigorate and yet plague modern civilization. Is instrumental activism really successful if viewed in the light of ultimate values? What are the costs of its successes? What are the costs of its failures? These and similar questions are usually asked in the context of the over-exploitation of natural resources and environmental degradation. The tensions brought about by the spread of instrumental activism cannot be limited to the interaction between science, technology and society in abusing nature. The risks rooted in the unequal distribution of wealth and income preserve their gravity. The steep distribution of power resources continues to shape present day civilization. This is the framework of social relations and processes in which the central question arises: What are the prospects for instrumental activism in the critical situation of global economic and political uncertainty?

The point should be clearly defined. Instrumental activism is by no means a *Western* value-normative and institutional phenomenon. It is part and parcel of everyday life all over the world and throughout history. What differentiates the historical case of Western European activism is the degree and manner of coordination of instrumental goals with ultimate ends. Western European culture pioneered their conceptual separation and the practical sophistication of inner-worldly oriented instrumental action. Thus Western European instrumental activism was able to motivate and to guide the conquest and domination of the rest of the world, which was up until then oriented towards the ultimate values of traditionalism, fatalism or escapism when handling practical problems. Consequently, the moving forces and effects of instrumental activism are at the very centre of the achievements and problems of modern civilization.

The discussions mostly concern the achievements and problems of industrialism as major incorporation of instrumental activism. Industrial organizations demonstrated an enormous capacity to motivate and maintain an accelerated learning process in solving increasingly complex problems. (Marx 1962 [1867]: 432f.) In the north-western part of the European continent, industrialism found its spiritual guidance in the religious ethics of Protestantism. Later on industrialism developed its own secularized ethics under the slogan "hard work and a rapid work pace at the work place". Industrialism is intrinsically bound both to *technology* and to *optimism* in assuming that all social and economic problems are basically technological problems and thus resolvable by the proper use of appropriate technology.

Whatever its ideological forms and institutional settings, industrialism is focused on the rules of action as well as on mechanisms of guidance and control which ensure the implementation of the rules. Its disciplining ethics has evolved into principles of formal organization based on the institutionalized practices of contractual rules. The market in all its modifications has become the major field for the implementation of these rules. Patterns of market competition and market contracts have expanded from economy to politics and culture. Geographically they have moved from Western Europe and later North America to other less advanced societies by re-modeling their social and economic organization. Thus the contractual philosophy and the market organization of industrialism have taken the lead worldwide. Both have been incorporated into technological and institutional infrastructures which have tremendously facilitated production and other activities.

This historical experience is inherently controversial. The spread of modern market mechanisms all over the world is undoubtedly a civilizational leap forward in social rationalization. That is why the evolutionary universal of the market economy cannot be suppressed in the long run without heavy losses in economic efficiency. But the "normal" functioning of market mechanisms and the re-establishment of market mechanisms is always full of tensions and conflicts. Social order based on market exchange always contains destructive elements of chaos and disorder.

Major constraints of market rationality are connected with the difficult balance between *autonomous* and *instrumental* ends. Profit-oriented market mechanisms are instrumental in principle. Profit may be presented as an autonomous end only in rather limited contexts, some of them with pathological elements. This is always a reason for theoretical and practical concerns since there can be no stable social order based on instrumental ends alone. The commercialization of social life brings about alienation and critically undermines the ultimate values of solidarity and social justice. This is fertile soil for many varieties of deviant behavior and crime.

These problems are closely related to the tension between *short-term* and *long-term* rationality in the functioning of market mechanisms. Market rationality is short-term as a rule since its guiding principle reads "maximum profit *now*". The mechanisms of postponed market gratification work only under rather specific cultural conditions and institutional arrangements. Thus, the compression of social time due to the search for profit *now* is the source of a wide range of social pathologies from mental disorders to criminal activities. Motivated by the search for maximum profit in the short-run, entrepreneurs tend to operate at the edge of what is morally and legally acceptable and what is a criminal or semi-criminal activity. This is not necessarily supporting societal integration and sustainability in the long run.

The historical success of industrialism is particularly questionable against the background of its impact on nature. The spread of instrumental activism permanently requires new rounds in the use of natural, social and human resources. Neither the limitless abuse of nature nor the over-exploitation of social and human resources could promise sustainable development. The studies on environmental imbalances, on social marginalization and degradation are helpful in illuminating the traps of instrumental activism. In the long run, it undermines social solidarity and societal integration.

Still another burning issue is the deepening technological and economic distance between the advanced societies and the rest of the world. The problem is crucial since the expanding demand for need satisfaction world-wide cannot follow the patterns of production and consumption which are already typical for the advanced societies. These societies make up some 20% of the world population but consume 80% of energy. This pattern of energy consumption cannot spread worldwide since it would bring about the total degradation of the Earth's ecosystem. This would threaten the very existence of global civilization by questioning the possibility for environmentally *sustainable development*. The disruption of environmental balances has the consequence of disrupting social reproduction. Basically, this was the style of thinking in the times of the famous Bruntland-Report to the United Nations. (Our Common Future 1987) Without neglecting the environmental issues, the discussions gradually shifted towards issues of economic, political and cultural development. Moreover, the debate is shifting from current concerns towards *visions* of what might be desirable to the *practical* steps needed to bring about the desirable states of affairs. The crucial point concerns the need for balance between instrumental activism and actions performed in the spirit of sustainability.

This is the most promising way to reduce the potential for a runaway socio-economic and environmental development. In positive terms, this would mean a 'win-win' situation for both instrumental activism *and* sustainable development.

These principles tend to develop into a 'secularized religion' which influences orientations, decisions and action all over the world by correcting the one-sidedness of instrumental activism. Laying stress on the unifying transcendence of the idea of sustainable development does not call instrumental activism into question. On the contrary, the very idea of sustainability *requires* instrumental activism in order to materialize the "concrete utopia" of sustainability. (Adam et al. 2005; Borghesi and Vercelli 2008)

The discussion on the spreading of instrumental activism in Eastern Europe will be hereafter focused on the following questions:

- What was or was not achieved in the market oriented reforms in Eastern Europe and why?
- What was or was not achieved in the management of the extremes of commercialization and why?
- What was or was not achieved in the preservation and further development of sustainability of Eastern European societies and why?

The global civilization has experienced an accelerated *universalization of value-normative systems* during the last decades. This trend has been mostly pushed forward by the global electronic media. However, the deeper causes of the process are rooted in the spread of universal technological standards, in the globalization of trade, in global political interdependencies as well as in the globalization of life styles. The same technological problems handled by basically the same technologies cannot but produce and support similar cultural patterns of problem management. The universal trend of individualization is bringing about strikingly similar cultural effects worldwide. However, together with homogenizing effects, the trend may also provoke counter-effects of value-normative particularism which may lead to various manifestations of the widely discussed "clash of civilizations". (Huntington 1996)

Behind the ideological overtones of discussions on coca-colonization and McDonaldization of the world lurks a simple fact. The organization of some companies in the service sector has proved to be economically quite effective. The explanation is that the fast-food work organization is replication of the fast-line organization of production along Fordist and Taylorist principles. These universalized organizational patterns bring about and sustain homogenizing cultural and behavioral effects among workers, managers and clients. (Meyer 2005) Cultural homogenization tends to develop its own inertia. 'Post-materialist' values mutually support and strengthen themselves. One might have good reasons to expect the further stabilization of these value-normative patterns worldwide after they have been already established among well-educated and well-to-do young people in the advanced industrial societies.

Cultural orientations permanently change. The present day uncertainty due to the global economic crisis seems shocking when contrasted with the optimistic mood of the 1950s and 1960s. At that time, no particular event could tangibly undermine the expectations for material improvement and cultural betterment on both sides of the Berlin Wall. It was widely assumed that big industrial projects, the concentration of resources and the achievement-oriented strength of political will would always bring about and sustain the desired breakthroughs in technology, economy and social development. Identifying these similarities in the ideologies of the opponents in the Cold War, analysts discovered the same strategies for mass industrial production, strong re-distributive state interventionism and cultural homogenization which were implemented on both sides of the confrontation line. It was this vision of the common path of modernization which guided Talcott Parsons' diagnosis of the achievements and prospects of the *one* system of modern societies (Parsons 1971). He expected their cultural convergence in a secular religion which was historically rooted in ascetic Protestantism but became deeply modified by modern consumerism.

The value-normative changes are deeply controversial. Together with the increasing cultural universalization which is resulting from technological and organizational homogenization, the world is becoming more and more diversified in value-normative terms. Economic well-being and increasing educational levels are bringing about specific individual and group aspirations. We may notice the proliferation of life-styles accompanying the global trend towards the individualization of preferences and actions. Efforts to assert group identities are nurturing the proliferation of 'tribal cultures'. They may substantially deviate from the global trend towards value-normative homogenization. Under the heading of diverging life-styles one might summarize rather specific cultural and behavioral patterns. Different religious identities are very much able to oppose the value-normative homogenization that comes together with global trends.

The universalization of value-normative systems worldwide has two pillars in the concepts of universal human rights and broadly understood sustainability. However, not even the best formulated legal norms are capable of controlling the problematic situations which arise from the social processes. Many open problems still concern the economic and social marginalization of vast social groups. In some cases the burning issues have strong ethnic connotations. They might lead the political and cultural life towards interethnic clashes. (Deutscher 2005) Inconsistency in the public mind together with the coexistence of mutually exclusive value-normative orientations may be other sources for tensions and conflicts. Thus, the elaboration on systematic analytical means for the diagnosis and prognosis of value-normative identities, preferences and inconsistencies seems to be in great demand.

The discussion on the universalization of value-normative systems in Eastern Europe will be hereafter focused on the following questions:

- What was or was not achieved in the strengthening of ideas and policies of universal human rights in Eastern Europe and why?
- What was or was not achieved in the spread and strengthening of the value-normative orientation of sustainability in Eastern European societies and why?

- What was or was not achieved in the management of the extremes of value-normative particularisms in Eastern Europe and why?

1.4 Controversial Social Trends and Cognitive Tasks

If scrutinized closely, each of the four global trends under discussion reveals a large and growing variety of manifestations. These tend to cause mutual reinforcement or hindrance. The same holds true for the four global trends themselves. Each of them provokes its own counteractive forces. The prospect is an immense increase in the complexities which individuals, groups, organizations and societies have to cope with in order to preserve their integrity while adapting to the stream of change. Competition is becoming fierce in all fields. Only the strengthening of moral and institutional regulations together with the retention of enough space for personal autonomy and creativity can prevent competition from getting out of control. The social sciences could offer promising insights into the causes and reasons for the new deficits in transparency and for the pathological developments. These insights are very much needed for the management of the ongoing processes.

The explanatory and predictive capacities of the social sciences could increase substantially, provided their theories would be consequently constructed by focusing on the sources, course and consequences of social development. In ontological terms, it always consists of mutual influences of micro-social and large-scale macro-social processes. Therefore, a combination of the research techniques which use the "telescope" of the macro-social and those which use the "microscope" of micro-social analyses is needed.

The implementation of this program for conceptual advancement in the study of socio-economic development presupposes interdisciplinary work, cross-paradigmatic interaction and a cross-fertilization of theoretical and empirical research. This is the only way to develop social sciences which have a clear cognitive value and are able to guide the practical management of social development.

A major reference point for the completion of this task consists of developing and applying concepts of social structures and functions. Today it is uncontested that a *range* of well-differentiated analytical concepts is needed to accumulate and systematically analyze empirical data, to make generalizations, to substantiate explanatory hypotheses and to carry out effective prognostic procedures. In addition, special attention paid to globalization has brought about a series of innovations in the study of social development. Globalization involves a large variety of actors and structures that are subject to change through different paths and logics. Against this background, the traditional teleological understanding of social development as a progressive improvement in social relations and processes gives way to a neutral definition. Nowadays it is pertinent to understand social development either as a substantial improvement in the adaptability of a social system to its environment *or* as a decline and dissolution of a system's structures and functions.

This re-definition of social development raises many questions concerning the linearity and progressive overtones of modernization theories. Another key issue concerns the concept of society. It is the major traditional point of reference in sociological theorizing and research on social development. More specifically, it is the concept of society understood as a nation-state. Recent studies on globalization, regionalization and 'glocalization' have revealed an extraordinary variety of micro- and macro-social causes of broader social processes as well as of their consequences. As a result, "methodological nationalism" is no more feasible. (Beck 2009) Trans-national and trans-cultural comparisons have become extremely important. The critique on "methodological nationalism" has good reasons, but contemporary social reality is still very much structured along the lines of nation states. Last but not least, as a result of the debates on the state and perception of the global environment, the concept of sustainable development has come into intellectual fashion. Currently, it is gaining richer and richer cognitive content and social relevance.

Could sociology successfully cope with the tremendous challenges of this rapid social and intellectual development? The answer should refer to the outcomes of the analysis of convergence and divergence in the controversial contemporary social development. The success and failure of Eastern European adaptations to global trends offer the perfect subject matter for carrying out this test on disciplinary performance. So far, the diverse and profound changes in Eastern Europe have one common denominator. This is the transfer of institutional patterns which have already proved their efficiency in managing industrialized societies. (Wiesenthal 1996) This transfer concerns value-normative orientations and institutional structures which embody major trends in the development of modern societies.

Is this development of Eastern Europe really unique? Undoubtedly, the experience of the regional transformation is as unique as every event in history is. As seen from a broader historical and conceptual perspective, the societal transformations in the region are just a special case of the worldwide change of everyday life and deep social structures. The overall trend of strengthening the individual initiative and responsibility cuts across social systems, functions and processes. Together with the increase of social complexity, social dynamics has put well-established patterns of hierarchic government on trial. The high complexity of processes brought about by numerous influential actors with diverging interests has come to the forefront. Efforts to cope with the growing social complexity by means of polyarchic frameworks involve state institutions and business organizations, political parties and voluntary associations, as well as social movements and groups. Their interplay fosters social change which questions established structures and roles. The crucial tasks now are the improvement of knowledge on social dynamics together with the improvement of the institutional mechanisms of its governance. (Bornschier 2008: 144f.) All of these processes offer abundant causes, reasons and consequences which might be well described and explained by the concept of risk.

Risk is hereafter understood as *the probability of dysfunctional effects of processes on social systems.* The stress on the risk concept does not imply any understanding of present-day societies as being especially prone to risks, as *risk societies per se.* Under circumstances such as natural calamities (volcano eruptions, floods or epidemics) or in cases of social crises such as wars or riots, societies throughout human history have always been "risk societies". The real point is that modern secularized, individualistic and achievement-oriented societies have developed a specific *culture of risk.* This lays the stress on the scientifically based *perception* and *assessment* of risk factors as well as on rationalized *risk management.* This culture of risk and its institutional frameworks are dominated by *calculations of risk factors* and by *accountability for risks.* The context of calculations and accountability is the *all-pervading competition* which is taking place under conditions of permanent *uncertainty and change.*

In order to cope with the new situation, advanced democratic societies have developed and are maintaining a tight safety net for the protection of individuals and groups who fail to cope with the competition. Protection from basic risks like illness, poverty or unemployment is increasingly regarded as a matter of universal human rights. The safety net includes state-supported welfare and private insurance. Both schemes socialize risk and thus strengthen social integration. However, they are also factors which diminish the propensity for risk-taking. Therefore, a special problem in democratic society is the balance (or imbalance) of the propensity for risk-taking and the lack of readiness to take risks. The *practical* problem is how to balance the need for the institutional management of risk with the preservation of enough space for autonomous decision and risk-taking on the part of individuals and groups. Stability and innovation in society depend on the way in which this balance is established and maintained.

As seen from this point of view, national transformations are major risk factors themselves. They always bring about uncertainty and instability. Marketization and democratization confront individuals and groups with the responsibility of making decisions and acting under permanent uncertainty. The paternalistic props of the traditionalist and authoritarian social and economic organization belong to the past. Moreover, there are good reasons to consider the *globalization of risk* (Beck 2007), since uncertainty and instability of current national transformations in Eastern Europe are brought about by global trends. Thus, there are important cognitive reasons for the special attention to the relationships between risk and national transformations. The concept of risk allows for the transparent coverage of major dimensions of change which shapes our present day and future social reality.

Chapter 2
Upgrading the Rationality of Organizations *and* Organizational Pathologies[1]

The adaptation of Eastern European societies to the ongoing globalization and European integration will continue. However, the crucial changes in the economy, politics and culture are already over. The immense pressure of accelerated processes requiring immediate cognitive and practical reactions no longer exists. Social scientists have thus reached the historical distance needed for a sober assessment of the profound societal transformations. The time has come to elaborate on this rich experience by focusing on its relevance to major theoretical debates and to broadly relevant practical issues. What implications might this experience have, for instance, for the present day assessment of the famous debates on positivism in German sociology? The debates were waged between representatives of the holistic critical theory of the Frankfurt school and the followers of the idea of piecemeal social engineering advocated by Karl Popper's critical rationalism during the 1960s. (Adorno et al. 1976 [1969]) The former insisted on the need for simultaneous changes of all action spheres of a society in order to achieve real advances in societal development. The latter criticized the visions of critical theory from a liberal point of view. According to the liberal Popperians, only well calculated partial improvements *in* action spheres could be rationally designed and managed. Only these rationally controlled changes might be legitimate from a social-technological *and* humanistic point of view.

Keeping in mind the recent Eastern European controversies between advocates of the "big bang shock therapy" and gradualism in managing societal transformations, who was right and who wrong in the German theoretical and ideological debate? Why? What could the new regional experience contribute to the better understanding and management of social development? (Kaelble and Schmid 2004) Can the Western European and North American social scientists and practitioners learn from the Eastern European experiments in this respect? The serious and systematic discussions on these complex issues are still ahead. Nevertheless, it is already clear that the societal transformations in Eastern Europe helped to develop knowledge of a broad theoretical relevance. There are manifold reasons for this spill-over effect. *First*, the Eastern European societal transformations occurred at a time when crucial political barriers on the way of

---

1 Some preliminary ideas of this Chapter were presented at a Conference held in Warsaw and will be published in a volume "New Europe: Growth to Limits" edited by Sven Eliaeson and Nadezhda Georgieva.

globalization of social relations and processes were removed. The regional change under scrutiny is the first in history to be directly influenced by full-fledged globalization. *Second*, this new quality of regional and worldwide processes was recognized in a timely manner by social scientists and practitioners alike. It is not by chance that the Eastern European transformations coincided during the nineties with the explosion of scientific and political debates on the content, the directions and manifestations of globalization. *Third*, the changes in the Eastern European region were influenced by the strategic visions and practical activity of powerful global organizations like the World Bank and the International Monetary Fund. These organizations relied on the huge intellectual capacities of their think tanks as well as on tremendous financial and political resources. *Fourth*, the processes in the eastern part of the European continent after 1989 became the most intriguing case of interaction between trends of globalization and trends of regional integration in the framework of the European Union. This latter process has global relevance, since the European Union is the most advanced supranational integration scheme in the world so far.

Thus, the achievements and failures of transformations in Eastern Europe became a test case for the availability, applicability and efficiency of conceptual frameworks and organizational mechanisms for managing profound societal changes.

2.1 Controversies on Upgrading Organizational Rationality

The profound changes were expected to bring about the rationalization of structures and functions of social organizations. This expectation was well rooted in the peculiarities of modern social life. It might have a wide range of connotations, one of which might be embraced without hesitation. This is the recognition of the fact that structures and processes in modern society are dominated by formal organizations. Organizations in the sense of goal oriented status-role complexes accompany, rule, support, limit or hinder individual and collective action in all walks of modern life. Therefore, a change in organizational frameworks is part and parcel of modernization in the form of all-embracing societal transformations. (Burnes 2009) One may even go a step further by assuming that *the changing rationality of organizations is at the very core of the transformations in Eastern Europe.*

This assumption immediately calls to mind Max Weber's vision of rationalization, which inspired generations of social scientists. The reference might be both helpful and misleading. It might be helpful, since Weber undoubtedly conceived of the civilizational breakthrough of capitalism in Western Europe first and foremost as a case of the upgrading of the rationality of economic organizations. The emerging capitalist enterprises introduced the rational assessment and control at all stages of production and distribution. Rational bookkeeping became the instrument of this historical innovation. The bureaucratic rationalization of state institutions and the emergence of competitive party politics became the political hallmarks of the innovations in the organization of economic structures and processes. Weber understood the profound changes in the economic and political organization of the Western European societies as part and parcel of a wider historical process. This included the move towards rational theological and legal reasoning, experimental proof in science, the dominance of the ethic of responsibility in all walks of social life and even the rationalization of architecture and music.

The overwhelming scientific relevance of this multidimensional approach to social processes notwithstanding, Weber's view on rationalization may be misleading. He used the concept of rationalization as a mere construct in his analysis of a specific historical situation in the Western European core of modernity. (Weber 1988 [1920]) The development of a generalized theory of rationalization was not his intention. He deemed this type of theory unattainable in sociology and related disciplines. Any effort to reconstruct and creatively use "The Weberian theory of rationalization" (Ritzer 2005) immediately provokes reservations and critical reactions. Nevertheless, there is hardly any doubt that Weberian ideas could be helpful in the attempts to put a diagnosis of trends in contemporary societies. This applies mostly to improving the knowledge base of organizational processes in order to optimize their implementation and output. George Ritzer's attempt at putting this kind of diagnosis by using indicators of calculability, predictability, control and efficiency is well rooted in this tradition. However, the label of the McDonaldization of the modern social world is merely attractive wording. The real innovators who introduced ideas and practices of calculability, predictability, control and efficiency in modern organizations carried out their path breaking work long before the McDonald's fast food restaurants appeared. The innovations were the Fordist organization of fast line production and the Taylorist scientific organization of work.

Elaborating on Max Weber's vision of social and cultural rationalization in the context of the Western European modernization, Talcott Parsons moved in a different methodological direction. He generalized the idea of rationalization in order to identify universal mechanisms of upgrading the adaptive capacity of social systems to their internal and external environments. (Parsons 1971: 11) In fact, present day social reality is marked by the omnipresent and decisive influence of organizational systems. They base their activities on the precise definitions of goals and procedures and on the dynamic control of goal implementation. Organizations learn from their own experience and adapt to changing environments by upgrading their knowledge base and the efficiency of their structures and functions patterns. Organizations which turn out to be unable to learn and to upgrade their rationality are doomed to vanish.

The concept of organizational learning and selection makes it possible to interpret the transformation processes in Eastern Europe in the sense of a broadly understood upgrading of organizational rationality. This option was considered at the very beginning of the Eastern European transformations. The objective of the debates was to establish the relation between polar types of rationality and the historical circumstances. The next step was the effort to develop explanatory schemes referring to the ongoing rationalization. The debate was intellectually intriguing and supportive to the practical efforts to rationally manage the changes in the region. (Genov 1991) The debate was also instrumental in identifying illusions concerning the state-socialist type of social organization and the imagined fast and smooth turn to a higher level of rationality in the organization of action spheres and actions. The debate considered scenarios according to which the re-organization of social life from collectivist towards individualist institutional arrangements might be accompanied by new organizational pathologies.

In this way, the concept of the upgrading of organizational rationality was among the few which made it possible to explain the accelerated and simultaneous changes. The concept allowed for a consistent analysis of the changing content, quality and relationships between collective and individual rationality, between the rationality of ultimate ends and instrumental rationality, between short-term and long-term rationality of action. In the strongly politicized environment of that time, over-simplified conceptual schemes like "a transition to democracy and a market economy" were more attractive for politicians, for the public at large and even for social scientists. In contrast, the concept of the upgrading the rationality of organizations proved helpful in the assessment of the impossibility to quickly restore the distorted balance between short-term and long-term rationality as well as between collective and individual rationality. It became possible to argue that the re-establishment of the above balance could not come about without organizational pathologies and without substantial social costs. Upgrading the rationality of organizations was included in broader conceptual schemes synthesizing ideas about global trends and visions of societal transformation as adaptations to these global trends. (Genov 1999) Following this line of conceptualization and analysis, the new task was to study variation, selection and stabilization of patterns of the upgrading of organizational rationality in particular action spheres. Another complimentary field of study concerns the mutual enforcement or hindrance of these processes. Following these tracks the analysis should check previous assumptions and facilitate conclusions which better correspond to the rapidly changing social reality.

Thus it became possible to revise the optimistic expectations at the beginning of the Eastern European reform processes that it could be fast and easy to correct the over-stretch of long-term and collectivist rationality in the authoritarian state socialism (Area 2, ellipse) and move by fast reforms of the organizational arrangements (see arrow) towards a real balance between long-term and short-term, individual and collective rationality (Area 1, circle). This organizational change was regarded as a pre-condition for the future sustainable economic, political, cultural and social development of Eastern European societies.

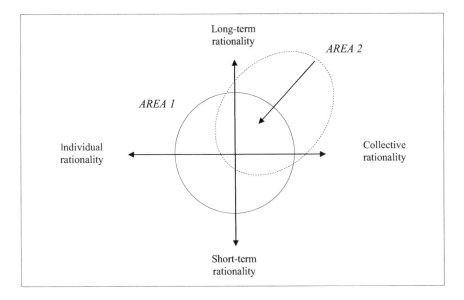

**Figure 2.1 Desirable upgrading of organizational rationality at the
beginning of the reforms in Eastern Europe**

Referring to other profound societal changes in history one could hypothesize that
the reforms of institutional arrangements might bring about new and probably
substantial imbalances in the organizational frameworks. Given this premise, one
could speculate that the expected triumph of individual rationality might come
about, at least temporarily, at the expense of collective rationality. The strengthening
of individual economic initiative could possibly be realized by undermining the
common good needed for the integration of society. The expected turn towards the
commercialization of social relations could bring about an excessive predominance
of short-term over long-term rationality, since markets are basically oriented
towards short-term achievements. The experts expected a turn towards short-term
rationality in political life as well. They knew the orientation of political decisions
and actions in established democracies on the short-term election cycle. Thus,
the realistic but rarely expressed assessment of the expected rationalization was
that it would bring about needed adjustments together with new distortions in the
balance between parameters of rationality.

The diagnosis of the situation and the prognostication of difficulties in the
course of the upgrading of organizational rationality turned out to be basically
correct. In times of profound changes the pendulum of ideological and political
preferences usually moves from one extreme to another. Some new distortions of
organizational rationality were the result of false or biased decisions. Consequently,
the achievements and failures in upgrading the rationality of organizations vary

considerably from country to country. The indications of divergences are obvious in the trajectories of the GDP development in Eastern Europe:[2]

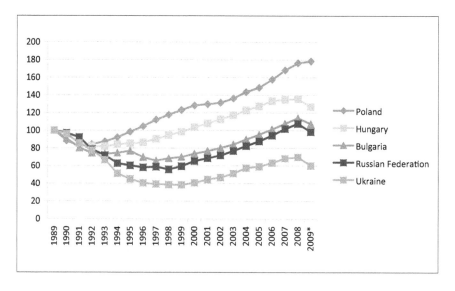

**Figure 2.2 GDP per capita growth of selected Eastern European countries
          1989–2009 (in %, 1989 = 100)**

The variations in GDP growth indicated above are impressive. In some of the national cases, the drop in the GDP was much deeper and lasted longer than was the case in the countries most affected by the Great Depression of 1929–1933. Explanations of this have to do with local specifics of structural continuities and discontinuities or with the quality of decision making and implementation of decisions at the local (national) level. Still another factor contributing to the diversity of local processes is the geo-strategic situation of a given country and the impact of the changing geo-strategic contexts on local processes. In addition, the variety is determined by the very complexity of the transformation processes understood as passive and active adaptations to dynamic global trends. Their effects vary considerably from country to country. It is alarming to notice that countries like Georgia, Moldova and Ukraine could not reach the level of GDP that they had before the start of the profound changes 20 years later. In most cases, this substantial delay can be best explained by the quality of the management of the transformations.

---

2   Data for years before 2004 stem from (UNECE 2005: 117, 128). Data for 2004 and further from the (EBRD 2009b) statistics. Data for 2009 are projections.

Another striking indicator for the long-term difficulties in the Eastern European societal transformations is the level of satisfaction with democracy as it functions in the national institutional framework. Even in Poland, which has achieved the most robust GDP growth since 1989, the level of satisfaction with the functioning of democracy in the country has been persistently low during the entire transformation period. (Opinie o funkcjonowaniu demokracji 2009:7):

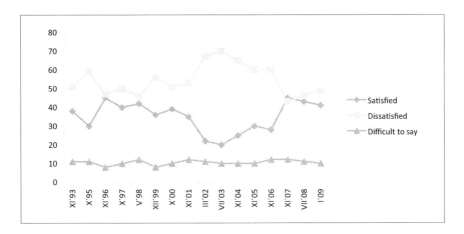

Figure 2.3 Level of satisfaction/dissatisfaction with the functioning of democracy in Poland (in %)

The difficulties in the development of the economy and politics of Eastern European societies are mostly due to the fact that the transformations in the region consisted to a large extent of adaptations to global trends and particularly to the global trend of the upgrading of organizational rationality. A wide range of tasks had to be managed. Hypothetically, decisions for handling these tasks could follow three major patterns: *First*, one option was the *adaptation of the domestic organizational structures* to the new domestic and global environment. *Second*, another option was the *transfer of organizational structures and experience* from abroad and their adaptation to the local conditions. *Third*, yet another option was the mobilization of domestic and international experience in order to implement *authentic innovations*.

Numerous studies on modernization show that the first pattern is *defensive* and implies a losing strategy of adaptation to international competition. The second pattern is *reproductive*. It also implies a losing strategy in the long run. What about the third and most promising pattern of active and creative adaptation to the global requirements for the upgrading of organizational rationality? This is the fundamental question that will guide the following analyses. In advance it may be said that the experience of two decades of Eastern European transformations seems to support a skeptical answer to this question. The lack of local resources and the high speed of the changes put objective limits on the capacity of local and international actors to manage the processes in an innovative way. Reforms were most often intentionally implemented as a reproduction of well known patterns in order "not to make mistakes". As a result, *authentic organizational innovations are rarities in Eastern Europe*. One might even ask if there are any genuine organizational innovations characterizing the profound societal transformations in the region or resulting from them.

If the above assumptions are well founded, then the crucial issue at stake is the long-term efficiency of the Eastern European adaptation to the requirements of the global rationalization of organizations. If this adaptation was basically of defensive and reproductive type, one may assume that the Eastern European societies will face substantial difficulties in their search for creative adaptations further on. Is the diagnosis adequate? Is the prognostication correct? There is no other way to properly answer these questions than by casting a glance at the systemic conditions at the start of the accelerated upgrading of organizational rationality in Eastern Europe. The best option for starting this analysis is to focus on the relationships between economy and politics. The domination of politics over economy was the core problem of state socialist societies. The efforts to free the economy from political over-regulation made up the very core of the push in the modernization of Eastern European societies.

2.2 Differentiation of Economy and Politics

The lack of organizational efficiency is widely identified as the major factor which determined the systemic collapse of state socialism. However, opinions concerning the organizational achievements and failures in Eastern Europe during the decades after the Second World War vary widely in the region. This is not exclusively due to political bias. Each individual country had specific experience in this period. The territory of the present day Czech Republic was already well industrialized before the war. The forced industrialization after 1945 was in many ways a repetition of previous achievements. In countries like Slovakia the industrialization was accomplished under state socialism. The period was marked there by technological progress and the development of the rationalized organization of industrialized society.

Whatever the diverging assessments of the post-war processes in Eastern Europe may be, there is at least one point of agreement: the major driving force of societal development in the region after the Second World War was the state. More precisely, it was the state whose institutions were merged with the institutions of the ruling party. Using the resources of nationalized productive assets, the state determined the structural parameters of technological and economic modernization by considering geo-strategic and domestic conditions. Due to the authoritarian fusion of the ruling party and the state, the political sphere was limited to the activities of the party-state. The state dominated the official culture. Mediators like autonomous market structures, independent trade unions and organizations of civil society were underdeveloped, suppressed or non-existent. The state had a tremendous capacity to influence everything and everybody. The end result of this political domination of society was an organizational failure.

The large foreign indebtedness accumulated during the eighties was a particularly convincing evidence of the failure. The crucial factor leading to this high level of foreign debt was the variety of administrative restrictions. These were imposed by the party-state on all kinds of creative deviations from the rules and thus undermined the innovations in the economy, politics and culture. However, this was the picture before the collapse of the state socialism. The over-concentration of resources and decision-making contributed significantly to the rapid industrialization and urbanization in Eastern Europe immediately after the Second World War. Thereafter decentralization of government, economic decision-making and cultural life became urgently needed in the region already in the sixties. The functional requirement for decentralization came from the growing complexity of Eastern European societies themselves.

Some strategic changes could have been introduced quickly, smoothly and with relatively low social costs at that time, since the Eastern European state institutions were still intact and functioning. The international situation was conducive for reforms. The United States was preoccupied with the Vietnam War. Left-wing political movements and organizations were strong in many advanced and developing countries. Confused by the turbulences of the Prague Spring and by other events of 1968, the leaderships of Eastern European societies missed the historical moment to move forward to the next step in the rationalization of organizational structures. The major task which remained not accomplished was the step-by-step differentiation of the state from the economy and culture.

In a variety of ways and to a greater or lesser degree of success, authoritarian governments in South Korea, Brazil and China managed this transition. But the core of Eastern European regional political power was not prepared to do this in the sixties and seventies. The attempts to break the patterns of political over-centralization during the *perestroika* period in the eighties came too late. The international environment was already unfavorable. It was obvious that Eastern European societies were losing the global competition in upgrading their organizational rationality. The technological gap between Eastern Europe and the West was deepening due to the incapacity of the Eastern European organizational systems to accelerate technological innovations. The lack of institutionalized competition in all action spheres precluded organizational innovations. The pathology of the administrative "soft budgets" of the economic enterprises used to undermine the efficiency of the national economies in the region. (Kornai 1992)

Thus, the rationalization of organizational structures and processes in Eastern European societies after the Second World War was marked by two discontinuities and by two radically new departures. Immediately after the war, a de-differentiation of action spheres took place as a result of the abolishment of the evolutionary universals of the market economy and the establishment of central planning. This was a radical societal transformation guided by state-socialist centralist organizational principles. Given these developments, the radical changes after 1989 focused firstly on the reforms of political institutions in order to prepare for the separation of the economy and politics. This differentiation of action spheres made up the core of the societal transformations all over Eastern Europe during the nineties.

There were no dramatic conflicts during the critical period of the collapse of the Soviet Union. In this sense, there are reasons to praise achievements in the establishment and functioning of markets free from excessive state regulation. (Åslund 2007: Chapters 2, 4 and 5) Taking a more realistic approach one has to acknowledge that instead of a well thought through and efficiently guided reduction of the scope and intensity of the political over-integration of Eastern European societies, in numerous cases spontaneous and destructive trends took the lead. The most visible part of this tendency was the state institutions' hasty and badly prepared desertion of their economic, cultural and social responsibilities. (Zaslavskaya 2003: 189–191) These responsibilities had to be taken for granted since they belong to state priorities in all countries with long and strong traditions of market economy and democratic politics. In a striking deviation from this tradition, the bulk of the problems facing Eastern European societies was and in some cases still is due to a paradoxical development. At least temporarily, the necessary dissolution of the state domination of society developed into the dissolution of the integration of society by the state. The end of the suppression of the evolutionary universal of the market brought about the suppression of another evolutionary universal, namely the organizational capacities of the modern state. The result was organizational chaos. In some cases it had creative capacities. In many other cases the organizational chaos had destructive effects. (Albert 1995)

There is one more paradox involved in the differentiation of politics from other action spheres in the Eastern European societal transformations. Under the existing conditions, there was no other agency able to rationally manage the withdrawal of the state from its dominant position than the state itself. At the end of the eighties and the beginning of the nineties some influential visions used to insist on the point that civil society organizations or movements could or should take the lead and become the major organizing factor in the expected transformation. Nothing like that happened. To the contrary, social movements and voluntary organizations – as far as they existed and were active in the Eastern European region – gradually lost appeal during the nineties. This experience strengthens the argument concerning the exclusive responsibility of the state in governing the transformation process. Due to numerous misunderstandings and a lack of coordination, the process often brought about degradation instead of the upgrading of organizational rationality in Eastern Europe.

The turning point in this direction was the liberalization of prices and trade at the beginning of the nineties. Following the ideology of neo-liberalism the economic reforms in Eastern Europe were guided by the assumption that market forces alone *would balance themselves in a spontaneous and efficient manner*. It was further assumed that market integration itself would become the stable foundation for the new integration of the economy, politics and culture. The experience of Keynesianism in Western Europe and in North America was forgotten. The post-World War II experiences in Eastern Europe were too easily declared irrelevant.

At the same time, under the influence of domestic and international factors, the organizational erosion of the state and its legitimacy took radical forms in a number of Eastern European countries. The wars in Bosnia, Moldova and Georgia, the riots in Albania in 1997 and in Macedonia in 2001 offer sobering examples of 'failed states' – at least temporarily. Under these circumstances, the motivation of state officials to design and implement developmental strategies faded. Frequent governmental changes caused the opportunistic narrowing of the scope of their decisions and actions to a level that did not allow any efficient management of long-term economic and social processes. However, it was very much needed because of the critical level of inherited international debt by Eastern European countries, the loss of major markets after the hasty dissolution of the Council for Mutual Economic Assistance (CMEA) in 1991 and the rise of unemployment and poverty. Therefore, state institutions had to take the lead in managing societal transformations. This is the only option for an organized and civilized change of the type of social order of contemporary societies. The issue was the necessity that the post-socialist states transform their nature by themselves.

This constructive option was gradually recognized by the local political forces as well as by international financial institutions. Due to the experience accumulated in Eastern Europe, neo-liberalism lost its dominating influence. New visions about the role of the state in democratic societies came to the forefront of national and international debates. (World Development Report 2007) The differentiation of economy and politics was carried out in the region together with efforts to reach efficient societal re-integration also by using the capacities of state institutions. Both processes invite careful examination. It shows that the major problems concerned the differentiations within politics and economy.

Thus, together with various structural and functional differentiations, other mechanisms for upgrading organizational rationality bring about new forms and a new quality of social integration. It is particularly needed in order to prevent the differentiation from moving into the extremes of social disintegration. This destructive development was possible everywhere in Eastern Europe in the course of the transfer of the means of production from public to private hands. At the end of the eighties, the societies in the region were marked by a historically unique high level of socialization of the means of production. The socialist states owned monopolies which massively precluded personal initiative and responsibility as the motor of economic development. The elimination of individual rationality based on economic interests and competition of individuals was the key factor determining the comparatively slow technological and economic development of Eastern European societies.

Therefore, the reasons for the then imminent rationalization of property relations seemed to be rather clear. The privatization of the means of production had to decentralize the economy and to open up opportunities for the development of economic competition. The intended effect of this development was to be the strengthening of the responsibility of economic actors. The 'soft budget' policy concerning economic actors was to be abolished. The socialist state used to intervene in order to support or save badly performing economic actors at the expense of those who were performing well. This type of redistributive economic policy used to facilitate collective irresponsibility. The introduction of market-based 'hard budgets' for economic actors was expected to bring about financial discipline for the improvement of the interest- and competition-driven performance of economic actors. The accelerated technological modernization of Eastern European societies was to be the major side effect from the change in property relations. In this way, the inclusion of Eastern Europe into the global division of labor and into the global competition had to be implemented on sound economic and legal grounds and was to lead to an increase of productivity, macroeconomic growth and an improvement of the standard of living and quality of life of the population. Small and medium size private enterprises were mostly expected to contribute to this result.

The situation was only seemingly transparent and the task only seemed to be clearly defined. Contrary to widespread views, property relations were rather complex under state socialism. The major part of the state ownership consisted of large industrial enterprises. However, Eastern European societies also had large cooperative ownership, particularly in agriculture and in the service sector. Under state socialism the legal status of cooperative property was very similar to the status of the state property. But the legal specifics had important consequences for the privatization procedures. In addition, municipalities also owned property. This was legally defined in a different way than state property. This legal difference became significant when the privatization appeared on the political agenda.

The picture of property relations in the region was even more complex. After unsuccessful attempts to carry out the collectivization of agricultural land and productive agricultural infrastructure, these assets had remained to a large extent private property in Poland and in Yugoslavia. To the greatest extent in Hungary, but also in Poland, Yugoslavia and Bulgaria, private ownership of the means of production of handicraft and in the service sector was also allowed. In the second half of the eighties, economic reforms in Hungary advanced to the point that small private industrial enterprises also appeared in the country. The famous cooperatives in the Soviet Union legalized the private property of the means of production in the last years of *perestroika*.

This complexity of property relations in Eastern Europe made it possible for economic and political actors to intervene in various ways into decisions concerning the privatization of public property. The actors often exerted influence and pursued their interests at the edge of what is legally possible or in direct contradiction to legal regulations. This was unavoidable in a historical context in which legal regulations concerning private property rights were rather underdeveloped and when there were unique opportunities to get rich quickly. The conditions were conducive to illegal activities since the Eastern European states and their control mechanisms were weakened. Even more important were factors connected to political confrontation and the institutional instability caused by rapid political change. There is abundant evidence that some state institutions and particularly the control mechanisms of post-socialist states were intentionally weakened in order to carry out privatization of public property in favor of particular groups.

The rational decision to get involved in corrupt policies concerning privatization was easy, since the risk of punishment had declined substantially. The typical procedure in this respect was the establishment of private firms, which supplied the state enterprises with energy, raw materials and components at artificially high prices. In addition, private firms took the initiative for the market distribution of the products of state owned enterprises by buying the products cheaply and selling them at a much higher price in national or international markets. As a rule, both schemes for the economic squeezing of state enterprises were established with the knowledge and usually with the active participation of the enterprise management. This was a highly efficient mechanism for privatizing the profit of state enterprises and for socializing the losses. The mechanism functioned efficiently since in most Eastern European societies poorly performing state enterprises continued to receive state subsidies for some time, thus reproducing the tradition of 'soft budgets'. In addition, there was the incentive that the financially squeezed state enterprises could be privatized at a low price by the managers or by political, economic or criminal groups related to them.[3]

Thus, the economic situation of artificially weakened enterprises, but also of many economically sound enterprises caused a strategic dilemma: Should the state enterprises first be restructured and stabilized and then privatized? Or, should they be immediately privatized, leaving the task of restructuring and stabilization to the new private owners? There could be no universal answer valid for hundreds of thousands of specific situations. In Poland alone, the dilemma had to be resolved with a view to the fate of about 8400 big enterprises. Some of them had to be closed because they could neither be efficiently restructured nor privatized. But many Polish industrial enterprises were at least potentially profitable and could survive a well designed and implemented stabilization and privatization.

Another factor making the privatization process in Eastern Europe a risky endeavor was the international economic situation at the end of the eighties and the beginning of the nineties. The international financial conditions were generally not conducive to large scale investments since the world economy was experiencing a slight depression at exactly this time. However, even in best times the international property market would not have the absorption capacity for favorable terms of trade

---

3   There is a large body of literature on the specifics of the Eastern European privatizations (Iatridis and Hopps 1998; Kalyuzhnova and Andreff 2003; Åslund 2007; Eckert 2008; Lieberman and Kopf 2008). The topic of the privatization of agricultural property is not dealt with here because of the variety of privatization schemes.

given the unusually large supply of productive assets offered up for privatization in Eastern Europe. The societies in the region themselves made this unfavorable international market situation even more unfavorable. They acted independently and in fierce competition, thus eroding the basis for favorable terms of trade in the biggest 'sale' in human history.

This 'sale' was conditioned by peculiar parameters. The key issue in sales is the price. Given the circumstances, the price of enterprises offered for privatization was calculated by referring to a number of variables that could not be clearly determined. It was extremely difficult to establish the value of the investments made into productive assets in Eastern Europe. The difficulty was conditioned by the specifics of industrialization in the region. Investments were made there on the basis of political decisions and not on the basis of precise market calculations. The price of land used for the purposes of industrial construction was not calculated in the value of the enterprise as a rule. Investments in infrastructure that supported the construction and functioning of productive assets were typically not calculated either. The price of the labor force used for the construction could not be known since labor had no clearly defined market value under the conditions of the very imperfect state socialist labor markets. Thus, the range of the announced or eventually negotiated price of the property 'on sale' could vary immensely due to intentional or unintentional miscalculations.

All of these conditions and considerations had to be taken into account in the design and implementation of strategies of privatization. To start with, it seemed to be most natural and just to consider returning private property that was socialized (transferred into state or communal property) back to the previous owners by applying the procedure of *restitution*. However, only in rare cases had the socialized property remained in the same shape after decades of large scale socialist modernization. The ensuing task was tremendous: How could the real value of the investments made by the socialist state in modernization be calculated if a given enterprise had to be returned to the previous private owner? To whom had the property be returned indeed? The former owners were usually not alive after forty years of state socialist management of their property. The heirs were often abroad or not known. If known, they were typically neither competent nor willing to manage the productive property. As a rule, they were only interested in seeking rent. This interest could be satisfied by offering the heirs compensation in terms of shares as it very often happened. The justice of this decision could not be substantiated since shares had very different real value from country to country and even from year to year in one country during the transformation period. Due to all these circumstances, the restitution of property was a rather difficult and protracted legal and institutional process. It hardly satisfied anybody in terms of economic and social efficiency as well as in terms of legal and moral justice. To the contrary, the restitution provoked massive protests on the part of the people who had contributed to the modernization of the socialized enterprises but were not compensated for their contribution in any way whatsoever.

At the beginning of the privatization it seemed that the *distribution of shares of public property* (mostly state industrial property) to the population at large would be the fastest and just approach to the privatization of state-owned productive assets. Countries ranging from Russia to Poland, the Czech Republic to Bulgaria instigated privatization via the distribution of shares. The procedure was usually called mass or voucher privatization. This turned out to be a quick method of privatization since the resulting transformation of state enterprises into share holdings and the selling of shares usually progressed smoothly. However, in terms of economic efficiency, the privatization by means of voucher distribution was questionable. No 'fresh money' came to the national economy or to the enterprises. The managers of the new corporations were usually unable to attract investments under the conditions of recession in the national economies and difficult international investment markets. Since the wide distribution of shares meant a wide dispersion of decision-making competences, the companies had organizational difficulties in mobilizing their internal resources to carry out the necessary restructuring. Due to these difficulties and the domestic economic recession they often failed to pay back the loans obtained from domestic or foreign banks. (Ellerman 1998)

Another strategy, which also seemed just in legal and moral terms, was the insider privatization. It was often called *workers-and-managers privatization*. Like mass privatization, this method could not provide privatized enterprises with fresh investments, since the accumulation of capital was more than modest in Eastern Europe at the beginning of the nineties. The savings of the population were annihilated by the high inflation following the liberalization of markets. However, depending on the local legal, economic and political situation, this type of privatization could distribute the property in shares to the persons employed in the enterprise and to pensioners previously employed there. In addition, if properly carried out, insider privatization could strengthen corporate identity and thus the economic efficiency of the enterprises. The critical point was that the profitable enterprises were constructed and equipped by investments from the state budget. Thus, the workers and managers of such enterprises were put in a privileged position at the expense of the tax payers in general since the rest of society that financed the construction and equipment of the enterprises remained without any reimbursement. Insider privatization could be also easily abused. In Russia and the Ukraine, it was the mechanism for the distribution of productive assets among managers, politicians, financial groups and mafia structures. (Kryshtanovskaya 2004; Steiner and Tamas 2005; Friebel and Panova 2007)

The best economic results could be expected by the *bidding strategy for the privatization* of productive assets. First of all, selling the enterprises to domestic or foreign investors would imply income for the Eastern European state budgets suffering perennial budget deficits. In most cases, the selling contract also implied fresh investments for the modernization of the enterprises. However, due to complicated ownership issues and bureaucratic obstacles the bidding strategy of privatization could often be implemented with substantial delays. Moreover, the experience of Eastern European privatization shows that only a rather small portion of the real value of the privatized assets was actually paid to state budgets. There were thousands of purchases at a price far below the real value of the privatized assets. Enterprises were intentionally bought to be robbed and then abandoned. Only in very few cases the income from bidding procedures benefited the millions of tax payers who had paid for the construction of the productive assets or the employees in profitable enterprises.

The considerations and actions outlined in this manner basically apply to the large scale privatization of industrial property regulated by the privatization laws. There were usually laws on the "small" privatization of communal handicraft and service enterprises. Most of them were already privatized in a 'spontaneous' way on the basis of arrangements between managers, employees, former owners, municipality authorities and local political forces. The privatization laws were revised many times in order to adapt to the large variety of specific cases. Nevertheless, it is possible in retrospect to identify national strategies and practices of the large scale privatization, which deviated substantially from country to country.

In Hungary, the privatization of industrial property had to be carried out under the pressure of a large foreign debt accumulated during the eighties. Therefore, the strategy of privatization was focused on selling property. The productive assets were mostly sold to foreign investors. The income had to cover the repayment of foreign debt and thus enable the credible integration of the Hungarian economy into the international financial system. In 1995 the cash privatization reached its peak with revenues of 438 billion Hungarian Forints. Some 411 billion was paid in foreign currency exchange. (Galgóczi 2001: 48) There was one more consideration determining the decision to focus on the cash privatization of industrial property. The expectation was that the selected strategic investors would truly be interested in modernizing the productive infrastructure and would thus make the Hungarian economy competitive under the new open market conditions. In general terms, both intentions were realized. The decision in favor of massive cash privatization was made earlier than in other Eastern European countries and was subsequently carried out under relatively favorable terms of trade. Particularly in the Budapest area, the modernization of privatized industrial enterprises moved forward quickly. The Hungarian economy stabilized early, its ability to compete internationally reached high levels. (Kornai 1997) But the differentiating effects of cash privatization in terms of deepening differences in property and income between groups and territories could not be avoided. Due to the preferences of investors, large territories in the country suffered rapid de-industrialization and economic decline. Only few significant industrial enterprises are currently owned by Hungarian companies. The banking sector is practically in foreign hands. The dependence of the local banking sector on drying-up capital flows from the parent financial institutions in the West contributed very much to the deep financial and economic crisis in the country in 2008–2009.

Privatization took an entirely different path in the Czech Republic. There the strategy was focused on mass privatization by means of vouchers. In two waves between 1992 and 1994 nearly two thirds of the industrial assets (more than 1,600 enterprises) were privatized in this way. This was the scheme of privatization which gathered the largest political support. The citizens wanted to participate in the distribution of state property. Voucher privatization seemed to be the best mechanism for satisfying this desire. In addition, the population and the political leadership did not want to sell out the national property to foreigners. Unlike in Hungary there was no need to do this since the international debt of Czechoslovakia was rather modest at the end of the eighties. Last but not least, there was a widely spread wish to avoid the transformation of the former political and managerial elite into new elite of owners. In order to avoid the wide dispersion of the property, Investment Privatization Funds were established where the vouchers had to be concentrated for the more efficient restructuring of the national economy. Thus, the privatization scheme seemed to be properly designed, legally well balanced and under firm institutional control. Up until the mid-nineties the Czech voucher privatization was praised as best practice by the World Bank and the International Monetary Fund. The reasons for praising seemed to be obvious – GDP grew, inflation and unemployment were low by international comparison.

Assessments of the Czech voucher privatization changed sharply in 1997 together with the currency crisis in the country. It turned out that the legal requirements for the founding of Investment Privatization Funds were too liberal. About 450 Funds were established mostly without capital of their own and without experienced personnel. Some of the funds used dishonest practices of advertisement in order to attract the accumulation of vouchers. Since the Czech economy was not profitable enough to secure the accumulation of capital, funds could only survive by taking out bank credits. Then, the Funds were unable to pay the credits back and came under the ownership of the banks. However, till the end of the nineties the banks remained state property in the Czech Republic. The surviving funds (one in ten) were practically re-nationalized through the banks. In the meantime, vouchers were devaluated by the macroeconomic processes themselves and by the dishonest practices of the Funds. The highly praised Czech voucher privatization turned out to be a modest success, and in some cases a clear failure. (Schütte 2000)

Due to economic and political considerations and under the pressure of the strong trade unions, the Slovenian Parliament decided in favor of the strategy of privatization by means of workers and managers buy-out of industrial property. The background for this decision was the strong tradition of economic and political self-management in the former Yugoslavia and particularly in Slovenia. Against this background it was relatively easy to transform the state property of the industrial enterprises into private corporations. Their shares were distributed among the workers and managers in a legally sound and well controlled way. The 'losers' were the international investors who were very much interested in buying portions of the Slovenian industry but managed to acquire some 5% of the privatized enterprises. The international financial institutions strongly criticized the Slovenian privatization strategy. However, at the end of the nineties, domestic and international actors had to recognize that this specific Slovenian path of privatization contributed substantially to the rapid stabilization of the national economy. (Peternelj 2005: 4–5) In addition, it precluded the overwhelming predominance of international capital as was the outcome of the Hungarian cash privatization. As seen from another point of view, the sound legal regulation and institutional control of privatization precluded the far reaching economic and social differentiation which took place in the Russian Federation and in the Ukraine in the course of insider privatization. (Stefancic 2005)

The privatization of state property started in the Russian Federation in the autumn of 1992, following a decree by the then President Boris Yeltsin. The strategy focused on voucher privatization under the assumption that it was to be fast, just and part of the shock-therapy intended to stabilize the Russian economy in due course. However, the legal regulation of the privatization was not elaborated in details, the institutional preparation and implementation of the process was hasty and full of uncertainty. Very limited efforts were made to explain the aims and means of the privatization to the public. For large groups of workers and employees it remained unclear why, how and with what intended effects state property was to be distributed to them by means of vouchers. One may assume that this was actually the wish of the managers of state enterprises, of some politicians and of mafia-like structures. After the distribution of the shares (vouchers) to the workers and employees, they were usually willing to sell them cheaply and did so. The concentration of property in the hands of managers, state functionaries and other interest groups became unavoidable. The voucher privatization turned out to be a tremendous cheating and robbery in Russia. This trend was confirmed in the next round of privatization by the sale of state property. The tiny strata of already rich 'oligarchs' made use of the weak legal and institutional regulation of the selling procedures and managed to amass large amounts of property. (Stiglitz 2003: Ch.5) The Gini coefficient of economic differentiation skyrocketed and reached the level of 0.47 in the late-nineties. This level is typical for deeply economically divided societies like those in Latin America.

Privatization in the Ukraine coincided with the difficult process of state building after the dissolution of the Soviet Union. The managers used the institutional uncertainty in order to legalize their ownership of the industrial enterprises by means of various mechanisms of transformation of property rights. However, they were usually pressed to share the newly acquired ownership with state administrators and politically relevant rent-seeking groups. Real entrepreneurs appeared as late as the end of the turbulent nineties. Step by step, the state managed to bring the economic processes under control. But the absence of efficient normative regulation of privatization in the nineties will influence the economic and political life in the country for decades to come. The concentration of property in the hands of several territorially divided economic and political clans makes governing the country difficult since the clans have specific economic and geopolitical interests. (Åslund, 2004)

The conclusion from the overview of privatization processes could only be that there is no clear-cut typology of privatization strategies which would take all above mentioned specifics into account. In very tentative terms, the positive and negative parameters as well as the uncertainties of the privatization procedures could be typologically presented as the following:

Table 2.1 Strategies for implementing the privatization of productive assets

Type of privatization	Speed	Economic efficiency	Legal and moral justice
Restitution	Low	Low	Unclear
Voucher privatization	High	Low	Middle
Insider privatization	Middle	Middle	Middle
Selling	Low	High	Low

Whatever strategies and mechanisms were used in the privatization, at the end of the nineties private productive assets already dominated in Eastern Europe. Hungary and the Czech Republic reached some eighty percent of the productive assets in private hands in 1999. As a contrast, in the same year only 20% of the productive assets in Belarus were privatized. (Transition 2002: 40) The rationalization of property relations by means of privatization had far reaching consequences. Modern management was introduced quickly in the enterprises acquired by strategic foreign investors. Production lines were modernized, new marketing strategies and evaluation techniques were developed and applied. Organizational flexibility increased. (Makó, Warhurst and Genhard 2003; Mikl-Horke 2004) Later, the same changes took place in the bulk of the enterprises despite the resistance of the inherited state-socialist organizational structures and patterns of authoritarian decision-making. Some of these remained quite influential, particularly in Russia. But the general trend of the rationalization of management took the lead there too, thus substantially contributing to the stabilization of the local market economy. For its part, the market attracts foreign direct investments, which bring about modern production lines together with the increased flexibility of employment and managerial practices. The newly established small and medium firms make the market more dynamic since they are typically prone to creative adaptations to the dynamics of markets. (Bogaevskaya 2005)

The well designed and controlled performance of state institutions was the key to the successful resolution of the complicated economic transformation of Eastern European societies. The task was difficult to resolve "on the rough sea", under the conditions of economic recession, political instability and cultural disorientation. The type and the outcome of privatization became the factor determining the economic performance and the prospects of sustainable economic development. A particularly important effect of privatization was the rise of unemployment and the ensuing impoverishment. The uncertainties surrounding privatization brought about and sustained a large segment of a shadow economy, marked by precarious working conditions, job uncertainty and a lack of health insurance. All Eastern European societies are affected by these negative developments, although to different extents. The external indebtedness is particularly high in Latvia, Estonia and Hungary. One may notice that Hungary was the most externally indebted Eastern European country in 1989 per capita. Twenty years later the country has the highest external indebtedness per capita among all post socialist countries once more. Another indicator for extreme cases of economic instability is the very high unemployment in Bosnia and Herzegovina, Macedonia and Serbia. After a slow and painful recovery almost all post-socialist economies are marked by negative growth. In several cases the economic decline exceeds the two-digit level (EBRD 2009b):

Table 2.2 Socio-economic results of the transformations in Eastern Europe

Country	GDP growth in 2009 (EBRD projection)	External debt as % of GDP in 2008	Unemployment as % in 2008
Albania	3.0	20.4	12.9
Armenia	-14.3	23.3	6.3
Belarus	-3.0	24.6	1.0
Bosnia and Herzegovina	-3.1	43.6	41.1
Bulgaria	-6.0	103.9	5.1
Croatia	-5.4	82.7	10.0
Czech Republic	-4.3	40.9 (2006)	7.1(2006)
Estonia	-13.2	115.7	5.5
Georgia	-5.5	35.6	12.9
Hungary	-6.5	113.5	7.8
Latvia	-16.0	124.2	7.8
Lithuania	-18.4	68.7	5.8
Macedonia	-1.6	49.1	34.0
Moldova	-8.5	68.2	4.0
Montenegro	-4.1	15.1	17.5
Poland	1.3	46.0	6.7
Romania	-8.0	35.4	4.1
Russian Federation	-8.5	36.0 (2007)	5.6(2007)
Serbia	-4.0	60.6	31.0
Slovakia	-6.0	53.3	9.6
Slovenia	-7.8	101.1	4.8 (2007)
Ukraine	-14.0	57.3	6.4

The dissatisfaction and disenchantment accompanying this development tend to preclude the mobilization of constructive political will. The experience of unsuccessful economic reforms aggravated the crisis of the legitimacy of state institutions. Painful measures of economic and administrative stabilization still have to be designed and implemented in conditions of a low level of confidence in state institutions. The confidence in the reform elite was exhausted rather quickly together with the first signs of unsuccessful economic policies. Most reform governments did not manage to serve their whole term. The rapid changes of governments made the functioning of the newly established market economic rules difficult. The observation of the international rules of property rights is rather different from country to country in Eastern Europe. Hungary is placed 30 and Russia 63 in the international ranking of 2007. (Horst 2007: 45)

The Eastern European national economies currently occupy a peripheral role in the economic relations and processes in Europe. Some of them have progressed more quickly in their adjustment to global and regional markets and have managed to occupy more advantageous positions in the international division of labor and in economic exchange. Others have moved more slowly and have had, or are still having, substantial troubles with the adjustment to the requirements of the global markets in terms of international competitiveness. The ranking prepared by the World Economic Forum is quite telling in this respect. (The Global Competitiveness Report 2008–2009: 12–13):

Table 2.3 Positions of Eastern European countries in the Global Competitiveness Index 2008–2009

Country	Ranking N	Country	Ranking N
Estonia	32	Montenegro	65
Czech Republic	33	Romania	68
Slovenia	42	Ukraine	72
Lithuania	44	Bulgaria	76
Slovak Republic	46	Serbia	85
Russian Federation	51	Georgia	90
Poland	52	Moldova	95
Latvia	54	Armenia	97
Croatia	61	Bosnia and Herzegovina	107
Hungary	62	Albania	108

The continuing challenges to the economic development of Eastern European societies invite innovations. Given the strong tradition of the developmental state in the region, expectations for improving the situation are mostly directed towards the state institutions. In spite of all the disenchantment, mass attitudes are clearly in favor of an active state. The reason is not just connected to the need for organizational rationalization. The real issue is the very desirable but extremely difficult to implement 'rationalization with a human face'. In the historical context this would be possible by a radical move from the hierarchical tradition of government under state socialism towards poliarchical structures of democratic governance.

2.3 The Development of Democratic Governance

Charles de Montesquieu and Alexis de Tocqueville insisted on the point that the decisive factor for the efficiency of modern politics was the division of the legislative, executive and judicial powers. Following their ideas, experts expected that the interaction of these autonomous powers in the sense of the famous 'checks and balances' would bring about and maintain the basis of efficient competitive politics in Eastern Europe after 1989. In turn, competitive politics was assumed to create systematic 'win-win' situations in the representation and mutual accommodation of different and often opposing interests. The pluralistic and competitive party system was regarded to be an inherent component of the representation and balancing of interests in free and fair elections. The active civil society was expected to be another major actor in the democratization process since grass-roots movements, associations and organizations had to allow differentiated interests to be incorporated in the interplay of political forces. Last but not least, the quality of this interplay and its outcomes had to be guaranteed by the structural stability and functional efficiency of rational bureaucracy in the form of a well-structured and functioning state administration. Due to its professionalized capacities to resolve organizational and social problems in a politically unbiased manner, modern bureaucracy was seen as a major precondition for the efficient preparation and implementation of democratic decisions and thus for the efficient democratic political integration. (Dahl 1998)

When analyzed in the light of these parameters of democratic politics, the development of Eastern European societies after the Second World War offers a rather controversial picture. The societal systems in the region were one-sidedly integrated through their political institutions and, to a much lesser extent, through their economy and culture. Moreover, societal integration was predominantly implemented by the executive power. The legislative and judiciary were subordinated to the role of mechanisms supporting the proper functioning of the executive. All state powers were actually integrated by the apparatus of the ruling party in a party-state ruling apparatus. No competitive party politics was possible under these conditions. The political opposition was institutionally or even physically eliminated. The checks and balances – as far as even possible under these conditions – were part and parcel of the party-state apparatus itself and subjugated to the party control. Aside from the formalized representation of occupational, gender, age, ethnic and other groups (the quota-representation), real political representation of specific interests could be established only as an element of the struggles of factions within the organizations of the ruling party. This type of competitive politics was always possible, although dangerous. Faction-builders in the ruling Eastern European parties could not, as a rule, expect a long political life. Political decisions and activities were very much reduced to administration. In spite of ideological slogans about the people's democracy and about very much needed political and social initiatives, grass-roots political activities did not have a recognized and respected place in the administrative politics. It replaced the articulation, public representation and coordination of group interests.

One may search for an explanation for this historically unique case of political over-integration in the clash between ideological visions and reality. Socialism emerged in Western Europe as an ideological vision for the resolution of its social problems. Due to historical circumstances, the practical proof of this ideological vision had to come about in the socialist transformation of Eastern European societies. They were underdeveloped in terms of productive infrastructure, organizational traditions and even in terms of general literacy. A high level of administratively imposed organizational discipline was needed in order to overcome the inherited deficiencies in the modernization of the countries in the region. Therefore, the socialist vision of societal organization had to be modified by stressing the need for the rapid development of the productive infrastructure under strict state planning and control.

As seen from this point of view, the political over-integration of the societies in the region made sense in the historical context. A high concentration of resources and their use in strategic projects was to be efficiently achieved under authoritarian rule. The crucial condition for the success of such endeavors is the professionalization and the efficiency of the state (and party) bureaucracy. Some achievements in its development in Eastern Europe cannot be denied. However, the over-concentration of uncontrolled political power made irrational decisions at the very top of the organizational hierarchy relatively easy. Due to local traditions, the Eastern European party-state bureaucracy was notoriously clumsy and intrinsically resistant to the efforts to introduce organizational innovations.

It might seem today that the democratic division and mutual control of the executive, legislative and judicative powers would be the most natural state of affairs in the political life of Eastern European societies. One may even speculate that the practical elimination of the autonomy of the legislative and judicative powers in the region before 1989 was an accidental break in the natural path of history. But the two decades of democratic rule in Czechoslovakia between the world wars notwithstanding, no other country in Eastern Europe had experienced flourishing democracy before the socialist transformation. Communist authoritarianism was merely another form of the continuity of undemocratic regimes in the region. The concentration of resources in the hands of authoritarian regimes seemed to be promising since the Eastern European societies needed to catch up quickly in the development of productive infrastructure, transport, communication, etc. If achieved, this very desirable rapid modernization of material conditions would be the excuse for the use of undemocratic political measures and of regional cooperation schemes that isolated the region from the world.

In each Eastern European country there were persons, groups and organizations willing to introduce or to support organizational changes in the direction of communist authoritarianism. Like in Italy and France, the local communist parties in Yugoslavia and in other Eastern European countries were able to raise support for their policies by referring to their victims during the resistance. This legacy was used to immediately initiate policies of forced modernization via the industrialization, the collectivization of agriculture and the stabilization of authoritarian political regimes.

The core of these policies was the excessive concentration of the power of political decision-making in the hands of the administrative apparatus of the ruling communist party. This concentration of power was legalized in the state-socialist constitutions passed after the war. They copied the Soviet Constitution of 1936. Later, the aspiration of the ruling party to fully dominate the political landscape was codified in the new socialist constitutions passed in the seventies. However, they included numerous codifications of universal human rights as well.

The irony behind these constitutional arrangements was their clash with key institutional structures and practices. The constitutional ideology stressed justice and human development. At the same time, the functioning institutions were guided by the simplified vision of the Marxist organization of society understood as a large industrial enterprise. In it the processes had to be based on precise time management in production and on collectivist need satisfaction in consumption. Both production and consumption had to be administratively regulated. This simplified understanding of social organization intrinsically suppressed the initiative and responsibility of individuals. The result was the development of a system that relied primarily on formalized discipline and much less on motivation for personal achievement. Thus, not the free development and realization of well educated individuals but institutional guidance and suppression of non-conformist patterns of behavior was the result of the socialist transformation. Aside from other economic, political and cultural circumstances, this was a key factor motivating the uprisings in East Germany in 1953, in Hungary and Poland in 1956 and the reform movement in Czechoslovakia in 1968. Due to domestic and international factors, these protest upheavals did not have the chance to change the system. However, they made its inefficiency and vulnerability manifest to both the citizens of Eastern Europe and the world at large.

Why was the political system established in the Soviet Union in the 1930s and all over Eastern Europe after the Second World War so inefficient?

First, the state socialist pattern of political organization was marked by a very asymmetric distribution of legitimacy for deviant opinion and action. The space for diversity was rather limited at the low levels of the organizational pyramid. Real grass-roots initiatives for organizational innovation were usually punished. On the other hand, the very top of the organizational pyramid could develop arbitrary initiatives without being controlled or punished. The political system itself required this excessively strong position of its leaders or even of a single person at the top of the organizational hierarchy. The position was occupied by the leader of the national variant of the communist party. He was the only person fully legitimated to develop initiatives at national level. The famous cult of personality was actually in-built in the state socialist political system and functioned with changing intensity from its very establishment until its demise. Other national sources of initiative and aspirations for responsibility could only survive if they were able to gain the support of the regional power in Moscow. The stress on collective responsibility was typically used to legitimate collective irresponsibility regarding decisions and actions.

Second, the asymmetric distribution of capacities for organizational initiative became possible in Eastern Europe under the conditions of the deeply unequal distribution of power. Its concentration at the top of the party-state administrative hierarchy made the control of the executive by the legislative and the judicative practically impossible. Democratic grass-roots control by means of free and fair elections was practically excluded too. The election rules typically allowed for one candidate for each incumbency. The numerous control bodies acted under the supervision of the state-party apparatus, which the control bodies were supposed to control. Major mechanisms of surveillance and control were incorporated into the well developed secret services, which were placed under the direct supervision of the leader of the ruling party.

Third, there was an excessive concentration of the right to organizational initiative and control at the top of the regional leadership in Moscow. The meetings of Eastern European national leaders were practically forums for formally supporting decisions taken in Moscow and for making them internationally known. This hegemonic system of international organization could in no way attract broad support in the region, which was traditionally known for the abundance of nationalistic ideologies and movements.

Fourth, the state socialist organizational framework could only function under the conditions of a well developed bureaucracy. This was the nomenclature system mostly based on personal loyalty to the national leader and to the international leadership in Moscow. This bureaucratic system could only function by applying the systematic threat of the use of violence or by openly using it at both national and international levels.

The critical stance towards the intentions, development and functioning of the organization of politics in Eastern Europe before 1989 should not preclude the recognition of the complexity of the issues under scrutiny. The concentration of political power made it possible to overcome the destruction caused by the war and to move towards industrialization, urbanization and the mechanization of agriculture in the region relatively fast. This achievement deserves attention today given the experience of the protracted economic depression and slow recovery in large parts of Eastern Europe after 1989. The achievements of the authoritarian regimes in Eastern Europe in raising the educational level of the population, in developing largely accessible health care systems and in establishing modern research and development institutions cannot be underestimated either. There were also efforts to make the system more open to innovations and to humanistic considerations. This was the strategy of the political reforms in Yugoslavia (the introduction of the system of self-management during the fifties and the sixties), the guiding ideas of the democratic political change in Czechoslovakia in 1968 (Ebbinghaus 2008), the cautious development of elements of competitive politics in Hungary in 1983–1985. The turbulent change of organizational visions and patterns during the *perestroika*-period in the Soviet Union between 1985 and 1990 was path-breaking for the round-table discussion in Poland in 1989 which signaled the end of the state socialism in Europe. The radical change in this form of political organization became historically inevitable since it was intrinsically hostile to innovation.

Nobody in the region or beyond its boundaries was set with a recipe for the content, sequence, coordination or timing of the looming political changes. This was actually a paradoxical situation since over the course of decades, numerous research centers for studies on the Soviet Union, Eastern Europe and communism were charged with precisely this task of preparing the conceptual and institutional tools for the change in the Eastern European authoritarian political systems. In reality, there was a tremendous deficit of expertise concerning the steering of the imminent political processes. The pioneering efforts were undertaken in Poland and Hungary. Other Eastern European countries were encouraged by the circumstances to follow their experience and the patterns of their institutional change.

The Polish innovation of Round Table talks between the representatives of the ruling Polish United Workers' Party, the Polish government and the representatives of the opposition in 1989 was a milestone on the road to institutional change in the Eastern European region along the path of negotiated democracy. (Mokrzycki 2002) The decisions of the Round Table became the general orientation for the steps in the way towards democratization all over Eastern Europe:

- The constitutional monopoly of the ruling party had to be abolished – if not immediately in constitutional terms, then at least in political practice.
- Consequently, oppositional political forces had to be legalized.
- A pluralistic party system of political representation had to be introduced.
- Democratic elections had to be prepared and carried out.
- The freely elected parliaments had to prepare constitutional changes or new constitutions allowing for the autonomy of the legislative, executive and judicative powers.
- The constitutional division of political powers had to be implemented in the establishment of new institutions and in profound reforms of existing ones.
- The mutual coordination of the newly developed institutions had to be achieved.
- The new balance of constitutional provisions and institutional arrangements had to be stabilized.

The changes indicated in the last point had to mark the end of a cycle in the upgrading of the rationality of political institutions and practices in Eastern Europe. The result was expected to be the functioning system of democratic competitive politics. The constitutional and institutional developments in Hungary after 1989 are a telling illustration of this process. The evolutionary establishment of competitive politics was well prepared during decades of cautious political reform which began in the first half of the eighties with the changes in the election law in 1983. They legalized electoral competition for the first time in Eastern Europe since the late forties. This pioneering legal act had the effect that independent politicians entered the Hungarian Parliament after the parliamentary elections held in 1985. In this way, the Parliament became a major factor for political innovations. It pressed for further reforms towards democratic politics by allowing the organized representation of oppositional forces. The path was paved towards a pluralist political system. This started to evolve together with the founding of the Hungarian Democratic Forum as oppositional party in 1987. The reforms immensely accelerated in the autumn of 1989.

The political changes took place in Hungary in a negotiated manner like in Poland. There were no intensive confrontations such as in Romania. There was no discontinuity in the political elite in Hungary as was experienced in Czechoslovakia. The major moving force of the pluralization of politics in Hungary was the reform wing of the ruling Hungarian Socialist Workers' Party itself. Close collaborators of János Kádár took the initiative for the National Round Table from June to September 1989. This decision was inspired by the events in Poland and by the experience of the Spanish transition from authoritarianism towards democracy (the Moncloa Pact). The outcome of the work of the Round Table was the fully fledged concept of a new democratic constitution of Hungary, which could be passed by the Parliament as early as in October 1989.

Being always influenced by temporary factors, the political reforms in Hungary during the nineties were strategically guided by the desire of the major political actors for the preservation and strengthening of institutional stability. With rare and temporary exceptions, they maintained this desire during the turbulent period of accelerated reforms. The oppositional forces refrained from intensive attacks against state institutions and avoided actions which would undermine them. The decisions to secure a majoritarian bonus of seats in the Parliament for the winner of the proportional representation in parliamentary elections, to have a strong Prime Minister and relatively weak President, to establish a respected Constitutional Court and to introduce and increase the threshold of electoral support to enter the Parliament were legal changes guided by the need to achieve and maintain institutional stability. It was materialized in a functioning system of 'checks and balances' between state institutions. In effect, the reform government of Antal/Boross was the only one in Eastern Europe which managed to serve its entire term in the first half of the nineties. During the same period between 1990 and 1994, four different governments served in Poland under the conditions of institutional confrontation and general political instability. The smooth change of the parliamentary majority and governments in 1994 and 1998 demonstrated the efficiency of the established continuity and stability of the political system in Hungary. An active civil society supported this institutional development and ensured the legitimacy of democratic institutional procedures. (Agh 2001)

A rather different picture of the development of political institutions and their interactions appeared in Russia during the turbulent nineties. Everybody who believed that the *perestroika* during the second half of the eighties had already opened the way to an active and influential civil society, to the establishment of 'checks and balances' between democratically legitimized and democratically functioning institutions was bound to experience profound disappointments. The putsch in August 1991 accelerated the dissolution of the Soviet Union, but not the democratization of the Russian Federation. The newly elected President of the Federation, Boris Yeltsin, continued the authoritarian tradition of ruling by decrees. Due to inherited circumstances (the composition of the Duma elected before the changes) but also because of the strong Russian tradition of resolving political issues by means of violence Yeltsin ordered the shelling of the disobedient Duma in October 1993. Acts of this type could not strengthen the public support for democracy. The supporters of non-democratic patterns of government were stronger than the supporters of the Western-type democratic organization of Russian society both before and after the violent clash between the presidential institution and the Duma. (Veber, Galkin and Krasin 2001: 181) This should not be surprising. Since the start of *perestroika* in the mid eighties, the very term 'democracy' became increasingly associated in Russia with phenomena of administrative chaos, economic decline, lack of political norms, value-normative uncertainty, rise in crime, unemployment, impoverishment and general disorientation in thought and action.

The propaganda and the organizational methods used to secure Boris Yeltsin's second term in 1996 additionally undermined the legitimacy of democratic political mechanisms in Russian public opinion and strengthened political apathy and cynicism. The elections demonstrated the powerlessness of civil society in all its educational, mobilizing, mediating, organizational and controlling functions. The shock of the economic crisis of 1998 provided evidence that the organizational foundation of the reformed Russian society was rather unstable. At this time, the majority of the population of the Russian Federation readily supported the view that the crisis was mostly due to the introduction of democratic political principles incompatible with Russian cultural and organizational traditions. Thus, at the end of the turbulent decade, Russian society was prepared to embrace a turn towards the strengthening of state institutions along authoritarian principles. Recent analyses of deviations from democratic governance in the country (Gel'man 2010) may sharpen the contrast in the overall picture of the political systems in Eastern Europe.

Applying the indicators of political rights and civil liberties, government turnover, war and political violence, the experts of the World Bank were correct in describing the political system in Hungary at the end of the nineties as "competitive democracy" and the organizational form of politics in Russia as a "concentrated political regime". (Transition 2002: 98) The Bertelsmann transformation index repeated this differentiation by dividing the post-socialist European societies in a large group of good performers and a small group of laggards in building up their national democratic institutions (Bertelsmann Transformation Index 2008: 94, 112):

Table 2.4 Bertelsmann Transformation Index: Democracy in Eastern Europe (2008)

Democracies	Defective democracies	Highly defective democracies	Autocracies
Slovenia	Montenegro	Russia	Belarus
Czech Republic	Macedonia		
Estonia	Serbia		
Hungary	Albania		
Lithuania	Ukraine		
Slovakia	Georgia		
Croatia	Moldova		
Poland	Armenia		
Bulgaria			
Latvia			
Romania			

The scientific objectivity requires a more differentiated analysis, however. Leading Hungarian political analysts raised a long list of open questions concerning the administrative efficiency of the newly established democratic political organization of Hungarian society. Open questions also concerned the global and regional (continental) interactions and the new relationships between economy, politics and culture. This new organizational constellation was described by Jadwiga Staniszkis as "the emerging enigma". (1999) It invites a discussion focusing on the fragility of the democratic political systems in the region.

Who would have dared to imagine at the end of the 1990s, for instance, that the reaction of the major oppositional party in Hungary, FIDESZ, to the lost parliamentary elections in 2006 could be the call for riots? Who could have assumed that this party which was established by young cosmopolitan and laic liberals would embrace a nationalist and clerical ideology? Who could even have dared to imagine that the party leadership would animate and support right wing rioters? Attila Agh praised the rationalized politics in Hungary during the nineties but was pressed by these changes to radically modify his assessment of Hungarian party politics. His judgment of the new situation is crushing: "After two decades the Hungarian party system can be briefly characterized as a socio-political 'senilisation' of the parties and the party leaderships, since they have no clear ideas and programmes ..." (Agh 2008) Agh sees the explanation of this confusing fact in the excessive focus of the Hungarian political debates and actions on securing the country's membership in the European Union. Once this goal has been achieved the Hungarian political parties turned out to be without any other mobilizing goals. The argument is certainly valid. But it is less persuasive than two additional explanations which Attila Agh briefly mentions himself.

The first argument concerns the social-structural implications of privatization and the concomitant differentiation of ownership and income. The differentiation of rich and poor introduced a differentiation of life chances in Hungary and in all other Eastern European societies. The perception that this is a long-term economic discrimination of large groups cannot be a factor of political stability. The second focus of explanation seems to be no less relevant. Not only in Hungary, but generally in Eastern Europe expectations were very high at the beginning of the changes. Now the political parties all over the region are encountering tremendous difficulties in explaining to the public why the expected substantial improvement of the living standard and quality of life could not come about 20 years after the beginning of the political changes. Millions of Hungarian consumers tried to resolve the issue by taking out easy credits. This turned out to be even more destructive than the inability of the political parties to explain the situation or to mobilize for action.

The global financial crisis surprised the Hungarian receivers of credit in Euros and in Swiss Franks. They have massive problems in repaying the credits after the devaluation of the Hungarian currency. Thus, both the inefficiency of party politics and irrational mass consumer behavior seem to be important explanatory factors for the critical situation of the Hungarian economy and the public mood in the country. The previously very much praised Hungarian best performers in the reforms turned out to be most disappointed by their results. Having been asked in the regular Europarometer survey at the end of 2008 about the financial situation of their households, 74% of the Hungarian respondents described it as "bad" and "very bad". (Eurobarometer 70/ 2008: A4a.5)

As compared to the current economic situation of Hungarian society and households, Poland is performing financially better under the conditions of the global economic crisis. There is no relevant political party or political group in Poland which would question the democratic arrangements in Polish political life as is the case in Hungary. Polish political parties actively try to mobilize, integrate and represent political will in the country. However, they rarely manage to draw more than half of the Polish voters to participate in parliamentary elections. This happened only in 1993 (52.1% participation of potential voters) and in 2007 (53.8%). (Polen-Analysen 2007/23:2) The desire of the activists of *Solidarity* to develop a society of politically mature, active and responsible people was thus profoundly questioned.

Even more relevant is another trend which concerns the ideology and politics of leading Polish political parties after the EU accession. The parliamentary elections of 2005 made it possible for the ruling coalition to use state institutions to spread rather conservative clerical and nationalist ideas. Both the socialist development after the Second World War and the liberal changes after 1989 were put under critical scrutiny as deviations from Polish traditions and interests. Contrary to the decisions of the Round Table which opened up the path to cultural and political tolerance in Polish society, a new wave of lustration of state officials came to the top of the political agenda. Various measures for future national consolidation around the conservative traditions of the Polish Catholic Church were undertaken in the educational system.

This development was interrupted with the early elections held in 2007. But the signal for a conservative turn in Polish cultural life and politics was given. It became also obvious that the conservative policies of the *Law and Justice Party* headed by the Kaczynski brothers mobilized mass support, thus hindering the ideas and practices of European integration and value-normative universalization. This became possible in Poland since "a political system rife with corruption and pathology, weak political parties and low electoral turnouts [had] crystallized" in the country. (Rae 2007: 222) The Hungarian case discussed above provides evidence that the so described phenomenon is not isolated to Poland. Various modifications of the same phenomenon can be identified in all other post-socialist European societies. Thus, the influential assumptions about the final victory of liberal political ideas and practices were questioned by the political development in the region. Surprisingly enough, this happened after the accession of eight Eastern European countries to the European Union in 2004 and two more in 2007. This development is only a small part of the broad issue of the impact of international organizations on the rationalization of economy and politics in Eastern Europe.

2.4 Impact of International Organizations on the Eastern European Transformations

The international organizations were caught by surprise by the implosion of the Eastern European socialist societies and their supranational integration schemes. Immediately after the fall of the Berlin Wall, the European Community did not have any vision as to how to react to the radical changes in the geo-strategic situation. There were deep differences among Western European national leaderships regarding the possible and desirable reactions to the changes in the Eastern part of the continent. The confusion was understandable since fundamental geostrategic issues and national interests were at stake. Even the unification of Germany was complex enough in itself. It took time for Western European politicians to reach national decisions and a tentative international consensus about the ways to handle the situation.

In a sharp contrast the World Bank and the International Monetary Fund already had rich experience in tackling all-embracing societal crises all over the world and numerous experts trained to do exactly this. Thus, both organizations could immediately fill in the gap by offering expertise and financial support to the reforms in Eastern Europe. Hundreds of experts of the World Bank flew immediately to Warsaw, Prague, Budapest, Bucharest and some later to Moscow and Kiev on field trips. They knew the diagnosis in advance and came with ready-made plans for handling the crisis. The various plans were actually one and the same plan called 'one size fits all'. This universally applicable strategy was called 'stabilization'. In the framework of the Washington consensus for dealing with critical national economic situations, the stabilization strategy implied four types of action (Åslund 2007: Ch.4):

- Rapid liberalization of domestic prices, foreign trade and currency exchange;
- Radical privatization of state owned productive assets and infrastructure;
- Monetary restrictions on investments and consumption in order to curb inflation;
- Radical cuts in social benefits and social support schemes.

The "Balcerowicz plan" for shock-therapy in Poland and later the similar strategy of market reforms in the Russian Federation were literally guided by these normative ideas. They were based on theories by Milton Friedman and other Chicago School neo-liberal economists. Proponents of Chicago School ideas were readily available for counseling in Eastern Europe since neo-liberalism was the intellectual fashion at that time. Moreover, there were strong political arguments for big bang liberal reforms. In this way any reversal of the political changes had to be excluded. Free play of economic forces had to be introduced immediately in legal and institutional terms. Full economic liberalization was expected to bring about the stable balance between supply and demand quickly. On the basis of the spontaneously attained economic stability, all other action spheres were supposed to reach their own equilibrium fast. Thus, the general stabilization of Eastern European societies had to be achieved in the course of months or in several years at maximum. Therefore, this was an all-embracing plan for upgrading the rationality of organizations in Eastern Europe.

The strategy for rapid economic and social stabilization by means of big bang reforms seemed to be coherent and transparent. But it was doomed to fail. It took the weakening of the Eastern European state institutions and the intensity of political confrontations only peripherally into account. Both underestimated factors were quick to undermine the ambitious plans for rapid big bang privatization in Poland and other Eastern European countries. The neo-liberal strategy also underestimated the capacity of the old *nomenklatura* and of organized criminals to act efficiently in taking over privatization processes in the Russian Federation or in the Ukraine. These actors spurred a unique criminal revolution by stealing state property which was the property of the whole population in each Eastern European country by constitutional definition. In effect, millions of Eastern Europeans had to struggle for mere survival. One of the major reasons for this critical development was the fact that the big bang strategists did not seriously consider institutional measures to support the large groups of losers in the neo-liberal economic reforms. In end effect, the contributions of the World Bank and the International Monetary Fund to the rational management of the Eastern European societal transformations were typically evaluated in critical terms. The criticisms were particularly strong in reference to their involvement in the management of the societal transformation in the Russian Federation. (Stiglitz 2003: 133f.)

The evaluations should be certainly differentiated with regard to processes in individual Eastern European countries. In some of them the financial expertise and particularly the financial control over budgeting offered by experts at the World Bank and the International Monetary Fund efficiently supported the transition to a more rational management of national finances. This was achieved in the course of negotiations of international with local experts. The international financial institutions made the transfer of their expertise rather persuasive by offering relatively modest, but very important financial support for the reforms. The real relevance of this support was the guarantee given by the experts of the World Bank and the International Monetary Fund that the reforms were on the right track in the particular country. This guarantee opened up links to other credit lines since the Eastern European economies badly needed fresh funding in order to continue the costly reforms.

Therefore, some critical assessments of the activities of the World Bank and the International Monetary Fund in Eastern Europe should be considered in this broader context. Both international financial institutions regarded the reforms in Eastern Europe as "business as usual" in the global context. They applied the incentives for reforms in Eastern European societies and controlled these reforms there in exactly the same way as in many other regional and national cases of crisis management. This was the way in which the World Bank and the International Monetary Fund handled the financial crises in Hungary and in the Ukraine in 2008 and 2009 as well. They did once more what they had done to handle the financial crisis of the Asian countries in 1997 or in Argentina in 2000.

The geo-strategic situation of the European Community was entirely different at the beginning of the changes in Eastern Europe. Eastern Europe was the hostile neighbor of the EC-12 in the Cold War and unexpectedly turned to a friendly neighborhood after 1989. After the shock of this rapid change was over, a tentative consensus was reached in the European Community for a pro-active position concerning the changes in the Eastern part of the continent. But the decisions for active measures were taken slowly. It took the Community one year just to design the PHARE Program. It was only intended to support the economic recovery of Poland and Hungary. Then the CEFTA integration scheme came about, increasing the European Community's economic and political impact on the processes in the Visegrad countries (Poland, Hungary and Czechoslovakia, later the Czech Republic and Slovakia). Behind these and some other activities lurked the idea that the enlargement of the European Community (later the European Union) to the East might bring substantial economic and political advantages to the EC member states. However, it took three years of intensive analyses, consultations and negotiations to prepare a tentative strategy for the enlargement of the Union to the East. In 1993 the turning point was reached. The Copenhagen Council opened the prospects for full membership in the Union to those Eastern European countries which were able to fulfill the membership criteria.

The northern expansion of the European Union in 1995 accelerated the preparation for the eastern enlargement of the Union but not the enlargement itself. At the end of the decade ten countries in Eastern Europe had the status of candidates for membership in the Union. In the course of the following decade they became full members. The accession was a protracted process because of numerous open questions concerning the mutual organizational adaptation on both sides of the European continent. The structures of the Union had to be prepared to accommodate the new members on the condition of minimal additional expenses of the Union's 15 member states. The adjustment of organizational structures in the accession countries to structures and processes in the European Union was more difficult mostly because it required the legal and institutional application of the 80,000 pages of the Union's *acquis communeautaire* in an intensive preparation process. (Orenstein, Bloom and Lindstrom 2008: 1–19)

The critical issues to be dealt with were defined in the Copenhagen criteria for European Union membership. The candidate countries had to demonstrate the presence of a functioning market economy, a stable political democracy and respect for human rights in order to be recognized as eligible for full membership in the EU. However, the "chapters" on negotiations included a much broader range of specific requirements for membership. They had to be opened and closed in the negotiations of each candidate country with the delegation of the European Union. Each candidate country was expected to introduce the necessary legal and institutional changes before and in the course of the negotiations. The country also had to provide evidence that the changes were successfully introduced. This was the condition for the continuation of the negotiations and for their successful conclusion. The Commission's annual reports on the progress of each candidate country registered the achievements and failures of its adaptation to the requirements for membership in the Union. (Pirhofer 2004)

The negotiations on the free movement of goods focused on the level of compatibility of national technical regulation, standardization, accreditation and certification with the requirements of the *acquis*. Closely connected to these issues were the negotiations on the speed and conditions of the adoption of European Standards. The transposition of the *acquis* pertained to goods as varied as mechanical devices, motor vehicles, gas-burning appliances, electrical equipment, recreational goods, chemicals, pharmaceuticals, cosmetics, foodstuffs, glass, textiles, footwear, toys, etc. Negotiations in the field of corporate law concerned industrial property rights and intellectual property rights, together with provisions on accounting. The chapter on social policy and employment contained the framework for negotiations concerning labor law, equal opportunity arrangements, occupational health and safety, the regulation of social dialogue between organizations of employers and employees mediated by state institutions, labor market policies, issues of public health, etc. In the field of education and training, the participation of the respective countries in the EU educational programs, the compatibility of the legal frameworks for the decentralization of educational responsibilities, the licensing of vocational training institutions and similar issues were the subject of negotiation. The chapter on financial and budgetary provisions included clarifications of the procedures and instruments required to manage public expenditure and stressed the need for long term budgeting. In the coordination of the legal parameters and institutional activities, the issue of strengthening the administrative capacity for dealing with accession was paramount.

Thus, the negotiations and the practical steps taken toward accession to the European Union had a far reaching mobilizing and disciplining impact on all action spheres in the candidate countries. They were negotiations by name only and had nothing to do with the pattern of communication free of dominance as envisioned by Jürgen Habermas. The positions of both participating parties were entirely asymmetrical. The EU officials set the conditions, required the fulfillment of these conditions and controlled their implementation. The reward was clearly defined – accession to the "club of the rich". Since this was the desirable goal for the Eastern Europeans, they had to comply. The punishment for non-compliance was also clear. The mild version was the protracted negotiation. The strong version could be the closure of access to the club.

Thus, the negotiations mostly concerned the time table for implementation – for instance the replacement of environmentally unfriendly public transport busses with less polluting ones. The negotiations were focused on the requirements of the candidate country only in exceptional cases. This was the case in the negotiations with Poland on the EU subsidies for Polish agriculture. The domestic pressure on the issue was so strong that the EU delegation had to make concessions in order not to prolong the accession process of this important country. This was one of the very few cases in which the public was really informed about the course and results of the negotiations. In most other cases the public in the Eastern European countries was excluded from the negotiation process.

In end effect, the preparation for accession provided a powerful impetus to upgrade the rationality of organizations in the Eastern European societies. The push reached all organizations in the fields of economy, politics and culture. The state institutions were most significantly affected. Paradoxically enough, the result of the rather undemocratic negotiations for accession to the European Union was the strengthening of democratic initiative and democratic control over governmental decision-making and implementation of decisions in the Eastern European candidate countries. They were put under pressure to comply with the requirements for EU membership and made substantial progress in this respect. The candidate countries did their best to introduce modern patterns of governance in the course of their preparation for membership in the European Union. They tried to change their image of belonging to the 'wild East' in which everything was organizationally and morally possible. In some cases the organizational changes affected ritualized interactions and caused a temporary decline of administrative efficiency. It turned out that the legal and institutional transfers from the EU-15 to the candidate countries had to be carefully adapted to the local conditions. The counter-productive effects of direct transfers had to be corrected by new time-consuming and expensive reforms.

The reform processes in Eastern Europe went hand in hand with reforms of the European Union itself. In the period after 1989, the twelve members of the European Community and later the fifteen member states of the European Union were under the constant domestic and international pressure to adapt to the rapidly changing conditions of progressing globalization. The legal and institutional frameworks of the Union and its members had to be adjusted to the challenges of the expanding global markets and to new global political uncertainties. The adaptations continued in the course of the eastern enlargement of the Union. The leaderships and the population at large in the Eastern European countries had to recognize the fact that the adaptation of the Union to global pressures and the deepening of the Union's integration were rather costly. There was not abundant funding for the enlargement itself. In addition, the newcomers had to learn that they had become part of an organizational framework which is permanently changing itself at national and supranational levels. This understanding implied the sobering conclusion that there was no 'final resolution' for the organizational adaptation of Eastern European societies to the organizational patterns of the European Union. They had to streamline their weaker organizational structures on the rough sea of the reforms of the Union in order to support the adaptation of the Union to the challenges of globalization. Moreover, measures had to be taken to prevent any diminishing of the organizational efficiency of the enlarged European Union by the deficiencies in the organizational rationality of the Eastern European societies.

The success stories notwithstanding, the Eastern enlargement of the European Union triggered complicated processes and raised a lot of cognitive and organizational problems in the Union itself. (O'Brennan 2006) Economic disparity increased immensely in the Union due to the enlargement. This development poses a serious challenge to the policies for deeper integration and particularly to the policies aimed at strengthening social cohesion in the Union's organizational framework. With the enlargement the average GDP per capita of the Union decreased. This development questioned the capacity of the Union to implement its Lisbon Strategy to transform itself into the most dynamic region of economic development on the basis of high quality research and technological innovations. This problem was already serious before the eastern expansion of the Union. Comparative data show that the United States and Japan consistently better managed their economic problems and achieved better economic results during the ten year period between 1995 and the enlargement of the EU to the East in 2004. This applies also for the years after the approval of the EU's Lisbon strategy for accelerated technological innovation and economic growth in 2000 (UNECE 2005/2: 59):

Table 2.5 GDP growth 1995–2004 (EU, USA and Japan, in %)

Country	1995	1996	1997	1998	1999	2000	2001	2002	2003	2004
EU – 15	2.6	1.8	2.7	3.0	3.0	3.8	1.9	1.2	1.1	2.3
USA	2.5	3.7	4.5	4.2	4.4	3.7	0.8	1.9	3.0	4.4
Japan	2.6	2.8	3.4	2.9	3.2	3.6	1.2	1.4	2.0	3.3

Intensive debates on deficits of democratic legitimacy of some organizational structures of the European Union accompanied its enlargement to the East. Deeply rooted economic and political problems hindered the efficiency of its functioning. These problems were well known before the eastern expansion. Nevertheless, it is difficult to deny that the economic and political difficulties experienced by the Union in the global competition were exacerbated by the accession of the weak economies and unstable political systems of the Eastern European societies. Critics even assumed that the eastern expansion of the Union may undermine its integration and thus its international competitiveness in the long run. (Alber and Merkel 2006)

No doubt, most new member states of the Union have a lower GDP per capita than the average GDP per capita in the EU-15. But all of them were marked by a substantially higher rate of GDP growth than the EU15 during the negotiation process. The newcomers to the Union have actually invigorated the economic development of the EU27 at least temporarily. The organizational crisis of the EU (the rejection of the project for the EU Constitution by the referenda in France and in the Netherlands as well as the rejection of the shorter version of the new Agreement by the referendum in Ireland) cannot be explained by the EU enlargement alone. The organizational tensions of the EU accumulated already in the framework of the EU15. There is no clear causal relationship between the enlargement and the organizational pathologies in the Union. (Jachtenfluchs and Kohler-Koch 2004: 112–113) No clear cut prediction is possible in this respect since the speed and effects of organizational learning in the member states and in the European Union itself might produce unexpected results. There are in-built institutional mechanisms of the Union designed to reduce uncertainty and to control negative developments. One of these mechanisms is the careful analysis of the organizational changes in Eastern Europe through the use of benchmarking and sound scientific criticism.

Both predictable and unexpected tensions are now accumulating in the new EU member states themselves. The efforts to overcome the high barrier of conditions for membership in the Union were accompanied and supported by many illusions. One of them was that the membership was the major and most difficult task to resolve. Once the accession treaty with the candidate country was signed it turned out that the tasks ahead were no less difficult for the respective new EU member. All conditions for the absorption of funds had to be clarified and the necessary institutions had to be set up together with the training of the personnel. The control of the absorption and particularly the control on possible abuses of funds turned out to be quite demanding as well. In the meantime, the Eastern European politicians, state administration and the public at large have been showing symptoms of accession fatigue. The membership in the European Union has been long regarded by the Eastern European public opinion as a major factor for the economic prosperity of the country and the households in the context of globalization and its uncertainties. The public mind has changed in some new Eastern European EU member states after their accession to the EU dramatically (*Two Decades after the Wall's Fall* 2009: 68):[4]

Table 2.6 "In the long run, do you think that in your country the overall
         economy has been strengthened or weakened by the economic
         integration of Europe?" (in %)

Country	Strengthened	Weakened	Neither/Nor	DK
Poland	53	28	15	4
Slovakia	41	33	21	6
Czech Republic	31	37	25	7
Lithuania	28	34	27	11
Bulgaria	14	63	16	7
Hungary	9	71	15	4

The crucial issue causing and reproducing accession fatigue in the new EU member states is the increasing understanding that the newly introduced legal arrangements and established institutions cannot start functioning without mutual adjustment. The new institutions have to be attuned both to the reformed inherited institutions and to the changing institutions of the European Union. These tasks are difficult and time consuming. They may take years and in some cases even decades as has been the case of the adjustment of the South European societies to the legal and institutional arrangements of the European Community. Enlargement fatigue can even become paralyzing in the moment in which it becomes clear that the changing global, regional and local conditions permanently require institutional changes and institutional adjustments in the enlarged European Union. Adjusting institutions means adjusting attitudes and behavioral patterns. This is particularly difficult for the Eastern Europeans who have already spent 20 years on reforms and adjustments. The same applies to collective actors such as political parties in the region. They have been restructured together with all other institutions. The new

---

4   Public opinion polls were not carried out in all new Eastern European EU member states.

challenge is to make the institutions perform efficiently. Individual and collective actors have to reach mutual arrangements in order to make the polyarchic system of governance work properly.

Aside from these structurally determined post-accession problems, the governments in the Eastern European new member states have to face the discrepancy between the highly raised local expectations connected with EU accession and the harsh economic realities. Various EU post-accession funds offer support to the newcomers. But the support is not sufficient to meet the widespread expectations satisfactorily. The specter of the effects of long-term postponed gratification haunts the governments in Eastern Europe. None of those who signed the accession treaty may hope to be re-elected. This is a strong signal that the discrepancy between the expectations raised by the much desired Europeanization and the social realities in Eastern Europe is quite substantial. The social convergence of the countries in the enlarged European Union is now the major issue of the EU as seen from the point of view of the people in the new Eastern European member states. If the EU administration were to underestimate this issue, it would certainly intensify social tensions in Eastern Europe together with the tensions between the former members of the EU-15 and the population of the new Eastern European member states. (Agh 2007)

Chapter 3
Individualization *versus* the Common Good

There is a widespread assumption that Eastern Europeans have been isolated from the global trend of individualization for a rather long period. There is some justification for this view since a collectivist ideology dominated cultural and political life in the Soviet Union since the 1930s and in the whole Eastern European region after the Second World War. However, reality was much more complex than this generalized assumption might suggest. In the course of the rapid industrialization and urbanization and together with the increase in the well-being of the population, all forms of modern individualization found their way to the Eastern part of the European continent. The enlargement of the pool of alternatives for personal realization coincided with the fast enhancement of personal capacities for rational orientation and adequate decision making in complex situations. The potential for conflict also increased in the region since the political over-centralization and the strong state interventionism into economic and cultural life put *narrow limits on individualization*. Together with the ideological and institutional flaws in the socialist organization of production and distribution, state interventionism undermined efforts to establish and maintain a meritocratic system of incentives and recognition of the achievements of individuals.

As seen from another angle, formalized official collectivism gradually eroded the communal bonds of state socialist societies. Aside from economic and political discontent, the search for genuine communal affiliations was the driving force of the *Solidarity* movement in Poland as well as of environmentalist and human rights groups all over Eastern Europe. The activities of the emerging civil society were very much caused and guided by a *longing for community*. The desired revival of communities was expected to bring about the best conditions for individualization. These had to include both higher economic and political efficiency *and* humanistic communal bonds between individuals freed from the grips of the state-socialist administrative system.

3.1 New Openings and Closures for Individualization

The rapid establishment of millions of private firms after the political turn at the end of the eighties was an impressive illustration of the speed and scale of the ongoing individualization in Eastern Europe. The registration of hundreds of political parties and thousands of non-governmental organizations in each country of the region would have been impossible without the initiative of individuals seeking new forms of personal development and realization. As seen in this context of the pluralization of economy, politics and culture, the dominance of private enterprises in the production of GDP in Eastern Europe at the end of the 1990s may be interpreted as an indicator of the *triumph of individualization in the region.* Previous limitations imposed by the state on mobility, self-expression, organization and communication of individuals disappeared. Millions cherished the hope that the core of all changes had to be the institutional support to the unrestricted development and self-realization of individuals. The institutional setting had to support the move from a situation, in which everybody was equally poor, to a situation, in which everybody would be well-off, although not equally.

In East-Central Europe the openings for individualization could already be celebrated at the beginning of the nineties. The availability of goods in the shops together with freedom of speech, organization and travel marked a break with the past of deficits and bureaucratic obstacles. Casting a glance at the whole Eastern European region during the nineties, the general impression would have been different. The institutional framework of most Eastern European societies was deeply destabilized and provoked widespread and intensive feelings of uncertainty. The vast majority of Eastern Europeans had lower living standards than before the political changes. At the end of the 1990s the share of the expenditures on food typically made up between 40 and 50% of the total income of Eastern European households. Public opinion polls regularly documented assessments of the financial condition of households which were characteristic of countries with mass poverty, serious economic problems and with a significant income differential. These parameters of the economic situation used to put strong restrictions on the space for individual development and self-realization. In the area of international travel the previous political obstacles gave way to financial restrictions which were no less effective. The Schengen arrangements became the symbol on the new political limitations of free travel and thus on the development and realization of Eastern Europeans.

In parallel with the spread of private entrepreneurship and political democratization, the principles of individualist ethics were embraced. They guided the activities both in the legal and in the black market. The crime wave was motivated by extreme individualism. However, the rise of crime was also related to the dramatic weakening of institutions that incorporated or protected the common good. The revival of traditional anti-individualist attitudes of extreme egalitarianism or state paternalism was the counter-reaction. It was strengthened by the growing understanding of the division of rich and poor as a major threat facing Eastern European societies. The universal values of individual human rights collided with the reckless pursuing of individual interests at the expense of the common good.

This critical development may be well recognized in the perceptions of typical problems facing the Eastern European societies. The assessments of crime and unemployment used to have stable and high values throughout the period of the transformation of Bulgarian society, for instance. The next most pressing issue was the concern about economic polarization and its effects. The intensity of the perception of other risks such as ethnic tensions gradually decreased mostly because interethnic problems had been suppressed by more intensive concerns:[1]

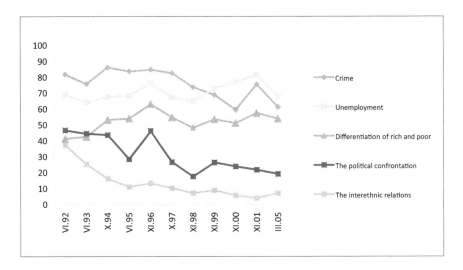

Figure 3.1 Dynamics of the perception of risks facing Bulgarian society, 1992–2005 (National surveys, five point scale, position 5 "A very serious problem", in %)

Some 20 years after the start of the changes one may strike the balance of the accelerated regional individualization. The effects of the global trend are most visible in the changes in legislation. The Eastern European constitutions passed after 1946 were based on an extreme collectivist legal philosophy stressing the relevance of the common good. While taking the common good as an important point of reference, the new constitutions and constitutional amendments passed in Eastern Europe during the post-socialist transformation have a rather different focus. This is the value and the normative regulation of *individual human rights*. The strategic difference consists of a profound shift from *collectivist institutional arrangements* towards *institutionalized individualism.* One might assume that the major problem of opening up opportunities for unrestricted personal development and realization had been thus resolved all over the region.

A closer look at reality helps to understand that the problems were and in many cases still remain much more complex than the generalized constitutional provisions. Across Eastern Europe, *individualization via privatization* brought about new forms of alienation of individuals. The expected revival of communities

---

1   This data stem from the national surveys on *Transformation Risks and Quality of Life* carried out annually by a team headed by the present author.

came mostly in the form of the revival of ethnic communities in the context of interethnic confrontations. The universal respect for the rights and freedoms of individuals only partly materialized in functioning institutions. Individualization turned out to be rather controversial, thus corresponding to the analytical type of an ambivalent and risk-laden process (Schroer 2008: 141).

What are the causes and reasons for this unpredicted and in many respects undesirable development?

Even the first glance cast at post-socialist reality recognizes that successful individualization came about in Eastern Europe during the nineties primarily *in the form of the looting of the common good.* The most impressive example is the privatization of state owned productive and infrastructural assets. No doubt, the socialist state did not effectively manage its large property in the increasingly differentiated Eastern European societies. That is why the introduction of market mechanisms and the privatization of state, communal and cooperative property became unavoidable. The main problems centered on the manner of transfer of public property into private hands. In many cases the transfer came about against modest compensation or without any compensation to the societal community. State institutions were substantially weakened and therefore not able to control the process. The variants of disrespect for the public interest in privatization procedures were numerous. They included the legalized selling of public property to managerial teams at low rates and ranged up to cases of large-scale criminal plundering. The high tide of crime became the most dramatic manifest pathology of individualization. Thus, the fundamental problem of 'transitional' societies was and in various ways still remains the *high intensity of structural risks* and the institutional incapability to manage them effectively. The resulting erosion of trust in public institutions has devastating effects on the moral quality of the ongoing individualization.

The typical individual reaction to risks incorporated in macro-social processes took the form of what is generally defined as *anomic behavior.* It had various causes and motives. Some of these, like the worldwide economic recession at the end of the eighties and the beginning of the nineties, were as objective as natural events. Others came about due to basically avoidable human error. The liberalization of prices was expected to unleash legally sound market initiative together with clear legal and moral responsibility. Little thought was given to the practically non-existent market-oriented banking system and stock exchange, insurance and pension schemes or provisions for unemployment.

Some exceptional national cases notwithstanding, the first reforms were carried out in the context of intensive political confrontation and lacking consensus on strategic issues. There were striking discontinuities in the policies of the successive short-lived governments. Dysfunctional relations between state institutions became everyday normality. Corruption became the unavoidable outcome. The economic polarization grew fast in conditions of institutional disarray. The destabilization of the institutional framework of Eastern European societies continues to provoke intense feelings of uncertainty.

Given the effects of the institutional and value-normative disarray, it is not surprising that the overwhelming trend in Eastern Europe is to search for individual solutions to problems which affect the majority of the population. It seems that it is precisely individualism which has taken the lead in thinking and behavior. Undoubtedly, individualistic liberalism is effective under such conditions as an ideology. Therefore, the former disputes about the advantages of the individualist 'American' or the institutionalist 'Swedish' model of social and economic organization seem to have been settled in Eastern Europe in favor of the former. Against the background of the overwhelming support to private initiative, a fundamental question immediately arises: *Can a stable social order be established and maintained by the efforts of extreme individualists?* Put in other words, *have the post-socialist societies already moved from the instability of a social order dominated by the rationality of collective needs and goals to another unstable social order dominated by the rationality of individual needs and goals?*

The question cannot be answered in generalized terms. It suffices to compare the strengthening of state institutions in the Russian Federation and the still inefficient management of the common good by the Ukrainian state in order to see the specific risks facing individualization in both contexts. If any generalization were indeed possible, then it should read that Eastern Europeans would like to have de-regulated conditions for private initiative of the 'American' type. But they would also like to have strong 'Scandinavian' state regulation of income levels in order to protect the economically weak groups. This is the typical controversial Eastern European situation after the difficult changes have reached the point of a relative institutional stabilization.

The practical problem does not primarily concern the desire to combine what cannot be implemented simultaneously. The crucial problem is that Eastern European societies are not as rich and institutionally well organized as the North American or Scandinavian societies. This is the major reason that *what is regarded as social and psychological tension, risk or uncertainty facing individuals in the advanced societies is being multiplied by a strong local 'stress factor' in most Eastern European societies.* The continuing deficits of transparency, efficiency and reliability of major social institutions determine and reproduce this 'stress factor'. So, the *tremendous opening* of the window of opportunities for individualization clashed and continues to clash with *tremendous problems* in the realization of these opportunities.

The major problem in this context concerns the limited space for autonomous personal decision under the conditions of widespread impoverishment. The general patterns of personal strategies for economic initiative are already well established in Eastern Europe. The opening up of opportunities for private entrepreneurship has found its followers. Some of them are truly successful. However, for large segments of Eastern Europeans the economic constraints on personal development and self-realization are substantial. It is sobering to notice that a very substantial part of the respondents in the PEW comparative study consider the economic situation in their countries in 2009 to be worse than the economic situation 20 years ago (*Two Decades after the Wall's Fall* 2009: 40):

Table 3.1 **"Would you say that the economic situation for most people in your country today is better, worse, or about the same as it was under communism?" (2009, in %)**

Country	Better	Worse	About the same	DK
Poland	47	35	12	6
Czech Republic	45	39	12	3
Russia	33	45	15	7
Slovakia	29	48	18	5
Lithuania	23	48	15	14
Bulgaria	13	62	18	7
Ukraine	12	62	13	12
Hungary	8	72	16	5

The above assessment of the economic situation in the respective countries together with the opening of borders make temporary or permanent out-migration a desirable form of escape from local restrictions on individualization. The decision to emigrate usually comes about as an outcome of the interaction of various factors. The strongest among them is currently the economic situation in the Eastern European societies. Due to the poor economic situation large groups have rather limited life chances there. This does not mean that the poorest persons and groups are those with the most intensive desire to emigrate and with the greatest numbers of emigrants. The desire to emigrate is often particularly intensive in groups in which the economic situation is relatively good in the national context. Nevertheless, the persons belonging to these groups see even better life chances for themselves and for their children in other countries. Since the substantial cleavage between the living standard and life chances in Eastern Europe and in the advanced societies will remain for a long time, there is no reason to expect a stop to the out-migration from the region in the near future. Moreover, it is no longer reasonable to cherish the expectations which were widespread at the beginning of the nineties. At that time many believed that out-migration from Eastern Europe would be a temporary phenomenon followed by a massive return of the emigrants to their countries of origin. There is no evidence supporting this assumption.

One may take the case of Poland in order to exemplify the controversies of individualization via emigration. Various estimates put the number of Polish citizens (registered and non-registered immigrants with their families) just in Great Britain and Ireland at between 1.5 and 2 million in January 2009. The explanation for this is that both countries opened their labor markets to Polish citizens immediately after Poland joined the European Union in 2004. Another explanation is the widespread command of the English language among the younger generation of Poles.

The reasons for the exodus are exclusively economic. Salaries and wages are still about 3 times lower in PPP terms in Poland than in the Western European countries. Migrants' remittances make up a substantial part of income for millions of households in Poland. Given the high level of unemployment and the low incomes in the country, mass emigration has generally had positive economic and social effects. It has reduced tensions on the national labor market thus making the necessary restructuring of the Polish economy at least partly bearable in social terms. In addition, due to the financial transfers of Polish migrants the survival of millions of Polish households and the further development of the human capital of the country has become possible. Therefore, without individualization in the form of mass emigration Polish society would have experienced more intensive tensions and conflicts in the course of the transformation than was actually the case.

Any stress on the positive effects of mass emigration from Poland after 1989 would distort the picture, however. The country lost – most probably forever – part of its best educated and most entrepreneurial labor force. The deliberate policies of Western European countries to attract the well educated Polish labor force caused intense discussions on the losses which the Polish economy is suffering or will suffer due to their emigration. The discussion mostly concerns the deficit of IT specialists in Poland which is currently estimated at around 30 to 40 thousand. These estimates together with concerns about the demographic trends in Polish society motivated the national program "Return" to attract Polish emigrants to go back to their country of origin.

Against the background of the intensive economic problems facing day-to-day life in Eastern Europe during the transformation period, the *low aspirations* in personal strategies have been of prime importance for the understanding of the cultural situation. Within the context of continuing economic pressure on households mass ambitions are reduced since they are related to the limited opportunities for choice and self-realization. The unavoidable consequence of this situation is the short time horizon of personal planning. This is in sharp contradiction to the requirements of the conscious and efficient management of personal development and realization. No doubt, the emancipation from the restrictive official party-state ideology imposed on the individuals was an evolutionary achievement. However, it brought about institutional insecurity and personal disorientation as well.

The conclusion is rather controversial. Instead of the desired rapid expansion of opportunities for choice for each individual, these opportunities have declined for substantial segments of the Eastern European population. Instead of the strongly desired increase in material standards, economic insecurity and deprivations have widely dominated everyday life of millions of Eastern Europeans for two decades. Instead of contentment with the effectiveness of democratic political institutions, large groups of the population in the region are suffering from their destabilization and the resultant expansion in crime. Instead of conditions for a higher quality of sustained personal development, in many cases the problems of recent years have led to personal and group degradation and to the destruction of human capital. This development provides abundant evidence supporting the point that "*rights, which impose demands on community members, are effectively upheld only as long as the basic needs of those community members are attended to*". (Etzioni 1996: 8)

The vast majority of Eastern Europeans have proved to be unprepared to cope with the challenges of societal transformation. This was the change from a society with restricted but clearly formulated opportunities for choice, to a society in which the orientation, choice and personal realization require intensive personal efforts under conditions of uncertain normative regulations. The moral and the institutional frameworks of communal life have come under pressure. Using the current terminology, not the Western European and North American societies, but the Eastern European societies are still *risk societies per se*. This is a mixed blessing for their participation in the global competition. It is widely acknowledged that developments, which throw a substantial part of the population below the standards typical for industrialized societies have to cope with detrimental effects on the national competitive power on an international scale.

3.2 Individualization and Communities

The reproduction of formalized organizational patterns of official collectivism had unintended and undesirable effects in the socialist societies. The politically imposed collectivism gradually eroded their communal bonds. Instead of fostering constructive individualization, the formalized administrative structures tended to foster social irresponsibility. Aside from the economic and political discontent, aversion to the over-centralized political formalism and the search for genuine communal affiliations became another major driving force in the search for change. Already in the late fifties the Yugoslavian leadership tried to counter the destructive effects of bureaucratization by introducing territorial and production-based self-government. It was intended to be an organizational framework supporting communal bonds and solidarity (Horvat, Markovic and Supek 1975). This was also the essence of the hopes for "socialism with a human face" during the short-lived Prague Spring. However, the high tide of the search for community came with the *Solidarity* movement in Poland. In its most enthusiastic and idealistic initial phase, the movement institutionalized itself in solidarity-motivated communities in territories and enterprises. The martial law abruptly put an end to this attempt to add community bonds to the organizational and cultural framework of individualization under state socialism.

The famous slogan of the Monday rallies in Leipzig in October 1989: "*Wir sind das Volk*" (We are the people) had exactly the same affective background. It expressed the need to re-vitalize feelings of communal belonging. The search for communal affiliation was the driving force of environmentalist groups and movements all over Eastern Europe. Longing for community guided the revival of national identities in the Baltic States and in other parts of the region. It animated the rallies in Prague, Budapest, Bucharest and Sofia in the late autumn of 1989.

The desired new and better organization of Eastern European societies had to achieve economic and political, dynamic and organizational efficiency *together* with the humanistic consolidation of strong communal bonds between individuals freed from the grips of the petrified state-socialist administrative system.

Eastern European intellectuals reflected on this *search for community* by modernizing the idea of *civil society.* Rather blurry in the theoretical tradition and in its more recent modifications, this idea used to convey a clear ideological and political message at the end of the eighties. Voluntary associations in economy, politics and culture had to replace the formalized organizations of state socialism. The association-like civil society had to offer the social space for the free development and realization of individuals.

The community-focused visions and desires of humanistic individualization could not but dramatically clash with the reality of individualization which came about with all forms of privatization of state, communal and collective property. The community-oriented visions also clashed with the shadow sides of the new competitive politics. The clashes were not obvious at the beginning of the changes. The mushrooming of political parties could be interpreted as the opening of a large window of opportunities for political initiative and responsibility and thus for creative and grass-roots based political individualization. The clash became unavoidable in the course of the formation of the new political elite and its distancing from its own grass-roots. The appearance of thousands of non-governmental organizations in the Eastern European societies was a clear sign of the success of efforts to invest personal time and energy for the enrichment of this common good of civil society. However, contrary to the expectations that community-based civil society would become the locomotive of the Eastern European societal transformations, civil society in the region still remains organizationally weak, leader-centered and dependent on the funding by foreign sources.

Thus, the search for new communities produced some positive results but also many disenchantments and anomic effects. These had two major determinants. The first one was the continuing instability of *formal organizations* due to the long-term mutual adaptation of organizational changes in economy, politics and culture. Anomie was also caused by the intensive uncertainties about the hanging organizational and community affiliations of individuals. Under the conditions of all-embracing transformation there are *many competing organizations and communities towards which each individual could orient his/her preferences, decisions and actions.* Eastern Europeans had to learn fast that the integration and functioning of organizations and communities could be mutually reinforcing or mutually dysfunctional and that the tensions and conflicts between organizations and communities are inherent to social processes. (Bauman 2004)

Under the conditions of organizational and communal uncertainty and instability, individualization became a risk factor for societal integration in Eastern Europe. On the surface, the first priority seemed to be the value-normative integration of communities. In reality, it was mainly the problem of organizational integration which had to have priority, since there was no time for organic value-normative communal integration *preceding* the organizational integration. Under the given historical conditions, only the reestablishment of organizational integration could bring about a long lasting repair of community bonds. The chance for positive changes is connected with the possibility to mobilize individuals, communities, organizations and the national society for the preservation and development of the common good. The prospect of *integration via mobilization for risk management* seems to be most promising in order to keep individualization, communities and organizations protected from anomie and pathologies.

Advanced Western European and North American societies manage the challenge of the progressing individualization successfully because they already have well established *organizational integration* of all major action spheres and between the action spheres. Parallel to the formal organizations they have various *community-type* formations. It has been recognized in the advanced parts of the world that communities do not belong to the traditional past alone. Communal bonds are an indispensable means of social integration in societies basically relying on mechanisms of functional differentiation and integration. The major outcome of the century-long debates between communitarians and libertarians on the issue may be summarized as follows: *Stable individualization requires personal autonomy and creativity in the context of well-integrated organizations. Stable social integration needs the informality, the affective relations and the human touch of community-type formations.* These are defined and dominated by we-identities which may be rather specific in their functions in the communal integration of individuals. Moreover, the communal formations may also be rather controversial in developing and reproducing we-identities of individuals.

Both the constructive and destructive effects of Eastern European individualizations may be illustrated well by changes that came about in the traditional *familial we-identities* during the transformation period. Economic grievances put strong pressure on families during the first years of the transformation. All over Eastern Europe divorce rates declined. The support of family members became existentially important for millions of unemployed who otherwise would not have been able to survive on the extremely low unemployment benefits. The return of urban families to small-scale agricultural production was also possible with the support of all able-bodied family members. This strengthened their family bonds as a rule. The struggle for survival of families also pressed family members to out-migration. This was usually intended to be short-term. It was widely expected that the transformation crisis would be short and the financial support needed would be accumulated abroad fast. Neither of these expectations came true. The legal or illegal short-term stays abroad had to be prolonged since unemployment and low incomes continued to dominate the everyday concerns of millions of Eastern European families. As a result, millions of children grew up without parents in Poland, Romania, Moldova, Bulgaria and Ukraine and in other post-socialist societies. In many families the generation gap became unbearably deep since the younger generations succeeded in their efforts to adapt to the dynamics of the new situations more often than their parents did. The older generation typically clung on to its nostalgic feelings about the egalitarian and secure socialist past. The trend of the fast rise in one-person households is another obvious effect of individualization at the expense of familial we-identities.

The variety of grass-roots political activities in small and large settlements during the first weeks and months of the Polish *Solidarity* movement rose expectations that one of its guiding ideas would immediately materialize. The activists of *Solidarity* wanted to establish communal solidarity not just at the level of enterprises, but also in the settlements. Many believed that the martial law would be just a short break in the implementation of the project. It was immediately re-vitalized together with the democratization wave in Poland at the end of the eighties. However, the enthusiastic rise of *we-identities within settlement communities* soon disappeared together with the rise of political rivalries and confrontations. The massive internal migration together with the large-scale out-migration from the Eastern European states undermined the local we-identities as well. This destructive development is particularly strong in rural areas where depopulation is advancing fast. The large cities which attracted the migrants from the rural areas are now becoming increasingly dominated by the economic alienation of commercialized relationships. Thus, we-identifications with settlement communities never reached the level of intensity which was desired and expected by the local activists of *Solidarity.*

The *Solidarity* movement protested against the lost sense of community in the state socialist enterprises first of all. Both the state bureaucracy and the official trade unions were identified as sources of alienation. Therefore, independent trade unions had to be established in order to revitalize the *corporate we-identities* in the industrial enterprises. The economic reforms after 1989 brought about results which radically deviated from the desires and expectations of the activists of *Solidarity.* In Poland like in all other Eastern European societies the new private owners only rarely allow trade unions within the enterprises. The unionization of the labor force declined all over the region from the standard level of just under 100% in the times of state socialism to the rather modest level of 15–20% mostly in the state run education and health care. The existence of the large army of the unemployed is the major factor explaining why it is not corporate communal solidarity but alienation and competition which dominates the organizational and cultural situation in Eastern European enterprises. The few exceptions to this are the enterprises which were privatized or built up by companies from countries where the corporate we-identities are high on the political agenda and on the agenda of enterprise management.

At the beginning of the nineties the expectation was widespread that religiosity and religious organizations were going to experience a massive revival after they had been suppressed for decades. This expectation was only partly realized in some cases like Russia. In most other Eastern European societies the *religious and church-related we-identities* experienced only a modest revival and strengthening, if any at all. A particularly interesting case in this respect is the development in Poland. Catholic religiosity and the Catholic Church remain as strong in the country as they have been for centuries. But contrary to widespread expectations, neither religiosity nor the Catholic Church received a strong new impetus after 1989. More precisely, religiosity and the Church had even lost some of their attractiveness since the times when the Catholic Church was the most important ideological and institutional competitor to the then ruling ideology and political party. A special case is the rise of *communal religious and institutional we-identities* in some newly established or expanded protestant communities or communities of new religions. However, these remain peripheral in the cultural and institutional life of the Eastern European societies as a rule. (Borowik 2006)

The rise of political pluralism and competitive politics at the beginning of the Eastern European societal transformations triggered beliefs about the future rich life of political communities. Many cherished the hope that imagined and imaginary political communities would be established in the region and would last for a long time. Contrary to these beliefs and hopes, political life in Eastern Europe has been marked by the rather dynamic rise and disappearance of parties and political coalitions. The fluctuation of voters has been very high. The major reason was and still is the continuing instability of social structures. No long-term definition of political preferences along the traditional distinction of "left" and "right" could be maintained by the voters. Their *we-identities concerning political communities* could only be stabilized step-by-step in the context of the fragile economic and cultural stabilization of Eastern European societies.

One could expect that the stability of political communities would be easily achieved on the basis of re-emerging ethnic identities. In fact, ethnically based movements and parties took the lead in the Baltic States and had a dramatic political dominance on the territory of the former Yugoslavia. But only there and particularly in Bosnia and Herzegovina and in Macedonia did the *we-identities of ethnic communities* take on a persistent political representation which still dominates political life in both countries. Ethnically based political parties have regularly participated in political coalitions in Romania and Bulgaria. It is still difficult to foresee what long-term consequences this ethnicization of politics might have for political life in these countries and in the region.

In the early stage of the Eastern European transformations the stress on politically organized *we-identities of national communities* was regarded with strong suspicion by the Western European states and other Western organizations. They feared that the nationalist propaganda and politics might get out of control and thus damage the emerging Eastern European democracies. It seemed that these fears were confirmed by the participation of the radical nationalistic *League of Polish Families* in the Polish coalition government 2005–2007. The *League* prepared legal acts in the field of education which deviated very much from the political philosophy and practice in the traditional European democracies. After the accession of ten Eastern European countries into the European Union was completed, it became politically correct to represent right-wing nationalist policies in the framework of the democratic political game. The argument of the Eastern Europeans is persuasive enough: there are nationalist parties and movements in most

Western European countries. The phenomena of nationalist political organization will still have to be carefully analyzed in Slovakia, Hungary, Bulgaria and in other new EU member states. The developments might be rather controversial since the strong identification with the national community may go hand in hand with alienation from the nation-state because of its inability to handle corruption, drug-abuse or crime successfully. There are serious signals coming from public opinion polls that the identification with the existing state administration in some post-socialist societies is very much disturbed because of exactly these reasons (*Two Decades after the Wall's Fall* 2009: 76):

Table 3.2 National problems today beyond the economy in the former Eastern bloc (2009, answers "yes", in %)

Country	Corrupt political leaders	Crime	Illegal drugs
Bulgaria	76	76	74
Czech Republic	71	55	51
Hungary	76	69	54
Lithuania	78	76	66
Poland	58	49	49
Russia	52	51	54
Slovakia	52	55	46
Ukraine	70	56	46

The *we-identities of belonging to the European Union* are underdeveloped in Eastern Europe. The advancements in this respect will very much depend on the development of the European Union itself and particularly on whether the perception gets stronger that membership in the EU has positive consequences for the individual Eastern European societies. This perception is not equally strong in all new EU member states. The *we-identities of the global community* are even less developed than identification with the EU.

The wide variety of potential or real we-identities only seemingly contradicts the global trend of individualization. The very possibility of selecting and making a choice in favor of specific we-identities under democratic conditions is a triumph of the autonomy of the mature individual. His or her liberty, dignity and self-realization could not come about outside of the interaction of various identities in various communities.

3.3 Individualization in Elite Change

The all-embracing societal transformations opened opportunities for extraordinary personal achievements in the change of political elites. All over Eastern Europe and at all structural levels of politics some individuals managed to take the lead and to fill in the newly created leadership positions or positions vacated by the former political elite. In some cases this happened just by chance. But the rule was different. Three unique and at the same time quite typical cases of taking over national political leadership will exemplify the point. The first example will be the fate of Boris Yeltsin who strongly influenced the domestic politics of the Russian Federation and thus the geostrategic constellation of the world during the nineties. This case exemplifies the *far-reaching continuity in the ruling elites* before and after the turn to market economy, democratization of political institutions and development of cultural pluralism. The second case of Lech Wałęsa exemplifies the sharp discontinuity in the political elite. The political career of Wałęsa shows *the emergence of political counter-elite from the low (working-class) layers of social stratification.* The last case of Václav Havel clearly exemplifies another pattern of *the development of political counter-elite from the higher (intellectual) strata of socialist society.* All these patterns might be generalized under Pareto's concept of "lions" in the circulation of political elites. (Pareto 2003 [1901]: 72ff.) The three persons and their biographies correspond to Pareto's type of political leaders marked by historical vision, strong will and the capacity to overcome tremendous obstacles. What their biographies share is perfectly well grasped by Pareto's view that real "lions" are needed by society for a rather short time. Their moment on the world stage expires fast.

Like Khrushchev, Brezhnev, Chernenko, Gorbachev and most other top functionaries of the CPSU Boris Yeltsin was born in a village. Like most of these party functionaries he profited from the rapid industrialization and fast increase in the educational level in the Soviet society. In his early thirties he already had a long record of membership in the ruling party und made his first step in the managerial *nomenclatura* as director of a construction enterprise. In 1968 he was already a party *nomenclatura* in the Regional Committee of the CPSU in Sverdlovsk (today Yekaterinburg). In 1976 he was elected first secretary of the party committee in this third major industrial region of the Soviet Union after Moscow and Leningrad (today Saint Petersburg). His steep carrier in the party apparatus continued in 1985 when he was promoted by Mikhail Gorbachev to the position of first secretary of the Moscow committee of CPSU and member of the party's Politburo. Thus, Yeltsin had all opportunities to be fully socialized in CPSU party life as one of the most successful party functionaries of his time. Yeltsin definitely must have had organizational talent in order to advance so fast in the party's authoritarian structures despite the fact that his father had been imprisoned as an enemy of the Soviet people.

The somewhat surprising move of Yeltsin against his patron Gorbachev and the *perestroika* politics has two popular explanations. The first one was Yeltsin's dissatisfaction by the content and the speed of reform processes. This reason was made publicly known by a provocative speech of Yeltsin in 1987 where he announced his retreat from the Politburo. His dismissal from the position of first secretary of the Moscow Party committee and the subsequent humiliation were the consequence. The second reason Yeltsin's growing critical attitude towards the party leadership was his embarrassment with the publicly known active involvement of Gorbachev's wife Raisa in party and state decision-making. One may only speculate about the third and probably the most important reason for Yeltsin's distancing from the person and politics of Gorbachev. Strong in-born political intuition, long experience in party life and the work in Politburo must have lead Yeltsin to the conclusion that Gorbachev's messy leadership could not endure for long. As seen in retrospect, Yeltsin profited very much from his timely exit from the circle of Gorbachev's supporters. He profited even more from his publicly expressed dissatisfaction with Gorbachev's policies and from his evolving public image as Gorbachev's rival. (Colton 2008)

The time for capitalizing on his image as persecuted radical reformer was approaching fast. Yeltsin himself strengthened this image by telling a widely publicized story about an attempt on his life. The official version of this story was that Yeltsin had fallen off a bridge when drunk. The public was inclined to believe Yeltsin and not the authorities. So he had public support and was elected a member of the Congress of People's Deputies in 1989 as a reform minded CPSU loyalist. Thereafter the events were accelerating. The Soviet Union has reached the point where immediate fundamental changes seemed to be unavoidable. The following stages in Yeltsin's political biography best illustrate the profundity and the extremely high speed of the turn to new patterns of organization and behavior. In 1990 he was elected Chairman of the Supreme Soviet of the Russian Federative Republic in the USSR. Yeltsin's public image as a dedicated and radical reformer was so strong that he received widespread support in the elections for the newly created position of the President of the Russian Federative Republic in June 1991.

The time of Yeltsin's rise to the top of the national and world leaders had come. However, there was still one major obstacle. The Russian Federative Republic was just part of the existing Soviet Union and the President of the Union was Mikhail Gorbachev. This last institutional and personal hurdle had to be overcome.

Most probably, Yeltsin did not know that his former colleagues from the Politburo of the CPSU were unintentionally trying to help him by preparing a *coup d'etat* against Gorbachev. The hardliners Kryuchkov (KGB Chairman), Yazov (Minister of Defense) and others wanted to stop Gorbachev's reforms which were running out of control. As they had all the power in their hands, it seemed that the organizers of the conspiracy had every chance to overthrow Gorbachev. They succeeded at the beginning of their attempt on 19 August 1991. Gorbachev was arrested during his holiday and the army supported the coup. However, its organizers had not properly calculated for "the Yeltsin factor". He had already acquired the real power in the Russian Republic as its legitimately elected President. His decisive actions against the *coup d'etat* and its organizers made history. The news about Yeltsin's speech on the top of a tank on the Red Square broke around the world.

This was the decisive turn in Yeltsin's biography. The world was ready to forget his impressive records as a CPSU party functionary. As if by miracle, he was already a true democrat and the most important democratic politician in the Soviet Union. The title of Yeltsin's first biography *Boris Yeltsin: From Bolshevik to Democrat* (Morrison 1991) published in the West at that time is a perfect illustration of the point. His rival Mikhail Gorbachev returned to his position of President of the weakened Union. But the power was already in the hands of Boris Yeltsin as President of the Russian Republic. He knew how to use power in order to eliminate his rivals. These could not have come from any anti-Communist elite since it could not have been consolidated in the Soviet Union. Rivals to Yeltsin's emerging monopoly of power could have only come from the Communist Party. So, it had to be outlawed as was done in October 1991. In this way Gorbachev was no longer head of the powerful party apparatus. But he was still the formal leader of the Soviet Union. There were certainly many reasons to think and act decisively in order to reform the Soviet Union. However, the better option for Yeltsin would be to dissolve it. The dissolution of the Soviet Union would immediately imply the elimination of the position of the President of the Union and thus the political death of the incumbent Mikhail Gorbachev.

The decision to proceed in this radical direction was taken by Yeltsin and supported by the Presidents of the Ukraine Leonid Kravchuk and of Belarus Stanislav Shushkevich. The three politicians met on 8 December 1991 in a strange location[2] under rather unusual circumstances and signed an agreement for the dissolution of the Soviet Union. The newly created entity of the *Commonwealth of the Independent States* was intended to become a confederation. Who has actually given the legal power to these three persons to make such a historical decision and to create a new international entity in the absence of most of the leaders of its parts – this remains the intriguing subject of historical novels. For the *Realpolitik* the result was that the Soviet Union no longer existed. Neither did the President of the Union. So, the only politician with real power in Russia was already legally and *de facto* Boris Yeltsin. Under these conditions he could freely use his monopoly of power in order to design and implement the profound reforms which were existentially needed for the modernization of Russia. There were no legal or organizational obstacles in the way of the materialization of the immense structural opportunities for his individualization.

There had been similar situations in Russian history in which a leader used the monopoly on power in order to radically modernize the country. Peter I and Catharina II were the most impressive examples. They managed to use these opportunities for extreme individualization and remain in history as great modernizers of the

---

2   The place was a natural reserve in the famous forests *Belovezhskaya Pushcha* some 50 km from Brest in Belarus.

country. However, Peter I had spent years learning ship building and navigation abroad in order to navigate the country towards the position of continental power. Catharina II possessed large knowledge of the reform projects of the European Enlightenment. Boris Yeltsin certainly wanted to introduce a market economy and political democracy into the Russian social institutions and everyday life. However, he had never really studied the way in which the market economy and political democracy function. He had never had the opportunity to really see the functioning of market economy and political democracy in practice. His education and his practical experience were not at the level of qualifications required for the management of profound reforms oriented towards market economy and democratic politics.

The situation was even more complicated. In a sharp contrast to Poland, there were no local experts in Russia possessing the knowledge and practical experience needed to design and rationally implement such reforms. Since Yeltsin wanted to keep to his promise for radical reforms after having acquired the power he needed, he had to rely on strategic planning and expertise from abroad. The invitation to experts of the World Bank and the International Monetary Fond was unavoidable. They seemed to possess the expertise needed to guide the profound reforms in Russia. The Harvard professor Jeffrey Sachs officially became Yeltsin's advisor in December 1991. Sachs already had working relations with two young Russian economists – Yegor Gaidar and Anatoliy Chubais. Both had key positions in Yeltsin's administration at that time and took on the responsibility of implementing the advice of the World Bank experts. They were headed by Sachs who already had practical experience from his advisory activities in Poland.

Events followed at the highest imaginable speed. At the very beginning of January 1992 prices were liberalized following the Polish example of 1990. But in striking contrast to the development in Poland, the hyperinflation did not stop soon in Russia and the shops received only a modest supply of goods which most Russians could no longer afford. Obviously, the liberalization of prices was not properly prepared for supporting the stabilization of production and trade. The next jump into unpredictable developments was the voucher privatization scheme which was announced in a Program of President Yeltsin.

The voucher privatization was prepared according to the Czech pattern and started in October 1992. Most inhabitants of the large country were surprised by the event. They did not know what the voucher privatization was for since the enlightenment campaign was badly prepared and implemented. The distribution of vouchers among the population was marked by many opportunities for massive cheating. Thus, the big-bang voucher privatization was designed and expected to become the model for the just way to privatize state property but turned out to be the opposite in its results. No fresh money came into the Russian economy. At the end of 1994 the formal status of Jeffrey Sachs as Yeltsin's adviser expired. At that point of time more than 40 million people in Russia lived on the brink of biological survival while a handful of other people managed to amass incredible fortunes. Having directly obtained large amount of shares in legal or mostly in illegal ways, directors of enterprises, politicians, state administrators and various criminal structures became the new rich people in the country. This was the time of the birth of the first economic oligarchs (tycoons) in Russia. They used the erratic presidency of Boris Yeltsin in order to privatize a large part of the former public property. The outcomes of the social differentiation were presented by the international scientific observers in a rather impressive manner: "Although the private sector has grown, self-employment is still rare. Incomes are down, and unemployment is up. Some entrepreneurs and managers have achieved dramatic success, while most of their compatriots have steadily lost ground to hyperinflation. The upshot is a distended income distribution and unprecedented income inequality". (Gerber and Hout 1998: 3)

The voucher privatization was presented in Yeltsin's Program for economic reforms as his personal major task. However, he had been only superficially involved in the process which had been moving out of control from the very beginning. But Yeltsin's distance from the implementation of the voucher privatization was only partly due to his lack of competence in the economy. Controversial political processes tended to take up a larger and larger part of his activities. The reason for this was the deepening animosity between Yeltsin and the Supreme Soviet of the Congress of the People's Deputies. This had been elected in the Soviet times and Yeltsin shared common values with many deputies at that time. But the cultural and political constellation has changed profoundly thereafter. The Supreme Soviet was against the dissolution of the Soviet Union, against the way that privatization had been implemented by Yeltsin's administration according the advice of foreign experts, and against Yeltsin's foreign policies of demonstrative cooperation with the West. The tensions between the President and the Parliament (Congress of People's Deputies) cumulated to the level of an almost successful attempt for the impeachment of Yeltsin. As a democrat he would certainly prefer that his adversaries would leave the Congress, as had happened with the opponents of the Bolsheviks in the Second Congress of the Soviets on 26th October (8th November) 1917 in Petrograd. However, the members of the Congress did not go but tried even to organize an armed defense of the parliament building.

Thus, the democrat Yeltsin decided to call tanks to shell the Parliament on the 4th October 1993. One may wonder if the way the bloody resolution of the conflict between two state powers came about was truly democratic or not. If John Morrison had published his book on Yeltsin not at the end of 1991 but at the end of 1993, he would have probably title it "From Democrat to Bolshevik" by referring to Yeltsin's *Realpolitik*. Another assumption might be that the former CPSU party functionary Yeltsin had never left the political platform of Bolshevik radicalism but has always tried to adapt it to specific circumstances. Whatever the interpretation, the major relevant historical fact in this context is the referendum on the Constitution of the Russian Federation held in December 1993. The new Constitution substantially enlarged the legal space for the individualization of Boris Yeltsin. He was called "Tsar Boris" before the new Constitution was approved. After the Constitution was passed there were already constitutional reasons to refer to him in this way by following the Russian tradition of government.

The inefficiency of the state administration to raise the funds needed for the functioning of the state belongs to the same long tradition of the Russian statehood. In 1994 and 1995 the state finances of the Russian Federation went bankrupt. The salaries of the state administration could only be paid with substantial delays. The presidential administration had no other rival institution or group to blame for the difficult reforms any more. International financial support for the Presidency of Yeltsin was substantial but not nearly to the degree which could have stabilized the Russian economy and the Russian state. Thus, there seemed to be only one legitimate way for resolving the issue which was becoming increasingly heated with the approaching presidential elections scheduled for 1996. Together with the drop in the GDP of the Russian Federation by more than 50 percent as compared to the level of 1989 and with the impoverishment of tens of millions of households in the country the public prestige of Boris Yeltsin was plummeting. At the same time, the Communist Party of the Russian Federation was strengthening its public support. The Chairman of the party, Gennady Zyuganov, was a very plausible candidate for the Presidency. The stakes were high. Action was urgently needed.

The action taken by Yeltsin's presidential administration to fix the problem and finance his re-election campaign belongs to the most mysterious chapters of the privatization in the Russian Federation. Officially it was called "Loans for Shares" and generally did not imply any wrongdoing. It is not unusual to guarantee the repayment of state loans taken from commercial banks with shares from state owned enterprises or other state owned assets. The relevant point in the given case was the publicly known inability of the Russian state to pay back the short-term credits. Therefore, the shares in the best Russian state owned primary industries (earth oil and gas production, nickel and steel works) offered as state guarantees were in practice gifts to the owners of the commercial banks. Their owners were the already well established oligarchs. (Blasi, Kroumova and Kruse 1997) They were very grateful and ready for friendly gestures in return. The richest people Russia's joined the initiative of the oligarch Boris Berezovsky to generously support Yeltsin for a second term in the presidential elections. This became the turning point towards the domination of oligarchs in the politic of Yeltsins Russia. (Gaman-Golutvina 2007) In addition, a special generous loan of 10 billion dollars came from the International Monetary Fund in a timely manner. Since all TV stations were in the hands of the oligarchs, Zyuganov had no chance, although his political rating was much higher than Yeltsin's at the beginning of the presidential campaign. Yeltsin's team, headed by his daughter Tatyana Dyachenko and Anatoly Chubais, managed to achieve the nearly impossible by applying the techniques of American presidential campaigns. The rival Zyuganov was presented as the person who would immediately re-nationalize the economy if elected. Nobody wanted the deficit economy back. On the other hand, Yeltsin's election team managed to "sell" his political failures as unrivalled historical successes. Yeltsin himself generously invested his personal time and energy into the campaign of his re-election despite his ruinous health conditions. The plausible explanation was his fear that a loss in the presidential elections would mean that he will be brought before the court. Each of his acts of dissolving the Soviet Union, the shelling of the Parliament building or the manner in which he waged the war in Chechnya could be fully sufficient for a serious sentence by the court.

Due to the large domestic and international financial support, Yeltsin succeeded in the presidential re-elections. This resolved his fears and the fears of his close collaborators. They were publicly regarded as corrupt persons and had good reasons to fear legal prosecution. However, the re-election did not resolve any of the burning issues of the continuing economic decline and political instability in the Russian Federation. A pragmatic definition of the new geostrategic situation of Russia after the dissolution of the Soviet Union was very much needed. The humiliating conditions under which the Federation had to conclude the peace in Chechnya after a bloody war was indicative of the grave problems of Yeltsin's policies of decentralization. The crippling financial crisis of August 1998 shone light on both the shaky grounds of the economic recovery and the Russian political and financial institutions' feeble way of handling the issue. The inadequate reactions of Yeltsin to the problematic war in Kosovo made it obvious that he and his advisers had not found the way to adapt Russia to the new geostrategic situation. Last but not least, the famous incident at Shannon Airport where Yeltsin could not meet the Irish Prime Minister due to acute health problems demonstrated how personally unreliable the ailing President of Russia could be. The repeated attempt at impeachment in the spring of 1999 was yet another signal that President Yeltsin had the control over Russian politics only loosely in his hands.

Therefore, the somewhat surprising stepping down of Yeltsin from his position as the President of the Russian Federation on the very eve of the new millennium could only have exceptionally been met by disappointment. Most probably, Yeltsin had good intentions for Russia, for the Russian people and particularly for democracy in Russia at the beginning of his service as a President. However, he was definitely not the best imaginable servant of the Russian state and the people in Russia in difficult times. His economic policy and particularly his policy of voucher privatization, later "Loans for Shares" privatization, was a failure both in terms of economic efficiency and in terms of its social consequences. Under Yeltsin's Presidency the Russian Federation went through an economic recession which was much deeper than the recession in the United States and Germany during the dramatic years between 1929 and 1933. Impoverishment and the related mortality in Russia reached levels which seemed to be impossible in industrialized societies. The values of the Gini coefficient measuring the economic inequality in the Russian Federation reached levels typical of Latin America. Due to the combination of the formally democratic organization of society with the openly authoritarian rule of Yeltsin, the very term "democracy" got in Russia despising connotations. In geostrategic terms Yeltsin left Russia with the territory which it had had 300 years ago and with the open task for his successors to properly define the new position of the large country in the world.

Boris Yeltsin was a person with unusually high aspirations. His steep upward career as a functionary of the authoritarian Communist Party of the Soviet Union as well as his firm political will to manage the processes after the weakening and disappearance of the Soviet Union provide enough evidence of his extraordinary personal qualities. Owing to historical circumstances, he received a wide range of structural opportunities to apply his qualities in extraordinary individualization. This was his historical chance and his tragedy. His personal level of education and organizational habits could not enable him to manage the challenges. Yeltsin's aspirations were high but his personal level of human capital did not correspond to the requirements of the historical opportunities. The mismatch was certainly clear for a person with such unusually high in-born intelligence as Yeltsin. So, announcing his step down from the position of the President of the Russian Federation he found it necessary to excuse himself on the national TV for not having achieved what he had intended and what the citizens of the Russian Federation would have expected. The intentions and expectations still remain matter of debate. But the need for a public excuse by Yeltsin was never questioned.

One may go to the extremes in the search for similarities and differences in the political carriers of Boris Yeltsin and Lech Wałęsa. Whatever the details, at least one similarity is unquestionable. Both Yeltsin and Wałęsa deeply influenced the regional history of Eastern Europe and consequently the global geostrategic situation. But they did this in rather different periods of their lives and in different ways. Yeltsin has spent the first decades of his political activity in the service of the ruling state-socialist ideology and politics. This was the period in which he did not have any influence on the broader historical context. Wałęsa spent the first decades of his political activities organizing the opposition to the state-socialist ideology and politics. This was exactly the period in which his name and political involvement became symbolic for the ongoing and forthcoming profound changes in state socialist societies and in the global political relations. Both Yeltsin and Wałęsa became presidents of states at the beginning of the democratization of their societies. This was the time of the most impressive historically relevant deeds of Boris Yeltsin. To the contrary, this was the period in which the political activities of Wałęsa began to lose historical relevance. At the end of their political carriers the political prestige of both men was approaching zero. Thus, both managed to occupy key social spaces in their extraordinary paths of individualization and left the political scene with very narrow spaces still open for socially relevant decisions and actions.

How and why did it become possible for a low-educated worker from a peasant family to profoundly influence political life in Poland, in Eastern Europe and even worldwide? The simplified answer might focus on the human capital of Lech Wałęsa. No doubt, in his public activities he could rely on his strong political intuition and analytical ability to simplify complex situations in order to identify major causes, actors and effects. In addition, he was able to surprise with fast reactions and to argue in front of smaller and larger audiences in a charismatic way. His straight-forward and sometimes rather undiplomatic style attracted attention and support. The worker Wałęsa also had the capacity to mobilize and apply a strong political will based on the remarkable psychological integrity of his personality. Last but not least, he was able to preserve his psychological integrity under complicated and rapidly changing conditions.

The extraordinary personal qualities of the electrician Lech Wałęsa would most probably have remained irrelevant in the broad social context if the structural tensions in Eastern European societies had not reached the point of permanent crisis. The economic reproduction in the region got slower and could not provide state institutions with the resources needed for the efficient reproduction of other action spheres. The political institutions were increasingly unable to innovate in domestic and international politics. The value-normative structures could not provide the economic and political organizations with the cultural legitimacy they very much needed. At the end of the 1970s Polish society was particularly struck by the mutual blocking of institutions. The ruling Polish United Workers' Party was increasingly losing space for political maneuvering after repeated crises. The illusion of wellbeing based on international credits could not last for ever.

Unlike in the previous crises of 1956, 1968 and 1970, at the beginning of the 1980s domestic and international analysts and advisers were very much involved in the consolidation of the Polish political opposition. As a result, there was already an expressed readiness for communication and cooperation between the two major oppositional actors who had acted separately before – the Polish workers and the Polish intelligentsia. There was nothing new in this insight. The necessary cooperation of workers with the revolutionary intelligentsia was a corner stone of the Bolshevik's revolutionary strategy and tactics, for instance. The innovation was in the new ideas concerning organization. The lessons from previous revolutionary practices were well adapted to the new circumstances.

Thus, the workers' unrests at the shipyard in Gdansk may have started spontaneously and by chance in Gdansk in August 1980. But the immediate arrival of advisors who joined the striking workers was already prepared in advance. The advisors represented oppositional organizations of the Polish intelligentsia like the Committee for the Defense of Workers (KOR). The gradually emerging demand of the striking workers to establish independent trade unions was actually widely discussed in oppositional circles in Poland and by experts abroad long before the events in Gdansk. What remained still uncertain was the authentic leader for the workers' uprising. The person had to come from the events themselves and to be identified with a particularly strong mobilizing message. This was the best imaginable chance for Lech Wałęsa. He grabbed it immediately. He became the authentic leader of the workers, bringing upon himself the massive attention of the media, politicians and analysts in Poland and abroad. He became the speaker of a movement which could have far reaching structural consequences in Poland, in Eastern Europe and possibly worldwide. At least, this was the perception of the active participants in the historical processes when the trade union *Solidarity* was officially recognized by the authorities during the hot Polish political summer of

1980. Well informed journalists immediately recognized the personal qualities of the new leader and his achievements. (Eringer 1982).

The achievements of Wałęsa did not concern the founding of the independent trade union *Solidarity* alone. Due to Wałęsa's skillful publicity campaigns the ruling Polish United Workers Party (PZPR) had to officially recognize that it no longer possessed the ownership of the idea of society dominated by solidarity. Moreover, this was the official recognition that PZPR has distanced itself from this idea in its practice. In fact, social reality all over Eastern Europe was marked at that time by bureaucratic inefficiency, technological and economic alienation and deficits of legitimacy. Therefore, it was entirely convincing to argue and to act in favor of new forms of social solidarity. At the beginning of the *Solidarity* movement the demand for authentic social solidarity could be understood as a demand for reforms in the framework of the existing political and economic order. However, the demand had the potential to lead away from the existing order as it happened some later.

Thus, the worker Lech Wałęsa became the symbolic bearer of the options for change. The social relevance of the link between the workers' movement and the demand for authentic social solidarity made him famous worldwide. His reputation increased following the imposition of the martial law in December 1981. At that time Wałęsa was no more a local, but an internationally respected symbol of the fight for freedom and human rights. The Nobel Price for Peace awarded to him in 1983 was understood by many as fully deserved and adequate considering his personal achievements in the organization of the workers' movement but also because of his sufferings under the martial law. Given this domestic and international recognition Wałęsa became most naturally the major speaker of the oppositional forces at the Round Table convened at the beginning of 1989. The Round Table was the last attempt of the Polish United Workers' Party to stabilize its regime. This was no longer possible as the results of the half-free elections of June 1989 demonstrated. The results surprised all the participants at the Round Table. The realistic task was no more to reform state socialism. The time was ripe to search for the ways to profoundly change the economic and political system.

The government of Tadeusz Mazowiecki had the practical opportunity to move in this direction and used the opportunity as far as possible. The Balcerowicz-plan for the switch to a market economy was announced and the profound economic reforms started at the beginning of 1990. Poland was the path-breaking force in the post-socialist development. But what had to be Lech Wałęsa's role in it? The experience from the French and the Russian Revolutions could be telling in this respect. Not a single person of low-class origin who stormed the Bastille could find a place among the leading personalities after 14 July 1789. Not a single worker or sailor who stormed the Winter Palace in November 1917 could find a place among the leading personalities in Soviet Russia thereafter. This could have been the fate of the worker Wałęsa after Tadeusz Mazowiecki was selected by some *Solidarity* leaders and organizations as their candidate for the position of State President. However, Wałęsa had his own logic of behavior and started his own election campaign. He moved against the historical experience that victory in revolutions is typically achieved by the revolutionary action of the lower classes but the new rulers come from the better educated and situated groups in society.

The smashing victory of Wałęsa at the elections for the President of the Polish state held in 1990 became the peak of his achievements in successful individualization. (Wałęsa and Rybicki 1992) At the same time, the victory marked the beginning of his political decline. He had already put his qualities as a political "lion" to a harsh test many times and had succeeded. Now he was expected to lead Polish society towards economic, political and cultural stabilization by implementing very much needed deep economic and political reforms. The task was tremendous. It required knowledge and experience in managing complex institutions together with sophisticated tactical skills. Wałęsa possessed neither the knowledge nor the experience and skills required. He falsely continued to believe that sound common sense and strong will would be sufficient to manage the complicated tasks. Even his famous political intuition would no longer suffice. In striking contrast to his behavior during the strikes and even during the Round Table discussions he repeatedly misunderstood situations as President of the state. He acted in an authoritarian way in cases requiring flexibility. In other situations he acted manifestly as an opportunistic "fox" when persistence and integrity had to be publicly shown.

Wałęsa inherited the constitutional provisions of the low profile of the President of the Polish State as it was negotiated at the Round Table. However, having been elected President he immediately initiated a public debate about the need for stronger presidential powers. He wanted larger areas for operation and a more decisive say for the President in governmental decision making. His demands had certain practical reasons. But raising them he immediately compromised himself. The memory was fresh that he was the person who insisted on the low political profile of the President during the Round Table. The reason was very well known. The first President was supposed to be Wojciech Jaruzelski as it actually happened. Wałęsa's fast change of mind implying the change of constitutional provisions according to his personal aspirations could not be easily accepted by the Polish voters. Moreover, Wałęsa's claim was inacceptable for most members of the parliament (the Sejm). In addition, Wałęsa advocated deep economic reforms. But he was strongly against the selling of Polish industrial enterprises to foreign investors in the same time. Thus he made the "big bang" privatization according to the Balcerowicz plan impossible. Wałęsa wanted prime ministers to be elected according to his wish but had to learn that the Sejm had other preferences.

There were various explanations for the institutional tensions and conflicts at the top of the political leadership of Poland during the first years of democratization. However, Polish public opinion perceived the institutional tensions and conflicts as mostly initiated by Wałęsa and other former activists of *Solidarity*. Jaroslaw Kurski had good reasons to hesitate in the title of his biographical work *Lech Wałęsa: Democrat or Dictator?* (Kurski 1993) Due to the controversial activities of Wałęsa the belief that persons and groups related to *Solidarity* could efficiently manage the difficult economic, political and cultural problems of Polish society was gradually undermined. The boomerang effect was predictable. Contrary to the declining trust in political actors related to *Solidarity,* trust in the newly established social-democratic organizations was growing. The veterans of *Solidarity* perceived their defeat in the parliamentary elections in 1993 as rather painful. But many of them contributed to this defeat by their own behavior after 1989. This applied first and foremost to the strikingly egomanic and authoritarian political behavior of Lech Wałęsa as democratically elected President of Poland.

The social-democratic government of Alexander Kwaśniewski could profit politically from both the mass dissatisfaction with the performance of the *Solidarity* governments and from the first signs of economic stabilization in Poland. Many voters understood it as a positive result which had come about despite the inability of the *Solidarity* governments to work efficiently. This was usually explained by the incompetent or misguided interventions of President Lech Wałęsa into the working of the executive power. At the beginning of his fifties he was increasingly regarded as the great man from the old battles who had become a nuisance under the new conditions. In the public debates his misbehavior and failure as a statesman was usually simply attributed to his low level of education.

This became the major argument in the campaign against Wałęsa's re-election as President of the Polish State in 1995. His adversary was the young and successful social democratic Prime Minister Aleksander Kwaśniewski who allegedly had a university diploma. He won the elections with a small margin but enough to send Wałęsa practically into the "graveyard of former elites" as Pareto metaphorically described the history. Wałęsa was later politically active in the re-vitalization of *Solidariry* in the form of the electoral coalition AWS, which won the parliamentary elections in 1997. But he did not want to take or was not allowed to take a position in the AWS government. His final effort for a political come-back was his candidacy for the presidential election in 2000. The attempt ended with the disastrous result of 1% of the votes.

Thus, Wałęsa ended his active political carrier exactly in the same infamous way as Boris Yeltsin. However, if analyzed objectively, Wałęsa's records were less dramatic. He did not leave the country convulsing economically, politically and culturally as Yeltsin did. Unlike the still uncertain situation in the Russian Federation at the end of Boris Yeltsin's second presidential term, the economic recovery of Poland was already completed at the end of Wałęsa's presidential term in the mid-nineties. Tensions between institutions notwithstanding, Polish society had established a functioning democratic political order as well. The division of powers was complete and their mutual control was basically efficient. This was a serious personal problem for Wałęsa during his presidency but a good omen for the future of democracy in Poland. There were cases of political corruption in the country but not to the extent to demoralize Polish society. The Presidency of Boris Yeltsin was marked by efforts to suppress the democratic division of powers by all means. The result could only be the flourishing of corruption. Yeltsin and his narrow environment were publicly regarded as corrupt. This could not be said of Wałęsa and his personal environment in such generalized way. At the end of the Presidency of Wałęsa Poland had a clear geopolitical definition of itself and of its interests. At the end of Boris Yeltsin's presidency, the new definition of the geopolitical situation and interests of the Russian Federation were yet to be defined.

The differences were not necessarily due to personal achievements or failures of both historical figures alone. Boris Yeltsin and Lech Wałęsa had to decide and act under rather different structural conditions. However, while the Presidency of Wałęsa could be generally judged as a failure, it did not inflict any substantial harm on Polish society. Whatever the personal intentions of Boris Yeltsin, this cannot be said for the impacts of his Presidency on the society of the Russian Federation. Yeltsin really needed a formal agreement with his successor that he and his family would not be persecuted for the harm inflicted to the Russian society. Under the Polish conditions an agreement of this type concerning Wałęsa was not needed. Moreover, it would not have been possible since it would be rightly understood as a grave perpetration against democracy. The strong signal about its maturity came from the accusations about Wałęsa's collaboration with the security services of the former regime (Cenckiewicz and Gontarczyk 2008). The sensitive issue could be freely and widely discussed in Polish society without any personal consequences.

However, there are also accusations against Wałęsa which go far beyond personal attacks. This mostly applies to the outcomes of the Round Table negotiations. One may certainly ask today why the decisions of the negotiations did not include a more radical ideological and political break with the former regime. This question might be serious or might just be intended to become the final destruction of a former idol called Lech Wałęsa. As seen in a broader historical perspective, this would not be a unique approach. Most revolutions tend to destroy their own idols. However, the serious reaction to the question should refresh one's memory. The previous regime no longer had legitimacy but still had control over the army and the secret services. One has also to remember that the Soviet Union was badly weakened but was still on the Polish border in the spring of 1989. It was the speaker of the oppositional forces Lech Wałęsa who was right at that time in his appeals for a cautious approach to complicated matters and not the present day heroes, who tend to forget the complexities of history.

Now it is widely known that Yeltsin's father used to be imprisoned as an enemy of the Soviet people. Whatever the reasons, this fact did not have a negative impact on Yeltsin's educational path or on his steep carrier as a CPSU party functionary. Thus, he did not have personal reasons to fight against the Soviet regime. To the contrary, he managed to successfully adapt to the Soviet economic and political order up until the moment when he understood that the regime itself was going to collapse. At this point his attitude towards the Soviet society and the CPSU changed abruptly. This was actually unavoidable since he had started the political carrier of radical reformer. Lech Wałęsa was also born in a village but he had the possibility to attend a vocational school for industrial occupations and later to join the huge number of workers at the "Lenin" shipyard in Gdansk.[3] The possibility was given by the same socialist educational and industrial policies carried out in Poland following the Soviet pattern of industrialization and raising the educational level of the population. Thus, Wałęsa did not have personal reasons to be against the socialist economic and political organization. His first oppositional activities had mostly to do with the bad payment and working conditions of those employed in the shipyard. His ideas concerning the dissolution of the socialist economic and political order developed later.

In contrast to the personal backgrounds of Yeltsin and Wałęsa, Václav Havel had strong personal reasons for a negative attitude towards the socialist regime. His family experienced sharp downward mobility in the course of the socialist transformation of Czechoslovak society. Due to the radical nationalization of big property the family lost large and valuable real estates in Prague. As the son of parents so strongly affected by the new regime Havel was not allowed to study and had to do casual jobs until he became technical assistant at a theatre. At this point of time his talent of playwright and essayist started to bear fruits. His literary works attracted attention since they largely deviated from the aesthetic standards of socialist realism. At that time Havel followed the style of the then trendy theatre of absurd. Under this aesthetic coverage his plays attacked the absurdities of bureaucratic socialism. Like Orwell, he managed to display the intentions and effects of the double speech in which the formal meaning of the sentence diverged from its real message. Havel's literary analysis of this schizophrenic distinction between meanings on the formal surface of communication and the hidden meaning led him to the generalization that there were plenty of lies in everyday life under real socialism. The lies made the communication paranoid and thus questioned the rationality of the state socialist economic and political order.

The issues raised by Havel did not concern the alleged rationalism of the state socialist transformation and organization of society alone. Following the philosophers Edmund Husserl and Jan Patočka, Havel questioned the scientific basis of modern civilization. His assumption was that the overwhelming impact of science on society had the consequence that the most important pre-reflexive basis of everyday orientations and actions of individuals tended to be forgotten or at least neglected. This fundamental mistake had been made under the influence of the rationalistic European Enlightenment. The mistake had misguided all efforts of social engineering. Havel's plays *The Memorandum* and *The Increased Difficulty of Concentration* provided evidence that the products of social engineering dramatically deviated from the pre-reflexive grounds of everyday life and destroyed

---

3   The huge shipyard was product of the socialist industrialization after 1945 and had some 17,500 employees in 1980. Having gone through various privatization and stabilization procedures after 1989, the shipyard employs currently some 2000 workers and specialists. As seen from this point of view the workers in Gdansk started a profound historical change under the leadership of Wałęsa. But they could hardly be called winners in this process.

them. The unspoken conclusion was that the state socialist social engineering was particularly effective in this destruction.

In the meantime, the issue concerning the causes and effects of state socialism had become the subject matter of intensive public discussion and political changes in Czechoslovakia in 1967–1969. The content of the discussions was rather different in the Czech and Slovak parts of the country. While the crucial issue in Slovakia was the ethnic autonomy, the discussions in the Czech lands had a more general content. The centralized planning could no longer be efficient in the highly industrialized Czech lands. The division of labor had reached a very high level of complexity there. Market mechanisms had to be urgently introduced to correct the shortcomings of the socialist planning. This was the guiding idea of Ota Šik who became the secretary of the Czechoslovak Communist Party in the area of the economy at the beginning of 1968. The new first party secretary Aleksander Dubček wanted that politics and ideology would be open to the people with a "human face". It seemed that new large social spaces appeared which were available for the individualization of millions.

Václav Havel was involved in this reform process known as the Prague Spring of 1968. However, the process itself was guided by the Czechoslovak Communist Party which had a very different history and different level of legitimacy than the Polish United Workers' Party. Therefore, this was not the reform process with which Havel could fully identify himself. His time came after the Prague Spring was crushed by the military forces of the Warsaw Treaty Organization in August 1968. The following period of "normalization" brought about the de-legitimization of the rulers under the new party secretary and President of the Czechoslovak Republic, Gustav Husak. In 1975 Vaclav Havel sent him an open letter which was a literary masterpiece and became domestically and internationally known. At this point Havel was already about to turn to the symbolic figure of the dissidents in Czechoslovakia. But the letter also had personal consequences for him. What followed were 15 years of arrests, sentences, imprisonment and sufferings which were much more brutal than the treatment of Wałęsa during the martial law. The sufferings strengthened the political and moral integrity of Havel and transformed him into the recognized moral standard for non-violent resistance in Czechoslovakia. His international reputation grew fast. His plays found the way to respected stages in Western Europe and North America. However, Havel rejected several suggestions to leave the country.

The famous open letter of Havel to Gustav Husak was actually a by-product of processes which followed the European summit in Helsinki in 1975. The Soviet leadership cherished the illusion that through the summit the division of Europe would be legitimized for ever. The effects were strikingly different. In the concluding documents signed in Helsinki the issue of human rights was emphasized. In reference to the Helsinki summit, leading Czech intellectuals prepared and signed the *Charta 77* which made history. The reform spirit of 1968 was obviously still alive. But the reform projects were not focused on the strengthening of the socialist economic and political order any more. The projects intended to undermine it. This was carried out at the beginning with a special stress on the human rights suppressed in state socialism. Later the intellectuals preferred the satirical analysis of everyday realities thus step by step stripping the socialist social order of legitimacy. Havel was particularly outstanding in these de-legitimizing activities. On its part, Mikhail Gorbachev's *perestroika* and *glasnost* heavily contributed to the rapid loss of legitimacy of the state socialist ideology and institutional framework all over Eastern Europe.

As a result, the public acceptance of state socialism in Czechoslovakia was so undermined that several mass demonstrations on *Václavské náměstí* in Prague in November 1989 were enough to prepare the radical institutional changes. The Parliament which had been elected in the times of Husak's rule accepted his resignation as President of the Czechoslovakian state and had only one alternative – to elect the former dissident Václav Havel to this highest position of state. Having been a free-lance intellectual for too long he had difficulties in adapting to the formal discipline needed for the good performance of the role as head of state. Some of his difficulties became the subject of widely circulating anecdotes. But there was no other person in Czechoslovakia with a moral statute even slightly approaching the moral recognition of Havel. In this respect, public opinion on Havel in Czechoslovakia was quite different as compared to the public opinion in Poland concerning Wałęsa and in the Russian Federation concerning Yeltsin. This difference was going to become deeper and deeper during the candidacies of these three persons for re-election as presidents.

The high public prestige Havel enjoyed in the 1990s could not make the role of the head of state easy. The Czechoslovak state was a federation and the head of the state was supposed to preserve the unity of the Federation. Havel highly valued the universal human rights of individuals and firmly believed that the federal political organization of democratic Czechoslovakia would fully satisfy the requirements for political and moral universalism. However, he did not understand that the new democratic liberties had strengthened not moral and political universalism alone. The liberties had also re-vitalized the spirits of the Czech and Slovak nationalism and chauvinism. The strong political gesture of Havel who left the office of President of the Federation before the end of his mandate was not strong enough to stop the powers opting for the separation of the republics. Having been completed in a civilized way, the dissolution of the Federation became a painful experience for Havel. He obviously could not influence a process which he believed was heading in the wrong direction.

The recognition of this fact was not an argument for him to decline the offer to become President of the newly established Czech Republic. In fact, there was no real alternative candidate in Czech political life. But times were difficult. This was exactly the period of the preparation and implementation of the large-scale transfer of state property into private hands. Havel did not have any reservations concerning the necessity of carrying out the privatization of state property. But he wanted an institutionally very well regulated process which would bring about maximum justice for the greatest number of Czech people. The organizational pattern could have been the functioning of the German tripartite tariff negotiations. This line of argumentation seemed to be convincing but it had strong opponents, first of all the Prime Minister of the Czech Republic Václav Klaus. He wanted "big-bang" privatization since each delay would mean that the reforms would cost more. Moreover, the vouchers of the mass privatization had to be concentrated in holdings in order to make the responsibilities clear and efficient management of the enterprises possible. The market implied economic and social differentiation but it was presented as unavoidable and actually not bad as compared to the de-motivating egalitarianism of the socialist economic organization.

The diverging opinions of the President of the Czech Republic and its Prime Minister continued to provoke public discussions after the voucher privatization was completed. This was a success for the Prime Minister despite the accompanying accusations about the lack of transparency in the privatization or about corrupt privatization deals. Klaus' key argument was that competition between individuals under the conditions of a free market would correct all the mistakes of the privatization or the deficiencies in the functioning of the market itself in the long run. Therefore, no special role of civil society in controlling or correcting the functioning of political or economic institutions would be needed. Havel argued differently. According to him the permanent reference to moral principles incorporated in civil society was very much needed for Czech society since it could otherwise be destroyed by the unlimited individualism and extremes of consumerism. (*Rival Visions* 1996)

This type of sophisticated public discussions would have been impossible between Boris Yeltsin and his prime ministers or between Lech Wałęsa and the prime ministers during the time of his presidency. Havel introduced intellectual quality in the political discourse. In his sometimes undiplomatic manner Václav Klaus also contributed to the intellectual quality of the political discussions by helping to clarify the variety of ethical backgrounds of the political strategies in a democratic society. Klaus was consequent in his individualistic neo-liberalism by stressing the point that the mutual control of individuals involved in competition would be the only framework to reach and maintain efficient economic interaction and democratic politics. Somewhat simplifying the complexity in modern democracies, he disagreed with all efforts to introduce universalistic ethics "from above". So he objected the style of thinking and acting of the social engineers guided by utopian visions about the relevance of communities. Havel argued that it is not in this simplified way that actions in the economy and politics can really be guided, performed and evaluated. His point was in favor of high moral standards which could keep present-day societies together and might keep them together for a long time.

As local and specific as this discussion between leading politicians in the Czech Republic might have been, they basically repeated well known discussions between individualists and communitarians in modern ethics and in the social sciences. Nevertheless, in the Czech debate an interesting element appeared which is indicative of the differences between the social positions occupied by Václav

Havel and for the intellectual implications of these social positions. At the beginning of his intellectual, literary and political career the dissident Havel did his best to delegitimize the rationalistic efforts to construct a "good" or "better" state socialist society. He insisted on the point that this type of rationalistic constructivism tends to neglect or to destroy the pre-reflexive experience as the most important factor for orientation, decision and action of individuals. Paradoxically enough, in the discussion between Havel and Klaus it was Václav Klaus who argued in favor of this philosophical and ethical position as the dissident Havel had done in the previous times. To the contrary, as President of the Czech Republic Václav Havel seemed to argue exactly in the spirit of the social engineers he so vehemently criticized in his younger years.

Havel tried to apply the principles of universalistic morality in his visions on international politics as well. By referring exactly to universalistic moral principles he fully supported the Kosovo war. However, he missed all opportunities to discuss the controversial non-universalistic legal and pragmatic bases for the war. Together with several other Presidents in Eastern Europe Havel fully supported the disarmament of Iraq from weapons for mass destruction. But he missed all opportunities to clarify his position after no weapons of mass destruction were found in the country. Obviously, Havel had learned in the meantime that in politics opportunistic pragmatism might be preferable to the risky implications of the consequent moral universalism.

Nevertheless, totally unlike Yeltsin and Wałęsa, Václav Havel retreated from active political life still enjoying the approval of the majority of the Czech population for his political activity. So, Havel could look back on the fulfillment of the historical options for his individualization. (Havel 2008) Both domestically and internationally he was and remains the symbolic figure of the successful societal transformation in the Czech Republic and in Eastern Europe. Due to a series of highly inspiring political speeches at home and abroad he is celebrated as one of the few leading present day intellectuals possessing strong moral integrity and attractive political visions. (Pontus 2004) Thus, there is at least one case in Eastern Europe which refutes the old wisdom that revolutions tend to destroy their own children. The precise conclusion should be different. Revolutions offer immense opportunities for extraordinary individualization. However, there are only few people who efficiently grasp the opportunity for individualization in times of profound changes. There are even fewer cases in which this extreme form of successful individualization continues for a long time. And in only very few cases is the successful individualization in guiding revolutions a life-long story.

3.4 Collectivism and Individualization in Urban Development

Urban development is inherently connected to present-day societal change in two ways. *First*, cities and in particular capital cities are key actors in preparing and leading profound change in the economy, politics and culture of contemporary societies. *Second*, changes in the structure and functioning of cities are deeply embedded in processes of societal change. Recent developments in Eastern European capitals offer perfect examples of this double contingency. In these capitals the whole variety of changes might be identified which marked the transformation of Eastern European societies after their opening to global trends. In particular, the global trend of individualization deeply changed human ecology and the patterns of organization in the Eastern European urban areas.

The recent urban changes in the region can be best described and explained against the background of the heritage of state socialism. The radical socialist idea of overcoming bourgeois individualism took on a variety of forms within urban planning and architecture. The decade after the civil war in Soviet Russia was marked by an extraordinary intensity of discussions about the ends and means in building the new collectivist society. The debates were particularly focused on prospects for the urban way of life since the desirable just and humane organization of social life was expected to be achieved in the highly industrialized urban environment. The urban settlements had to stop the reproduction of class cleavages and other pathologies of capitalist industrial centers in Western Europe and North America. The new socialist urban settlements had to be garden cities, as close to nature as villages, and at the same time with highly developed urban infrastructure, transportation and communication means. It was assumed that the feelings of belonging to the so-planned community would be very strong due to the collectivist way of thinking and behavior of the inhabitants. Thus, the need to strengthen individuals' identification with their settlement community had to become the guiding collectivist idea of urban planning. Urban architecture had to efficiently support the feeling of belonging to community life, both in housing architecture and architecture of urban infrastructural designs.

The time seemed to be ripe to immediately transform these normative ideas of desirable urban and architectural development into innovations in town planning and urban architecture. However, there were no financial resources for large-scale restructuring of cities in Soviet Russia. The victorious revolution could only be reflected in few new public buildings. The housing issue was also high on the political agenda. The practical task was rather complicated: How could the best urban conditions be achieved for individual development and realization by not allowing social space for bourgeois individualism? Obviously, the task could not be resolved at once. But could it be resolved at all? Could the conditions for a personal development and realization be strictly separated from individualism which was supposed to belong to the decadent bourgeois culture alone? Could constructive individualization become so inherently connected to socialist collectivism in the socialist urban environment?

Pioneering Soviet architects could not rely on any clear recommendations by Marx, Engels or Lenin for the collectivist architectural design of housing or public buildings. The only meaningful reference point could be Charles Fourier's ideas about the harmony of *phalanstery* organized according to socialist principles. The reference was ideologically easy to make since Engels himself had briefly mentioned the relevance of Fourier's vision of the collectivist organization of the future good society. The idea was well known in the Russian circles of the intellectual avant-garde since it was further elaborated by Nikolai Chernyshevskiy in his programmatic work *What Is to Be Done?* (1989 [1863]) In the mid-twenties the idea seemed to be particularly attractive since various visions of garden cities uniting urban life and the rural environment were high on the agenda in the discussions among Western European and Russian architects.

The full-scale implementation of the idea of a self-sufficient urban-rural *phalanstery* would have required large investment which was not available. On the other hand, there was a burning need for housing after the destructions of the civil war and the announcement of ambitious plans for rapid industrialization. This had to be accompanied by the internal migration of large masses from the rural areas to the new industrial centers which still had to be built. In addition, rapid industrialization had to go hand in hand with a fast increase in the educational level of millions of the Russia's badly educated population in order to enable them to take part in industrial production. In infrastructural terms, the achievement of both aims required the construction of hundreds of large dormitories. They had to accommodate the labor force mobilized for the construction of the new industrial centers. Dormitories were also very much needed for the accommodation of pupils and students coming from the villages and the small towns to study in the big cities. Due to historical circumstances dormitories had to become not just facilities for accommodation. They also had to become the most important places for collectivist civic education.

Thus, the historical situation of profound changes in the social structure of Soviet Russia gave architects a unique chance to carry out large-scale experiments. They could limit the private space of rooms in dormitories to several square meters but design instead large public facilities like clubs, libraries, cinemas, self-service restaurants, etc. The inhabitants of the dormitories were expected to leave the rather modest conditions of private rooms and to move to the generous infrastructure and equipment of the areas reserved for collective activities. The best known early example of this socialist collectivism in architectural design is the constructivist dormitory for students of the Institute for Textiles constructed in Moscow in 1929–1930 (architect I. Nikolaev). The architecture of the dormitory was intended to serve the needs of education in a collectivist way of life by practicing it.

The ideological background of this and numerous other architectural designs aimed at the introduction of the collectivist way of life in housing during the 1920s and 1930s was the concept of the *kommunalka.* This concept appeared as a reflection on the way of life in the large nationalized houses of former aristocrats, merchants and other wealthy people during the first years of Soviet Russia. Due to the extreme housing deficit in the large cities several families had to inhabit these houses or apartments turned into *kommunalka*s. Every inhabitant of the *kommunalka* had to comply with the rules of collective life, particularly in sharing spaces with other members of the community (kitchen, sanitation facilities, etc.).

If the collectivist rule would not be followed, communal life would be endangered by conflicts. They used to accompany the co-habitation.

For a while, *kommunalka* was seen as a temporary situation. But due to ideological and political considerations the collectivist arrangement of co-habitation in nationalized houses or apartments was interpreted as organizational innovation. Later the innovation turned into normative principle for collectivist architectural design in housing building. New programs for housing construction had to reflect on the experience of *kommunalkas* in various forms. Behind the ideological principles of alleged collectivist humanism there were also rational economic calculations. The use of a kitchen or of a dining room by several families implied real economy of construction materials and housing space.

Dormitories were particularly suited to the purposes of architectural experimentation along *kommunalka* principles. It was exactly in the building of dormitories where these principles had to be implemented in full. But hundreds of thousands of blocks of flats were also designed and constructed in the Soviet Union with shared kitchens facilities, eating areas and sanitation facilities for several families during the 1930s and after the Second World War. Later the *kommunalka* principles became increasingly regarded as artificial and could not be successfully applied on a larger scale under the conditions of the relative stabilization of the economy and step by step satisfaction of housing needs in the Soviet Union. They were indeed only rarely applied in other Eastern European countries. Nevertheless, in present-day Moscow there are still thousands of blocks of flats of the *kommunalka* type. (Pott 2009)

Experiments focusing on collectivist architectural design continued in Moscow in the 1960s. The best known example is the famous *House of the New Way of Life* which was designed by architects N. A. Osterman et al. and built in 1968–1969. The complex of 812 apartments in two 16-storey buildings was intended to minimize housework for young families. The time saved on working in the apartments would persuade the young families to extensively use the services and all kinds of collective entertainment facilities. This was the modern variant of the slogan from the 1920s: out from the private spaces, go into the spaces designed for collective life. The experiment failed. The continuing housing crisis notwithstanding, young families preferred apartments in which kitchens and dining rooms were in the apartments and not in the spaces for collective use. The experimental complex had to change its function from accommodation for young families to a dormitory for doctoral students and guests of the universities in Moscow.

This was the last large-scale experiment to test the viability of the *phalanstery*-like organization of housing under socialism. Some smaller experimental houses of this type were built in other towns of the Soviet Union and in other Eastern European countries. In many cases the inhabitants of the experimental collectivist housing evaluated their new living conditions as much better than their previous conditions of housing. The simple reason for this evaluation was the fact that the previous housing conditions had been rather bad as a rule. The social processes themselves made life in collectivist housing rather exceptional. Together with the industrialization, urbanization and the rapid increase in educational level, Eastern Europeans tended more and more to prefer the private spaces as the main area for their progressing individualization. *Kommunalka* housing was rejected by the historical development itself despite some humanistic and rationalistic ideas underlying it.

The same fate had the ideological and political efforts to get people out of the private space of housing and to attract them to public buildings. There they had to socialize in the spirit of collectivism. These efforts were motivated by influential socialist visions during the early years of the Soviet Union. Most of the visions turned out to be based on illusions. The major illusion was the expectation that everyday life might be easily constructed or reconstructed by political decisions. It was expected that the decision to build palace-like clubs for workers would immediately change public attitudes in favor of spending leisure time in the clubs. The impressive constructivist buildings like the Zuyev Workers' Club (architect I. Golosov, built 1926–1928) or Rusakov Workers' Club (designed by K. Melnikov, built 1927–1928) are now seen as pioneering achievements in Soviet architecture. Some of these buildings are highly valued internationally as achievements of architectural constructivism. (Kopp 1985) Due to the generally primitive housing conditions in Moscow during the 1920s the internal design and the functionality of the workers' clubs really attracted a mass audience. The clubs offered cinemas, rich libraries, cheap self-service restaurants and many other facilities with infrastructure and equipment which was regarded as luxurious in the twenties and the thirties. Most services and entertainment were subsidized. One could draw the conclusion that the desired utopia of collectivism in spending the leisure time was thus put into practice.

The attractiveness of the workers' clubs gradually declined with the improvement of housing conditions in the Soviet Union. Modern means of communication and entertainment radically diminished the attraction of the collectivist organization of leisure time. Even in cases when the same halls are used nowadays for public events such as disco evenings, the type of entertainment offered there is far from the collectivist spending of leisure time as it was ideologically and politically envisaged in the twenties and thirties. The numerous workers' clubs or similar establishments in other Eastern European countries had basically the same fate. Those still in existence today are now used for entertainment dominated by free individual choice and according to individualist commercial principles.

The next variant of the efforts to steer urban life in the direction of collectivism was the large-scale experiment with Soviet city planning. This happened first and foremost in the development of the new master plan for Moscow during the 1930s. Work on the plan provided an opportunity for international competition. This turned into a clash between extremes of architectural radicalism and variants of moderate traditionalism. What was at stake was the desired domestic and international acknowledgement of Moscow as the leading centre for new ideas and practices in urban planning and architecture worldwide. The new Moscow had to become the symbol of the successful proletarian revolution, as the status of the city was defined at that time. Accordingly, the revolutionary drafts of N. Ladovsky, Le Corbusier and E. May were all guided by the vision of the need to construct an entirely new capital city of the Soviet Union marked by rationalism, progressivism and universalism. In this way they all wanted to underline the revolutionary break with the past, including the break with the Russian tradition of city planning and urban architectural design.

At first glance, the key arguments against these radical visions were the rather limited investment available and the requirement for visible effects in short periods of time. In reality, the issues at stake were much more complex and profound. At the time of the competition the Soviet leadership no longer cherished illusions about an imminent worldwide proletarian revolution. The identification with the universalistic collectivism of the worldwide proletarian internationalism was no longer relevant. Stalin had already taken the strategic decision to foster the building of socialism in the Soviet Union first and then to leave this example to irradiate all over the world. This change in the political strategy had direct implications for the master plan for Moscow. Instead of stressing rationalism and universalism, the plan had to be rooted in the Russian tradition. This was the project of the architects V. Semyonov and S. Chernyshev. It was guided by the idea of continuity with the available buildings and infrastructure in Moscow. At the same time the project opened up possibilities for innovation by focusing the new master plan and future everyday life in the capital city on several symbolic centers.

This vision was further elaborated and became widely known as Stalin's master plan for Moscow of 1935. Moscow was intended to become an impressive imperial centre promoting the intensive identification of its inhabitants with the city. The socialist collectivism had to have a clearly defined national specific. Indirectly, this was already the recognition that the universalist appeal of proletarian internationalism could not manage to establish itself as a key factor of value-normative integration. Therefore, the decision in favor of traditionalism in city planning and architectural design had to strengthen the factor which was already regarded by the Soviet leadership as more effective in the integration of Soviet society, namely the continuity of national cultural traditions.

The architectural style of new Moscow was already indicated in the architecture of the first stations of the Moscow metropolitan. The buildings to be erected on symbolic places had to convey the message of the uniting and mobilizing power of an empire of world relevance. The prototype of the symbolic irradiation of state power via architectural design from the times of the Roman Empire till the times of Napoleon I was architectural classicism. The architectural style of the Moscow metropolitan was unofficially but properly called *socialist classicism*. It was intended to convey monumentality, uniformity and discipline, whatever the specific functions of the buildings constructed by following this pattern of architecture. In everyday life the huge uniform buildings had to impose feelings of respect for the state power on the citizens and demand compliance with it. The state power had to be understood as the most important bearer of the collective identity of individuals. The classicist buildings of the Moscow State University, Hotel

Ukraine or the similar apartment houses in Barikadnaya and in Kotelnicheskaya Street had to incorporate the same symbolic meaning and to bring about the same ideological effects. These were all designed to suppress individualism and to demonstrate the collectivist framework of individualization under the intensive supervision of the party-state. (Chmelnizki 2007)

The imitation of the same classicist pattern in the post-war architecture of Warsaw (Palace of Science and Culture, Constitution Square), Berlin (Karl-Marx-Alley), Sofia (Party House), etc. had to convey the same meaning under the local conditions. It was the all-mighty party-state that was impressively symbolized in the city planning and in the early socialist architecture beyond the boundaries of the Soviet Union. The copying of the Moscow imperial style of the fifties had to express a new form of collectivism inspired by socialist internationalism. The message had to be well understood: All socialist societies had the same economic and political system together with the same internationalist ideology and architecture. The shaky background of this latter idea became visible later in the most impressive copy of the Moscow imperial style in Ceausescu's Romania. Paradoxically enough, the House of the Republic (today Palace of the Parliament) built in Bucharest as late as the second half of the 1980s was intended to incorporate the uniting power not of socialist internationalism but of Romanian nationalism.

Stalin's gigantic skyscrapers and the imitations of these built all over Eastern Europe were impressive but they could not resolve the most burning social problem of Eastern European societies – the housing deficit. Skyscrapers were extremely expensive and took too long to be built. Cities in the western part of the Soviet Union, in Poland or in the GDR were destroyed during the Second World War and had to be re-built fast and without large investment, as this was simply not available. Everywhere in the region the accelerated industrialization was a state priority and this had consequences in the development of settlements. Millions of peasants moved to industrial centers and had to be accommodated there. Thus the major task of state planning and architectural design in the mid-fifties was clearly defined as deviation from Stalin's monumentalism. It was necessary to introduce industrial methods of the mass construction of blocks of flats. The technological innovations needed had already been introduced in France in the form of industrial systems for the production of pre-fabricated parts of the buildings and then for the assemblage of the parts on site. Eastern European societies completed the transfer and the adaptation of this progressive technology by the late 1950s. Large areas of the socialist capital cities and industrial centers became increasingly dominated by uniform, monotonous and grey pre-fabricated blocks of flats. There the rationalistically calculated function of the housing was incorporated in full but the creativity of the architectural design was close to nil. The architecture in itself could not convey any strong ideological meaning of collectivism since it was dominated by pure functionalism. The housing usually did not reproduce the *kommunalka*-pattern in any way whatsoever. The apartments were designed to meet the needs of nuclear families and not of communal living. Thus, the ideological task to spread collectivism could only be implemented in city planning provided the task would be taken seriously.

In fact, there were numerous and serious efforts to introduce and reproduce socialist collectivism through the city planning and design of housing complexes. This could be achieved above all in the planning of the smaller districts of the huge housing complexes. Each district had to have specific traits as a specific settlement with all the required kindergartens, schools, shops, services, entertainment centers, sport facilities, etc. In most cases these were really included in the projects. However, the construction of housing at the fastest rate and for the greatest number of people possible had absolute priority. Thus, all additional tasks in the construction of local monumental specifics, of social facilities, green areas, etc. were postponed for better times ahead. These did not come. The local specifics in planning and architectural design tended to be forgotten indeed. The socialist housing complexes consisting of pre-fabricated blocks of flats became typical "sleeping-room" areas and powerful sources of alienation. Instead of satisfaction with the general quality of life in the modern urban environment they produced and reproduced dissatisfaction. Instead of a community-like way of life they dragged the inhabitants into depressive social isolation. No slogans about the possible or desirable human face of the sleeping-room-like housing complexes could be persuasive and efficient. In these complexes it was difficult to develop and maintain feelings of identity and patterns of behavior guided by solidarity. Most inhabitants of the pre-fabricated blocks of flats could enjoy a better quality of life there than in their previous housing. Nevertheless, the alienation accumulated fast. It became a strong motivating force for the support to movements, which made the political changes in the autumn of 1989 and later unavoidable. (Wagenaar et al. 2004)

The failure of the socialist industrialized housing construction to satisfy the growing aspirations of the Eastern European population is only one specific case of the many failures of the planners of the socialist transformation of the region. The planners believed that the efforts of state institutions to resolve the housing problem would bring about recognition of the state as a manifestation of socialist collective identity. Thus, the individualization in this collectivist context would produce, reproduce and strengthen socialist collectivism. Twenty years later we have the necessary historical distance to objectively evaluate what happened in Eastern Europe in city planning and architectural design. Their achievements and failures paved the way for individualization which began to deviate more and more from the patterns of socialist collectivism. At the end of the 1980s these deviations were ripe for profound social changes.

The profound socio-economic and political changes in Eastern Europe were largely prepared in the urban areas and became particularly visible in the capital cities. Huge demonstrations took place there. They signaled expectations for profound changes. The ideologically and politically imposed collectivism of state socialism had to be abolished. Individualism was no longer heresy or an anti-social phenomenon. To the contrary, neo-liberal individualism became the dominant official ideology which was gradually opening up and legitimizing a large variety of options for individualization in economic, political and cultural life. Some individuals were successful at identifying and taking advantage of the new life chances. Others became losers in the differentiation of life chances.

The effects of the far-reaching social differentiation are immediately visible in the Eastern European capital cities. Whatever the average economic situation in the particular countries, all of the capital cities' economies are now booming. This is not due to local economic activities alone. International financial transfers usually go through the capital cities and the lions' share remains there. The presence of foreign capital is easily visible in the numerous skyscrapers of multinationals, Western banks and insurance companies. Hilton, Sheraton and other global hotel chains have buildings in all Eastern European capital cities. The few old-fashioned luxury cars of the former *nomenclatura* have been long since replaced by the powerful limousines of the new rich. Whole new districts have appeared with luxury detached houses or with big and guarded blocks of large flats inhabited by the new economic and political elite. These districts themselves are usually called "elite" since they impressively demonstrate the new socio-economic cleavages when compared with the dilapidated socialist housing complexes. The shopping malls have become the new cathedrals of the commercial spirit of consumerism. It is the value-normative core of current Eastern European individualization.

The capital city of the Russian Federation has been particularly affected by these developments. Under the extraordinary active and efficient leadership of the city mayor Yury Luzhkov a new master plan for Moscow was elaborated and passed in 2004. The plan takes into consideration the substantial changes already introduced in the city's landscape and foresees possible and desirable urban developments up to 2020. Aside from the appearance of respectable commercial centers, quite unimaginable in Stalin's time, it is striking to notice the very high level of continuity of the new master plan for Moscow with Stalin's plan of 1935. The new plan preserves the medieval concentric planning which puts stress on the political relevance of the Kremlin as the traditional core of the capital city. The second guiding idea of the radial prospects was clearly outlined in the plan of 1935 and is being elaborated further in the new plan. Taking into account the territorial expansion of Moscow far beyond the city boundaries of 1935 and repeating one of its major ideas, the new master plan foresees a third and a fourth concentric highway around the Russian capital.

The only substantial difference between the two plans lies in the firm economic grounding of the new one. In contrast to Stalin's master plan, which was mostly guided by political considerations, the new master plan introduces the principle of a precise commercial evaluation and re-evaluation of territories. This applies in particular to territories which became available for urban planning and architectural design due to the massive de-industrialization. It hit Moscow just like all other capital cities in Eastern Europe. All of them had and still have to dismantle large parts of their inefficient industries and to re-orient their economies from industry towards financial, cultural and administrative activities.

The substantial changes in the size of the population of Moscow and in the branches of the city's economy notwithstanding, the new master plan for Moscow fully preserves the symbolic centers of urban space as they were defined in the plan of 1935. This particularly applies to Stalin's six skyscrapers. In the new plan they receive an additional accentuation. No higher or larger buildings will be allowed to be built close to them. A special lightning underlines their relevance in the city landscape. The transportation strategy basically follows the same scheme as in 1935 with stress on the extension of the existing metro lines. Most of these were included as projects in the previous master plan. The continuity in the city planning of Moscow is thus not a formality, but concerns the substance of urban development.

Even more striking is the obvious continuity in the architectural design of some of the new buildings which co-define Moscow's present-day urban landscape. The recently erected and already famous "Triumph-Palace" with 1000 apartments (architect A. Trofimov, completed in 2004) is currently the tallest block of flats in Europe. The architecture of the building clearly resembles the style of Stalin's six "vysotki" (skyscrapers). The Palace building is even somewhat ironically called the seventh of them. The architectural design of other new buildings goes even further in stressing the continuity of styles. Some architects use elements from traditional Moscow architecture in combination with elements of the Russian constructivism of the 1920s and Stalin's socialist classicism in post-modernist fusions.

The stress on continuity in city planning and the architectural design of major buildings in Moscow is not at all by chance. This continuity is a product of the guiding ideology in present-day Russia as this was impressively demonstrated in the new-old anthem of the Russian Federation. The post-socialist Moscow conveys the message of continuity with the imperial status of Stalin's Moscow which was intended to become the capital of the victorious world proletariat. However, there are some nuances in the new master plan, which differentiate and enrich the monolithic idea of a city fully dominated by state philosophy and politics. The centre of collective ideological identification is no more the Palace of the Soviets which was designed several times but never constructed. The very centre of collective cultural identification with the Russian capital city is now conceived to be the Cathedral of Christ the Savior. It was flattened in 1931 to make place for the Palace of the Soviets and was re-erected in 2000 to put an end to the intended symbolic relevance of the Palace. This change of the centre of symbolic mass identification has a very deep historical meaning as a cultural frame of the ongoing individualization in Russia. The cultural frame is no more provided by the cosmopolitan ideology of the world proletariat. In addition, the centre of spiritual identity was moved out from any direct link to the centre of political power as symbolized by Kremlin. The message is clear. The Russian Orthodox Christianity is at the very centre of the new value-normative identification. In the Orthodox tradition the Church has always been divided from the centre of political power but subordinated to it. This is the new and rather old interpretation of the relations of powers as incorporated in the new master plan for Moscow. No less important is the obvious stress on the political and architectural heights reached by Moscow in the time of Stalin. The clear message is that the present day Russians should be proud of this.

As for the new market individualism and individualization in business activities, the settings for their performance are already numerous and dispersed throughout the whole territory of Moscow in the forms of shopping malls, business centers and local branches of banks. But the core location of business is very clearly defined in the new urban landscape of Moscow. This is the area of Moscow City. In symbolic terms the City is a territory at a distance from the centre of political power (Kremlin) and from the centre of spiritual power (the Cathedral). The City is a power in itself. This is already visible in a number of impressive skyscrapers housing office space, hotels and dwellings together with entertainment facilities. The Federation Tower is intended to become the highest office building in Europe. In symbolic and practical terms no doubt remains that the new development of Moscow under market conditions has already reached the level of full-scale opportunity for individualization in business life.

A remarkable characteristic in the rapid development of the urban landscape of Moscow is the deep involvement of the state in city planning and development. The preparation of the new master plan for Moscow and its step-by-step implementation would not be possible without the far-reaching participation of the state in the funding and managing the reconstruction of the city. Thus the spirit the new city planning is simultaneously the spirit of the rising new political self-confidence of the Russian state. It is the driving force for the new definition of the status of the Orthodox Church in Russian society as well as of the new symbolic relevance of church buildings in the urban landscape of Moscow. A substantial part of the construction of Moscow City and the continuation of the project was made possible by massive state financial and logistical support.

All these indicators substantiate the assumption that the institutional framework of individualization in the present day Russian Federation and particularly in Moscow is rather complex. There are always clear signs of the connection of religious, economic and all other institutions in Russian society to the state institutions *under the dominance of the state institutions*. There are various terms such as "sovereign democracy" or "guided democracy" used for designating this specific situation in the development of polyarchic institutional relationships. The specifics of these relationships are clearly identifiable in the urban landscape of modern Moscow and in the institutional and cultural framework for individualization in Russia. (Dmitrieva 2006) The culture, political institutions, city planning and architecture of Moscow emanate the self-confidence of a capital city which has much to be proud of and nothing to hide or to be ashamed of.

One may get an entirely different impression when looking carefully at what has been already done and what is planned for the development of the modern centre of Warsaw. This is known as Parade Square and has been clearly dominated by the Palace of Culture and Science for decades. Since the Palace is known to have been the gift of Stalin, there are certainly some historical and political reasons for the city planning projects which aim at knocking it down. One project suggests an artificial lake on the area currently occupied by the Palace building. However, suggestions of this type seem too radical. The Palace is most probably going to stay. But already before 1989 there were efforts on the part of city planners, architects and certainly of politicians to diminish its symbolic dominance. This was only partly accomplished by the selection of the location of the tall Marriott Hotel very close to the Palace. After 1989, the booming economy of Warsaw attracted the skyscrapers of the Bank of Austria and Mercedes-Benz on the other side of the Parade Square. Higher skyscrapers adding stress to the new geo-strategic orientation of democratic Poland are going to complete the modern center of Warsaw in which the Palace will be just one of the high buildings. But it will definitely not be the highest and not the dominant building any more. Among other things, the current and forthcoming architectural dominance of business centers is a special message. Obviously, this is not a philosophy of city planning and architectural design which stresses historical continuity. To the contrary, this is a philosophy which is focused on diminishing the historical relevance of some parts of the capital's architecture. The symbolic context of the present day individualization in Warsaw has different architectural domination than the Palace of Culture and Science. (Kula 2007)

Thus, there are substantial differences in the strategy of city planning and architectural design in the central areas of Moscow and Warsaw. But there are substantial similarities in the planning and architectural design in the suburbs of both capital cities where the new rich tend to establish their housing. Following American examples rich Russians and Poles as well as representatives of international organizations and multinational companies search for a clean environment, comfort, better education for their children, prestige and security in *gated communities*. As compared to the luxury castles in the gated communities "Serebryannyi bor" or "Knyazhne ozero" in the suburbs of Moscow, the former dachas of the top Soviet party and state functionaries look like housing for the lower middle class. As compared to the large number of luxury houses in the present day gated communities in the Warsaw's districts "Ursynow" and "Mokotow" the two dozen villas of the former top Polish *nomenclatura* in the times before 1989 only provoke condescension. This is all the more so since the Soviet and Polish *nomenclatura* functionaries had to leave the villas after having lost their posts. This happened often in the Soviet Union and in socialist Poland.

Much more important than this historical specification of the new developments in housing is the structural relevance of the process. The gated communities belong to the major symbols of structural change since Russia and Poland are not cohesive societies in economic, political, social or value-normative terms. To the contrary, due to the specifics of the Russian post-socialist transformation, the population of Moscow is deeply divided in economic terms with far reaching consequences for the stability of community life. This is obvious in any comparison of the present day clients of Moscow's Central Department Store (CUM) with its clients in the times when CUM used to be demonstratively accessible to the purchasing power of everybody. The comparison could be even more telling if one were to compare the clients of CUM with the clients at the bazaars around the metro stations in Moscow's periphery. Polish society is not divided to the same extent economically. But the cleavages between winners and losers in the post-socialist transformation of Poland are very well documented statistically and by the results of public opinion polls. Having collected some impressions on Polish everyday life from a walk past the luxury shops of Marszalkowska Street one may collect rather different impressions in a walk through the streets of the Praga district of Warsaw.

The rise in the social relevance of the gated communities very well exemplifies these socio-economic cleavages in Moscow and in Warsaw. The post-socialist gated communities reproduce the socially divisive characteristics of their American prototypes. Following this pattern, the inhabitants of gated communities in Moscow and in Warsaw are physically isolated from the outer world and guarded by their own security services. Thus, the gated communities are an impressive example of the privatization of public space. Since the inhabitants usually have to follow strict rules of communal life, there are ironical hints that the present day gated communities actually reproduce the communal pattern of the Soviet *kommunalka* housing. However, this ironic remark arises from a false understanding of the background. The Soviet *kommunalka* were intended to socialize the inhabitants in openness to society at large by means of local communal life. In clear contrast, the gated communities tend to close their inhabitants off from society at large. The controversial consequences of this concern both the inhabitants and the outsiders of the gated communities. (Gated and Guarded Housing 2009)

As for the inhabitants, most gated communities in Moscow and in Warsaw have full scale services like kindergartens, primary schools, shopping facilities, medical and dentist services, etc. So, they are self-sufficient in many respects. Some of the inhabitants, mostly children, may spend months without leaving the gated community. It becomes the organizational framework of the socialization of well-to-do representatives of the young generation. These young people are socialized not in conditions of social opening but of social closure to society at large. Given this type of socialization, one may only speculate about the sensitivity of the future elite of the Russian and Polish society to the social problems in their environments.

As for the outsiders, many of them belong to the strata in Russian and Polish society which feel increasingly alienated from their national economic and political elites. The elderly Poles still remember that *Solidarity* became so popular and influential because it appeared with the requirement for true communal life in the enterprises as well as in the settlements. These elderly people see their positive expectations gravely disappointed by the territorial self-isolation of the successful entrepreneurs and politicians in the gated communities.

The same holds true for the Muscovites who sincerely expected that the *perestroika* would help to end the bureaucratic isolation of the Soviet elite from the average citizens of the country. Now they see that the economic and political elites are hiding behind the walls of the gated communities from the poverty and crime of the Russian capital city. They also see that the self-isolation of the elites in the gated communities came about together with the weakening of state institutions and the commercialization of all walks of social life in the Russian Federation. In a broader historical context, the self-isolation of elites from the masses is not a new phenomenon in Russian economic, political and cultural tradition. The major negative effect of similar developments has usually been the search for a radically new direction for social development in order to radically overcome this isolation. The historical effects of radical re-orientation have rarely been constructive in Russian history.

Thus, what is at stake with the organization of social space is not a matter of short-term considerations. What is at stake in the long run is the social-structural and cultural ramification of individualization and therefore the future of Eastern European societies.

Chapter 4

Instrumental Activism *and* Sustainability?

To what extent have the Eastern European societies moved towards an economic, political and cultural sustainability since 1989? The answer cannot be brief and simple. The reasons are manifold but one of them is particularly important. The outcomes of Eastern European societal transformations diverge considerably from country to country due to differences in path dependency, quality of decisions and geostrategic specifics. The diversity holds true to the outcomes of the spread of instrumental activism as a process determining achievements and failures of sustainability in industrial societies. Together with many commonalities in this respect, Eastern European societies brought about a variety of patterns of commercialization of economy and all other action spheres. This fact will guide the further discussion since commercialization is the very core of the global trend of the spread of instrumental activism. (*A Fair Globalization* 2004: IXf.)

The trend itself has a much broader range of driving forces, manifestations and effects than the commercialization of individual and collective action. The driving forces of instrumental activism include the strengthening of the relative autonomy of economic calculability and technological efficiency in the course of industrialization. Some extreme manifestations of instrumental activism can be detected in the efforts to dominate the natural and human environment whatever the long-term consequences might be. The typical effect is the disconnection of technological development from moral and social considerations as well as the disembeddedness of markets from their social environment. This is the diagnosis which Karl Polanyi put on the great transformation from the feudal agrarian to the industrial capitalist social and economic order. Last but not least, the spread of instrumental activism has a manifestation which belongs to the major characteristics of present day advanced societies. This is the powerful orientation of society towards consume in its large variety of forms. Consumerism is thus a key feature of modern instrumental activism.

Complex and interrelated processes accompany the spread of instrumental activism on the global scale. The processes became manifest in various ways in the Eastern European regional history after the Second World War. For several decades this history was marked by tremendous efforts to achieve technological modernization. In the end of the state socialist development these efforts resulted in a total failure. Eastern European societies lost in the fierce international competition in the field of technological innovations. The failure was definitely not due to the lack of political will. At a given point of time the Soviet leadership cherished the ambition to elevate Eastern Europe to the position of one of the leading centers of the modern industrial civilization. There were even efforts to establish the Soviet Union and its allies as the leading force in the area of technological and economic development worldwide. The goal lurking behind these ambitions and efforts was clear. In this way economic, political, ideological and military advantages for Eastern Europe had to be achieved in the Cold War. In reality, besides some respectable breakthroughs in the military and aerospace industries, Eastern Europe retained its status of global technological periphery or mostly semi-periphery during the whole period between 1945 and 1989. How did this become possible given the historically unique concentration of resources in the hands of the over-centralized leadership of the Eastern European states? Why did the massive propaganda campaigns in favor of the scientific and technological revolution not bring about the cherished results?

The answer might be simplified for the purposes of clarity. *The economic and social organization of Eastern European societies used to neglect and even to suppress the motivational power of commercial mechanisms.* One may convincingly exemplify the whole multidimensional issue by one quite telling case. The famous submachine gun designer Mikhail Kalashnikov created the small arm which became the most successful one in commercial terms in the whole world history. Various versions of his famous AK-47 have been produced, purchased and used in more than 100 countries. However, his invention has never been patented. Consequently, Kalashnikov has earned fame and glory but never received financial returns. The famous designer of weaponry lived a living like all other low paid Soviet military officers. In his public appearances he used to stress the patriotic motives for his achievements. However, no modern society could prosper on the basis of the patriotic motivation of its best minds alone. The suppression of the commercial motivation for activity in all spheres of social life and particularly in the field of research and technological innovations did have long term negative consequences for the technological and economic development of the Eastern European societies. The desire for more high quality goods and services did undermine the real socialism stronger than the disenchantment by all economic, political and ideological principles of the socialist organization of society. (Althanns 2009: 8)

These conclusions only seemingly clash with some outcomes of the profound change in the value-normative orientations and behavioral patterns in Eastern European societies. At the beginning of the socialist transformation the official ideology there had two clearly distinguishable centers. The first and guiding one used to include the ultimate values of humanism, egalitarianism and social justice as they were incorporated in the socialist revolutionary ideals. A new humane and just society had to emerge by means of overcoming class divisions and antagonisms. The second value-normative center evolved around the instrumental goals of industrialization, mechanization of agriculture and the development of the infrastructure and consume of industrial society. The achievement of the instrumental goals had to make possible the establishment of the "good society" marked by a high living standard and quality of life. Since everyday life turned out to be dominated by issues of economic deficits, low living standard and quality of life the moral impetus of humanism and justice lost gradually its appeal and ideological relevance. It became more convincing to inherently connect the desire for "good society" with the achievements of the accelerated socialist industrialization.

This was the state socialist version of the spread of instrumental activism. By focusing exclusively on this instrumental goal the Eastern European countries realized a substantial economic growth during the 1950's and 1960's. The large-scale industrialization enforced by centralistic states brought about egalitarian mass consumption. Eastern Europe as a region had high rates of economic growth in worldwide comparisons. The region was able to reduce the gap in its gross domestic product per capita to the Western European and North American core of the modern civilization. (Berend 1997: 11) For millions of Eastern Europeans the modest but stable rise of consumption was a good reason to put up with the inherently repressive nature of the system.

The aims and practices of a catching up modernization qua industrialization were closely linked to the technological conquest of nature. It brought about the increase in living standards together with a massive disturbance of the ecological balance. It was this spirit of the time which animated the projects to redirect Siberian rivers to Central Asia in order to intensify the agriculture there. The technological and economic effects of the project were initially its only relevant parameters. The environmental consequences appeared as a topic for discussion long after the project was rejected due to economic reasons. Another dimension of socialist industrialism was the rationalization of industrial work by following the principles of the Taylorist scientific organization of work. Together with the enforced socialization of property on the means of production, the Taylorization of industrial organization very much contributed to the suppression of the individual initiative and to the economic and technological alienation in the societies of *real socialism.* They gradually stabilized value-normative and institutional patterns which precluded the prospects for sustainable technological, economic, social, political and cultural development.

Under these conditions the economic growth slowed down all over Eastern Europe. However, only in the republics of former Yugoslavia the growth reached the level of stagnation in 1980s. The national leaderships in Eastern Europe lost all illusions about the possibility to join the leading forces in the scientific and technological revolution world-wide. The major reason was the obvious inability of the Eastern European societal organization to deal successfully with the challenges of the information and communication technologies. (Castels 1999: 9) The Eastern European societies did not manage to establish a motivational system corresponding to this qualitatively new type of industrialization. The simple industrial mills could be constructed and managed at the beginning of the massive industrialization in the region by using commands and threat of violence. Effective development and production of information hard- and software cannot be achieved by externally imposed discipline. The efficient production and use of

modern information and communication technologies requires subtle motivations
which include massive commercial incentives.

Could the Eastern European societies develop more dynamic economic and
social organization by reforming their institutional framework but retaining
basically their state socialist characteristics? Unlike in Asia, this proved to be
impossible despite the market oriented reforms in Hungary and the innovating
effects of the *Solidarity* movement in Poland. The East European state socialist
societies turned out to be generally unable to efficiently manage the new
challenges of the technological modernization marked by the production and
use of information and communication technologies. This development and its
impacts on living standards and quality of life became the major factor for the
widespread discontent which finally triggered the political implosion in the region.
Instrumental activism had to come to dominate the economy and all other action
spheres by means of full scale commercialization of action patterns and social
structures in the region.

4.1 Globalization and Commercialization

The all embracing commercialization was expected to become the panacea against
the stumbling blocks on the way of further modernization of Eastern European
societies. Privatization of productive assets in industry and agriculture had to be
the major content of the commercialization. Privatization of trade had to go hand
in hand with the privatization of banking. All communal services had to be put
on sound economic ground by offering them to private entrepreneurs as well.
Research and technological development, tertiary education, health care, social
services and media had to follow the trend. Commercialization was regarded as
the adequate answer to the challenges of globalization. Only few dared to openly
question this neo-liberal euphoria.[1] It seemed that everybody had willingly
forgotten the innumerable failures of market self-regulation, the Great Depression
being the most outstanding one.

Twenty years later the Eastern European neo-liberal orthodoxy and the stress
on the universal medicine of commercialization is mostly discussed in critical
terms. However, the issue of market regulation is still with us in most impressive
ways. It was in September 2008 that the then United States Secretary of Treasury
Hank Paulson insisted on the point that the American financial institutions were
fully prepared to meet any financial challenge by their own commercial means.
The occasion was the bankruptcy of the *Lehman Brothers* bank. Paulson's reliance

---

1   As editor of the first UNDP *Human Development Reports* for Bulgaria (1995,
1996 and 1997) the author had to "briefly and in details" answer many questions about the
meaning of statements like the following: "The strategic path to sustainable development
goes through the creation of a *dynamic balance between the market and the state regulation
of economy*". (Genov 1995: 89)

on the self-cleaning capacities of commercial institutions was false and practically disastrous. He repeated the mistake made by Andrew Mellon who happened to be the US Secretary of Treasury at the beginning of the Great Depression in 1929. Only gigantic efforts of national and international public and private institutions rescued the global economy from a similar collapse in 2008–2009. In the most liberal (commercialized) national economy of the United States the public rescue operations included state bailouts for the *Citigroup* Bank and the *Bank of America*, the insurance giant *AIG*, the Federal National Mortgage Association (*Fannie Mae*), the Federal Home Loan Mortgage Corporation (*Freddie Mac*), the car producers *Chrysler* and *General Motors*. The list is longer. Obviously, the market forces of demand and supply turned out to be unable to balance themselves. It is clear now that commercialization cannot be the universal medicine for resolving economic bottle-necks. Society has to use public institutions efficiently in order to save itself from the destructive effects of the extreme commercialization. The global society has to use global public institutions in order to cope with the global estrangement of markets from their social settings. (Altvater and Mahnkopf, 2007: 90f., 517f.)

Public control on the introduction of markets was not organized efficiently in the Russian Federation during the 1990s. The Russian state administrators turned out to be professionally unprepared and not properly motivated to manage the complicated introduction of full-fledged commercialization. The state institutions were weakened by chaotic political reforms and turned out unable to neutralize the destructive over-commercialization of the national economy during the decisive decade of privatization waves. Thus, Russia could be described as a risk society at the end of the twentieth century. Natural and human resources were over-exploited. The typical attitude of state institutions to the problems caused by the extreme commercialization was only reactive. Power dominated over law. There was no consensus in society about past, present and future. (Yanitskiy 2001: 34–35)

Similar effects of over-commercialization became widespread all over Eastern Europe at the turn of the century. The institutionalization of commercial principles of societal organization was widely accompanied by disenchantments and anomic behavior. The rapid privatization of public property was supposed to offer the fast and efficient solution to the accumulated economic and social problems of state socialism. The economic decline due to the reforms of property rights was expected to be minimal and the recovery was believed to come in months. The expectations turned out to be utterly unrealistic. Even the best business analysts were far from the prediction of an imminent economic collapse in large areas of Eastern Europe. Without devastating military defeats or dramatic natural disasters most Eastern European national economies suffered a deeper decline in their GDP than the most affected Western countries during the Great Depression of 1929–1933.

The deep drop in the GDP development and the slow economic recovery in Eastern Europe are due to the combined differentiating effects of the global commercialization and the commercialization in the national institutional frameworks. The comparisons of the global distribution of FDIs, foreign trade, communication, transportation, tourism, etc. show that the effect of both the global and local commercialization is not the homogenization of positions and roles in a global village. To the contrary, the effect is the deepening differentiation of regions and states in the already divided human civilization and in internally divided societies. (Kessler 2009: 45ff.) What are the consequences of this development for Eastern Europe?

Problems of delayed and inefficient technological innovations permanently plagued state socialist societies. This is the reason why technological development was often openly debated in Eastern Europe in critical terms. As seen from another vantage point, the repeated political statements in support of the scientific and technological revolution did not remain statements alone. In the average, the societies in the region used to spend some 2% of their GDP on research and development. The effect of the comparatively high investment in R&D was usually modest. The high percentage of generally low national GDPs did not offer too much economic support for science based technological innovations. However, there were more relevant reasons for the modest effects of the relatively generous investment in research and technological innovations.

As hinted at with the famous case of the gun designer Kalashnikov, the first and most decisive reason was the lack of market incentives for efficient work in all stages of innovation activities starting from basic research to the commercialization of new products. Until its collapse the state socialist organization of R&D did not manage to establish adequate economic incentives for remuneration of efforts in this area of high risks. The reference to patriotism could mobilize some human resources for risk taking but only temporarily and modestly. The second reason was of structural nature. The principles of the state socialist economic organization did not support risk-taking in general and risk-taking in bottom-up initiatives in particular. Promising initiatives for technological innovation could only come about top-down from the political bodies dominating the economic processes. But the political functionaries could usually not take any direct personal advantage from successful innovations. Why should they ask for troubles by politically initiating or supporting technological innovations? Researchers, developers and managers of enterprises implementing successful technological innovations were so moderately remunerated for their success that innovations were not attractive for them as well. R&D institutions were modestly remunerated for successful technological innovations but were only rarely punished for not initiating and implementing innovations. Being on a soft budget, R&D institutions could even afford to neglect the purpose of their own existence. Some small shares of the profits from successful innovations used to remain with the innovation-friendly enterprises. Thus, neither the managers as individuals nor the R&D centers or enterprises as organizational units were interested in taking initiatives and risks of technological innovations.

The new way of thinking provoked by the neo-liberal ideology raised high expectations at the beginning of the reforms. Politicians, managers, economic experts believed that both the motivational and structural barriers hindering technological innovations could be easily overcome by spreading the unlimited commercialization. It was expected to strongly motivate and guide the R&D activities and particularly the technological innovations at the level of enterprises. The arguments in favor of unlimited commercialization seemed to be transparent and convincing. The R&D units which used to be financed directly or indirectly by the state budget had to provide the evidence that they were really needed under the conditions of market economy. The assumption was that the R&D units which were needed for the markets would manage to find out their market niches, to survive and flourish. The R&D units which would not succeed in identifying their market niches would go bankrupt. The "survival of the fittest" strategy had to be applied to the enterprises in the same way. After the "big-bang" privatization they had to demonstrate their adaptability to the new market conditions. If they would not be able to do this efficiently they had to go bankrupt.

Twenty years later this philosophy of "shock without therapy" and the related practical measures look like tasteless jokes. Researchers, managers and politicians in Eastern Europe are currently well aware of the fact that in all economically and technologically advanced societies state institutions and companies have special strategies to protect and support organizational units preparing and implementing technological innovations. These units most often enjoy long-term financial stability for the R&D activity which includes high risks in its very nature. Technological innovations are literally raised under incubator conditions in technological parks generously financed by states, regional governments, municipalities, companies, private foundations, etc. Institutional conditions of this type could not be available in Eastern Europe at the beginning of the reforms. At that time Eastern European societies were just moving into economic recession. Enterprises did not have absorption capacities for technological innovations. Thus, the very call for putting the numerous inherited R&D units directly under the market pressure was actually a call for their extermination. This is what actually happened. The investments in R&D dropped in the region dramatically from the average of 2% of GDP to 1.4% in the Czech Republic, 0.8% in Hungary, 0.7% in Poland, 0.4% in Romania, 1.0% in the Russian Federation and 0.9% in the Ukraine during the years 1996–2000. (Human Development Report 2003: 274–275) These percentages are actually misleading since most Eastern European societies had much lower GDP than in 1989 at that time.

The consequences of neo-liberalist market strategies are well known today. The Eastern European societies were generally technologically underdeveloped before 1989. But they were also global competitors in some fields of research and production. After the radical commercial turn of their economies they became just consumers of technological innovations. With Hungary as the only exception, the share of high-tech products in the overall exports of the new Eastern European member states of the European Union is much lower as compared with the average of high-tech share in the exports of the EU-27. This parameter has improved in all new member states after 1999 but their distance to the EU-average is overwhelming. The international competitiveness of the European Union itself has declined after the passing of its ambitious Lisbon strategy in 2000 (Eurostat 2006):

Table 4.1 Percentage of high technology exports in all exports of Eastern European societies

	1999	2006
EU-27	20.41	16.65
Bulgaria	1.71	3.34
Czech Republic	7.85	12.74
Estonia	10.13	7.99
Hungary	19.45	20.32
Latvia	2.33	4.20
Lithuania	2.06	4.65
Poland	2.26	3.11
Romania	2.81	3.85
Slovakia	3.50	5.43
Slovenia	3.75	4.66

The typical counter-argument concerning the technological development in Eastern Europe reads that strategic investors have modernized the production, radically improved the organization of work and thus contributed to the making of the national economies in the region better adapted to the international division of labor and more competitive on the global scale. The argument has good reasons. The example of Hungary on Table 4.1 above is in itself a telling argument. However, the issue is more complicated. At the same time Hungary is hardly hit by the current economic crisis. The key explanation for this discrepancy is quite simple. After the substantial investments in modernizing Hungarian production facilities, the investors have now the legal right to enjoy the returns without reinvesting in difficult times. The issue is well known: "Though FDI was, on the one hand, an indispensable modernization lever, it resulted in dependent economic position with strategic decisions made at Western company headquarters and profit repatriation practices having a negative impact on current account balances. This factor adds to the vulnerability under stormy conditions". (Galgóczi 2009: 4)

Another dimension of the same problem might be well exemplified by the activities of companies which are large investors in the food processing and beverages industries all over the world. Unilever, InBev and Nestle belong to them. They are active in all Eastern European countries. After having privatized leading enterprises in the region, these companies invested largely in the technological modernization of the local production lines. The organization of work was modernized there to be compatible with the work organization in the production units in Western Europe. Special programs were implemented for improving the vocational training of the local workers and managers. In this sense, the multinational companies substantially contributed to the improvement of the international competitiveness of the Eastern European national economies. Moreover, the companies usually have substantial social programs. They are involved in cooperation with the municipalities where their enterprises are located and contribute to the modernization of the local infrastructure as well.

Without questioning these achievements due to the opening of the Eastern European national economies to international investments, one has to notice the peculiarities of the process as well. None of the three above mentioned global companies has established any research centre in Eastern Europe. None of them has made any contract with local universities and local research centers for implementing cooperative projects in the sense of R&D so far. The only contacts with Eastern European universities concern the selection and attraction of the best qualified personnel for employment in the local production units of the companies. (Inovatsiite 2009: 664)

These findings require interpretation. The starting point might be the refreshment of the memory in the sense that all Eastern European countries did have relatively well developed R&D units in the areas of food processing and beverages production before 1989. The explanation is twofold. *First*, the countries in the region had large agricultural sectors in their national economies. Food processing and production of beverages was part and parcel of their technological and economic production chains and had to be served by state supported organizational units for research and technological development. *Second*, the countries from the region were important suppliers of food and beverages to the international markets before the reforms. The Eastern European states were deeply interested in these exports and supported them generously with research end development services.

The situation changed profoundly after the massive privatization of the food processing and beverage industries by powerful global companies. They do not need the local expertise in terms of R&D. The same basically applies to all large international investments in Eastern Europe. There are large factories within the car industry in most East European countries, for example. Without exception, these factories rely only on know-how from abroad.

This development has spill-over effects. It makes national investments in local R&D capacities meaningless since there are few local producers who would rely on products of the local R&D activities for the modernization of their production lines. In the short run, the positive effects of this development might predominate since foreign companies transfered advanced know-how. In the long run, this development turns the Eastern European societies to losers in the global competition between knowledge based national economies and societies. The brightest Eastern European researchers and the most inventive engineers are pressured by the circumstances to leave their countries since the local labor markets do not need them. Even the best conceived national strategies for fostering research, development and technological innovations are thus doomed to fail. There are no real consumers and absorption capacities for locally made technological innovations. The innovation needs are served by products of R&D centers located abroad. One may take this development as unavoidable in the context of globalization. The counter-argument might read that the effects which we observe now as unavoidable are the results of policies implemented in the past. If so, some of these policies might be reconsidered and changed. The crucial condition is the political will.

The issue raised in this way does not concern the new East European member states of the EU alone. The rather uneven national investments in R&D, the concentration of R&D activities in the EU-15 and the de-institutionalization of R&D in the new members of the Union are not promising prospects for the stability and the global competitiveness of the whole European Union. One cannot imagine a successful implementation of its ambitious Lisbon strategy for the transformation of the Union into the leading power in R&D worldwide if a substantial part of the Union member states is so dramatically lagging behind in this respect. The economic, political, cultural and territorial cohesion of the Union would be questioned if its Eastern European part would remain only consumer of R&D products.

Given the rather sobering percentage of high-tech in the Polish exports, the recent discussions in the country are indicative for the direction and the content of the desirable changes in Eastern Europe. In Poland they include legal improvements of the status and functions of the research and development centers. The step is needed since between 2004 and 2006 23.2% of the Polish enterprises were evaluated as innovative while in the EU-27 this applied to 42% of all enterprises. The reasons for the discrepancy were identified, the major one being the low share of GDP invested in R&D in Poland as compared to the EU average. This particularly concerns the low level of financing of R&D in Poland by the business sector. This source of financing R&D makes up just 0.18% of the GDP in Poland but 1.17% of the GDP in the EU-27 average. One explanation of this alarming situation might be that the businesses in Poland are not very much interested in technological innovations. This hypothesis could be easily falsified since the businesses in the country are exposed to all kinds of international competition. The realistic hypothesis seems to be different. Most probably, businesses in Poland do not rely on products of Polish R&D institutions. This mostly concerns businesses owned by foreign investors. Thus, the efforts to strengthen the national commitment to R&D have to be connected with efforts to increase the national absorption capacities for products of research and development.

As seen from another angle, the Polish national R&D institutions could be strengthened by an active participation in EU research programs. They are expected to contribute to the general improvement of the quality of the Polish research and development, to facilitate the transfer of knowledge and technologies to the country and to make careers in R&D in Poland more attractive for the Polish young people. Whatever the intentions in this respect, it is a sobering fact that Poland remained a net payer in the Sixth Framework Program of the European Union. This means that Poland as a relatively poor country financed the R&D institutions of the more developed EU countries. In order to change this unfavorable situation, state support was allocated for the establishment of technology transfer centers, technology incubators and technology parks. (5 Years Poland in the European Union 2009: 185–199)

Referring to the strong dependence of the Russian economy and society on the exports of raw materials and energy resources, O.N. Yanitskiy outlined scenarios for the research and development sector in the country. Provided the exports of Russia would continue to be mostly raw materials and energy resources, he foresees an additional decline of research and high technologies in the country. The focus of local research might move to applied projects servicing needs of foreign investors. Yanitskiy assumes that this trend would be strengthened by the rise of consumerism as attitude and behavioral pattern among the population. He notices that consumerism currently thrives in Russia on the nexus between corrupt state officers and the market power of the new rich. Both groups are particularly interested in fast and easy profits from the exports of raw materials and energy resources and much less interested in productive investments with long-term and generally uncertain profitability. (Yanitskiy 2007: 36–37)

The issues dealt with above are so complex that simplified descriptions, explanations or policy recommendations might be misleading. The chains of mutually dependent processes of academic research, its technological application and commercialization of its results include many institutional actors and their interactions. Both the underdevelopment of actors and interactions might sustain the technological underdevelopment of Eastern Europe. The consequences of the underdevelopment of local R&D activities for the wellbeing of the societies in the region and for their successful integration in the global division of labor are particularly far reaching. It is undisputable that Eastern European societies definitely need regularly updated national programs for research and development. The programs should use the mechanisms of indicative planning thus stimulating the private sector to be more active in funding R&D activities on commercial basis. However, there are no neo-liberal illusions in Eastern Europe any more that the states could or should abdicate from their legal, organizational and financial obligations concerning the national R&D systems. To the contrary, an active position of the Eastern European states concerning technological innovations is currently regarded as a matter of a very desirable normality. For the Eastern European member states of the European Union the expectation also applies for an active participation of the national R&D institutions in the scientific and technological programs of the Union.

One of the major obligations of the state institutions is the spread of knowledge about the specifics of R&D and its links with production, markets and consumers. The future politicians, academic leaders and corporate elites in Eastern Europe are expected to acquire this knowledge in the course of their academic education. This is the condition for successful partnerships between academic research institutions, business corporations and territorial political elite. The partnerships might bring about concerted actions followed by astonishing outcomes like these of the cooperation between Stanford University, Silicon Valley business companies and various levels of administration in the state of California. Partnerships of this type need a long-term institutionalization with clear mutual obligations and controlling. It is not easy to achieve a stable institutionalization of such partnerships since the

R&D activities and business-related technological innovations are marked by high risks and low level of predictability.

In order to cope with the risks, reforms are needed in the Eastern European academic institutions. The academic leaders in the region have to be encouraged to support research facilities carrying aggressive policies for fund raising at supranational, national, regional and local (company) level. Clear priorities in the cooperation of academic institutions with the local businesses should be pursued. One well known mechanism for stable and purposeful cooperation is the involvement of representatives of the local businesses at all levels of decision-making and controlling of academic research activities. This is possible in places where the parties in these interactions keep to the culture of mutual respect and support. Particularly in Eastern Europe this is an extremely difficult task due to the traditions of doing research for its own sake. On the other side, the new rich people in the region usually lack the knowledge about the commercial potentials of academic research. Last but not least, both the academic leaders and the representatives of the new business elites do not trust the local politicians since they are not believed to be willing and able to promote the local academic activities and businesses efficiently.

The mistrust has good reasons since state administrators and politicians are used to "sell" the decision power of their positions. These typical stumbling blocks facing the public-private partnerships in the region are particularly hindering in the complicated commercialization of the products of research and development. The process might be successful and profitable for each participant but may also end up in an intellectual, economic and political disaster as many efforts to bring about technological innovations in the region have actually ended up. This is not necessarily due to the lack of competence or good will but more often due to the bad management of the very risky nature of the innovation activities.

Actors, structures and cultural patterns in Eastern Europe are still far away from smoothly approaching and resolving the tasks outlined. This is a long-term learning process. Fast learners are being remunerated. Laggards have to pay a high price for learning and acting slowly. Some academic institutions, businesses, local and national governments in Eastern Europe are or will be successful, others not. The differentiation might put the sustainability of businesses, economic branches, region or states in question. Commercialization means competition. It is ruthless. One may be somewhat skeptical about the prospects of the Eastern European societies to succeed in the global competition. They neither have the advantage of low-income and well organized open economies like China nor the advantage of well established knowledge based economies, such as the Western European and North American ones. The future will show what real options the individual Eastern European countries will have in the global competition and what the outcome of their efforts to compete might be.

4.2 Challenges to Social Cohesion and Sustainability

The Hungarian economy experienced a successful re-industrialization already in the early nineties. However, large territories in the country and all over Eastern Europe suffered rapid de-industrialization. One may interpret it as a correction of the socialist over-industrialization. It was guided by the idea of a relatively homogenous development of diverse territories. This was a matter of planning guided by political and ideological but not by market principles. The full reliance on market principles during the transformation had consequences. The technological and economic cooperation predominantly with the Eastern part of the European continent was replaced by a radical westward re-orientation with all implications for large territories. Whatever the causes, the effect is the emergence of deep territorial disparities.

In most Eastern European societies the privatization in agriculture brought about small peasants' agriculture. The effect was the *return to low-productivity agriculture*. Mechanization, the usage of fertilizers and the functioning of the irrigation systems collapsed. Thus, commercialization of agriculture is flourishing around the capital cities and other centers of re-industrialization and services in Eastern Europe. Large rural areas are currently dominated by technologically underdeveloped small peasants' agriculture and will remain most probably laggards in the modernization during the decades to come.

Thus, the territorial division in economic prosperity has already deep traces. The outcome is not promising for social cohesion in the Eastern European societies defined as "the capacity of a society to ensure the welfare of all its members, minimising disparities and avoiding polarisation". (A New Strategy for Social Cohesion 2004: 3) The *territorial differentiation* has far reaching implications for social structure, research, education, labor market and the infrastructure in the disadvantaged territories. Large territories in Eastern Europe lost the best educated and economically active segments of their population due to the out-migration. It was very much believed to be a temporary solution of personal problems. Out-migration was even praised since it used to decrease the pressure on the local labor markets in the times of mass unemployment. However, the temporary out-migration turned out to be a permanent emigration causing scarcity of educated and trained labor force after the recovery of Eastern European economies. This makes the recovery of the underdeveloped territories particularly difficult.

The problem is burning in the enlarged European Union. Its regional policies used to be guided by the vision of step by step territorial homogenization of the whole area of the Union. The enlargement of the Union to the East has sharply increased the share of the underdeveloped territories. Making their development a real priority in the enlarged Union would require tremendous financial means and concentration of political will. Given the pressure of global competition, one can hardly believe that both conditions could be met simultaneously. The manifold issues of distorted territorial social cohesion in the Eastern part of the European Union will most probably remain a long-term challenge to the Eastern European states *and* to the Union. The issue of disturbed territorial cohesion took particularly dramatic dimensions in the Russian Federation. Huge territories were supported there by policies of the state planning before 1991. Later they became practically de-populated or are suffering various disadvantages due to the disruption in the territorial social cohesion.

The spread of instrumental activism in Eastern Europe implies, above all, the accumulation of capital in private hands. The transformation of property relations had immediate consequences for the level of real wages in the region. Their decline went further than the decline of the GDP during the nineties (UNICEF 2001: 159):

Table 4.2 Index of real wages in Eastern Europe 1990–1999 (1989 = 100.0)

Country	1990	1991	1992	1993	1994	1995	1996	1997	1998	1999
Armenia	107.7	72.3	39.6	6.3	16.8	20.0	29.0	26.2	31.9	35.1
Bulgaria	111.5	68.0	76.7	77.6	63.7	60.2	49.6	40.1	47.0	52.2
Czech Republic	96.3	68.9	76.0	78.8	84.9	92.2	100.4	102.3	101.0	107.1
Estonia	102.5	68.2	45.2	46.3	50.9	54.0	55.2	59.5	63.5	66.2
Hungary	94.3	87.7	86.5	83.1	89.1	78.2	74.3	77.1	79.6	81.0
Latvia	105.0	71.9	49.0	51.8	57.9	57.7	54.1	60.7	63.0	65.0
Lithuania	108.8	75.3	46.6	28.4	32.5	33.5	34.8	39.5	44.6	47.8
Macedonia	79.2	67.9	41.6	56.5	51.2	48.6	48.8	49.4	50.9	53.0
Moldova	113.7	105.2	64.4	41.8	33.8	34.3	36.3	38.2	40.4	35.1
Poland	75.6	75.4	73.3	71.2	71.6	73.7	77.9	82.4	85.2	95.8
Romania	105.2	88.9	77.3	64.4	64.6	72.7	79.8	62.3	61.1	62.3
Russia	109.1	102.4	68.9	69.1	63.7	45.9	52.0	54.5	47.2	38.2
Slovakia	94.2	67.3	76.6	69.2	71.4	75.3	81.9	87.4	88.8	86.1
Slovenia	73.8	61.8	61.3	70.4	75.4	79.4	83.1	85.4	86.7	89.4
Ukraine	109.3	114.2	123.7	63.2	56.4	62.2	59.3	57.7	55.7	48.4

In no one country which was affected by the Great Depression 1929–1933 has the real purchasing power of salaries and wages declined so dramatically like in the most Eastern European countries during the 1990s. But this is only one side of the critical processes in the region since the above statistical averages do not tell the whole story. The privatization brought about and stabilized very substantial differences in property. This had immediate consequences on the *differentiation of incomes*. In contrast to the egalitarian distribution of incomes under state socialism, they became rather unevenly distributed under the new market-dominated conditions.

Table 4.3 Change in East European Gini-coefficients between 1987 and 2003

Country	1987	1996–98	2002–03
Belarus	0.23	0.26	0.30
Bulgaria	0.23	0.33	0.29
Czech Republic	0.19	0.25	0.24
Estonia	0.24	0.37	0.36
Georgia	0.29	0.43	0.40
Hungary	0.21	0.25	0.27
Latvia	0.24	0.32	0.38
Lithuania	0.23	0.34	0.36
Moldova	0.27	0.42	0.33
Poland	0.28	0.33	0.36
Romania	0.23	0.30	0.31
Russia	0.26	0.47	0.40
Slovenia	0.22	0.30	0.28
Ukraine	0.24	0.47	0.28

The fast rise of the Gini-coefficient all over the region became alarming because of its social consequences (see Table 4.3).[2]

The economic differentiation in the Eastern European societies has long-term consequences for their social structure, political stability and cultural integration. As seen from a broader point of view, the processes in the region correspond to processes of growing differentiation of per capita incomes world wide. Both in the Eastern European societies and at a global level the negative effects of the economic differentiation mostly concern the middle class which is regarded as the key factor for the stability of the democratic political order. (Milanović 2005: 31f.)

Various *monetary experiments* became an important factor for the downward mobility of broad layers in East European societies. The experiments were mostly conducted according recommendations of the international financial institutions. The first experiment consisted in the sudden liberalization of prices and commercial regimes. The effect was skyrocketing inflation, lack of transparency and calculability in economy and society. Both measures were basically necessary in order to introduce disciplined market competition. But their execution began at a point of time, when the state institutions were weakened. Under these circumstances the measures which aimed at strengthening the financial discipline paradoxically contributed to the criminalization of the

---

2   The data on 1987 and 1996–98 stem from (Transition 2002: 9). The data on 2002–03 stem from the (Human Development Report 2007: 281–283).

economy. The outcome was the criminal concentration of wealth and incomes. The policy of monetary stabilization brought about stagnation, unemployment and poverty.

The economic differentiation mostly operated not by the mechanisms of supply and demand alone. The process used to be the outcome of *political* initiatives as a rule. The key motivation of the initiatives was the separation of politics from the economic processes. However, it was already too late when the international financial institutions realized that the multi-dimensional and profound transformation cannot be administered rationally without carefully planned and conducted state interventions. They had to be replaced by the self-control and the mutual control of actors in commercial transactions. This expectation turned out to be unrealistic. The emergence of a broad shadow economy was thus facilitated.

Putting aside many national specifics, at the end of the century the consequences of all these processes for social cohesion could be summarized as follows:

First, the economically active population decreased substantially. This was to a large extent due to the *unemployment* caused by the commercialization of the property on productive assets. The impact of privatization and the following unemployment on the living standard and quality of life is still far reaching in the region. The most impressive drop in employment and consequently rise in unemployment came about in Eastern Europe in the first half of the nineties. However, at the end of 2008 the unemployment still remained at the level of 41.1% in Bosnia and Herzegovina, 34% in Macedonia and 31% in Serbia. (EBRD statistics) It would have been very high also in Poland and in Romania provided there was no opportunity for mass labor migration to Western Europe after the two waves of the enlargement of the European Union to the East. The majority of persons, who remained one decade or longer on unemployment benefits lost the links to normal working life and remained hopeless marginalized. The poverty related to unemployment together with the imposed social isolation throws a long shadow on the attitudes and behavioral patterns of their children. Due to unemployment women were forced into the position of housewives. Some of them unwillingly remained in this position during the phase of economic stabilization since they have also lost their occupational qualification and did not dare to get a new vocational training.

Still another group dropped out from the employment statistics because it drifted to the shadow economy. The composition of this group and its share in the working population vary substantially from country to country. Estimations revealed that the production of the shadow economy reached over 50% of the GDP in the Russian Federation and Ukraine. Whatever the exact calculation of the share of the shadow economy in the GDP of particular East European countries might be, there is no doubt that it has a strong negative impact on social cohesion due to illegal transactions, tax evasion and accumulated risks. They mostly concern the lack of medical and old age insurance of the people employed in the shadow economy. The issue has still another dimension. The large scale move of employment into the shadow economy has destructive impacts on the institutionalized solidarity as well. Persons involved in the shadow economy evade their social responsibility of supporting the elderly, sick and disabled, mothers and other people in need.

The number of employed persons substantially decreased in all Eastern European societies also due to the massive temporary or permanent out-migration. Some territories in the region are particularly affected by out-migration and will remain problematic concerning the local social cohesion in the long run. The social cohesion at micro-level is being disturbed in millions of Eastern European families due to the absence of some of their members working abroad for short or long. Most affected of such absence are the children. They suffer particularly in cases in which both parents stay abroad for long.

Secondly, following the decline in GDP and the deepening differentiation of property and income most Eastern European societies were strongly affected by a general decline in the living standards of large groups of the population. On average, some 15 to 30% of the population in these societies enjoyed an upward mobility in the course of the 20 years of market oriented reforms. The remainder has to cope with the effects of downward mobility or with stagnation of the socio-economic positions. During the first half of the 1990s the impoverished Eastern European societies could hardly offer decent unemployment benefits. In some cases they provided for about 1 USD per day for household member. According to the UNO criteria this was the level of extreme poverty. The effect was the total economic marginalization of the unemployed. Since unemployment and the ensuing impoverishment particularly affected some ethnic groups, the less educated, the youngest, the elderly, etc. became marginalized in all dimensions of social exclusion. The situation changed in the course of time. Together with the economic stabilization most Eastern European societies increased the level of unemployment benefits. But the long-term unemployed still remain out of connections to working life and many other dimensions of sociability due to the local incomes. However, the effects undermining social cohesion reached not the impoverished unemployed alone. Due to the differentiation of wages and salaries in the course of the privatization large segments of employed people turned to *working poor* as well.

The differentiation between winners and losers of the economic transformation is the major characteristic of the current social structures in the Eastern European region. These structures condition the specifics of the political and cultural processes. Apart from the unemployed, the young, the old and the ethnic minorities, the groups involved in research, technological development, education and arts also belong to the major losers in the transformation. The latter groups used to form a specific middle class which was respected under state socialism because of the possession of cultural capital. This capital was largely devaluated in the course of the transformation. Given the key position of these professionals for the cultural integration of societies, the loss of prestige they suffered had specific destructive consequences for social cohesion in the Eastern European societies in the long run.

The spread of poverty in Eastern Europe at the end of the twentieth century had substantial national specifics. In 1990 only 2% of the Czech population was poor according to the official definition of poverty. The differentiation of incomes in the Czech Republic was rather modest in the course of the transformation. Thus, no underclass of very poor and marginalized people evolved in the country. However, this happened in most other Eastern European societies. Large groups of unemployed and working poor remained out of the widely praised post-socialist revolution of consume. (Althanns 2009) A tendency appeared of deteriorating the socio-economic situation of the upcoming generations. This was an entirely new phenomenon of intergenerational downward mobility in the region since in socialist times the general trend was the slow but stable increase of living standards from generation to generation. (Derczynski 2004: 9)

One can certainly speak of winners of the transformation in value neutral or in morally positive terms. There were individuals, groups or organizations, which succeeded in adapting to the changes actively by generating genuine achievements and thus managing to change their life for the better. However, the expression *winner of the transformation* has a specific connotation in Eastern Europe. The expression usually points out to those individuals who managed to take advantage of a situation dominated by normlessness for fast and undue enrichment. Such winners are to be found throughout the region. Their achievements are only exceptionally commented with moral respect. The reasons are very well known. Even in countries like the Czech Republic where privatization could be kept basically under legal control the *nouveau riches* are typically regarded with mistrust. During the 1990s there were hardly any legal opportunities in Eastern Europe to become rich quickly – the national lotteries notwithstanding. This is the background reason of the influential view that property was usually accumulated in the region in illegal and immoral ways. This widespread public opinion will remain a strong factor hindering social cohesion in Eastern Europe. Cohesion cannot efficiently be achieved and maintained on the basis of the observation that leading personalities in society do not deserve moral respect. If corroborated by facts, this observation undermines the moral legitimacy of the newly established social order.

The Russian Federation is the most prominent example for rapid economic and social differentiation leading to the emergence of a tiny layer of particularly strong winners in the post-socialist transformation. In the Soviet times there were certainly small groups of rich people in the country due to political corruption, criminal networks, or to niches in the distribution within a society marked by permanent deficits. Nevertheless, the Soviet society was not too much different from the other basically egalitarian state-socialist societies. The top-earners in the regulated economy could rarely earn more than three- to fourfold of the average income. During the 1990s there were cases in post-socialist Russia in which the enterprise director in a still state owned enterprise could receive 1000 times the average salaries and wages in the same enterprise. How was this possible? The short answer reads: By means of a criminal revolution in the course of which the directors managed to legally accumulate the capital needed to buy the enterprise at a manipulated low price.

There were two major institutional reasons of this extreme redistribution of property and income in the Russian Federation at the expense of the cohesion of Russian society. The first reason was the administrative way in which the privatization was implemented in the country. Intentionally or unintentionally, Russian society remained badly informed about the aims and the means of the voucher privatization. State administrators and economic managers were able to use and abuse their positions and to acquire lion's shares of the privatized state property. The second reason was the intentional or unintentional delay in the modernization of the legislation in the country. Together with the weakening of institutional control by the state the insufficient or outdated legal regulations fostered the concentration of property and income. The strengthening of state institutions in Russia after the turn of the century raised the expectation that the episode of oligarchic structures in the country might have been over. A close look at the more recent distribution of ownership and income in the country shows that this is not the case. The concentration of property and income remains high. There are elements of oligarchic structures also in other Eastern European societies. *An economic order, which is to a considerable degree based on economic inequality, cannot support cohesive institutional arrangements in society.*

Thus, without the painful adaptation to the modern requirements of instrumental activism Eastern European organizations and institutions could not become adequate partners in the global markets as well as in global politics and culture. It was practically unavoidable to go through these deep institutional changes and re-arrangements without putting strains on social cohesion or causing disturbances in it. However, in many cases the disturbances in economic relations and in the commercialization of non-economic relations took extreme forms.

The fast economic differentiation had far reaching consequences in the divisions concerning *the availability and quality of housing*. Housing was on average of relatively low quality in Eastern Europe before the changes. This applied to the rather small apartments in the monotonous industrial pre-fab blocks of flats first of all. They became the symbol of the uniformity and monotony of life under state socialism in Eastern Europe. However, the statistics of Eastern European societies provide clear evidence that the period between 1945 and 1989 was the time in their national history marked by the most active building of housing indeed. Housing was strongly subsidized. This applied to the building of housing itself, to the rents for housings, energy supply, the price for water, communal services, etc. All communes had special housing for needy people where the rents were particularly low.

The situation changed literally over night with the fast privatization of state and communal housing, of housing owned by enterprises and of social housing. The new owners rarely had the means needed for modernizing the privatized housing property. Twenty years after the privatization one may observe whole housing complexes which have not been renovated ever since. The widely discussed boom of housing construction in the beginning of the new century is very much misleading. Construction was concentrated in the capital cities, in the centers of regions or in some specific areas like holiday resorts. The concentration of high quality of modern housing in small areas is not conducive for strengthening the social cohesion in the Eastern European societies. Very well conceived, financed and implemented sound state policies are needed in order to reduce this disparity. The issue of providing social housing to the newly emerged large underclass is particularly burning.

Basically the same controversial processes mark the development of *transportation*. The economic and social differentiation of Eastern European societies is most obvious in the quality of cars on the streets of the capital cities. In a sharp contrast to the times in which only few officials could enjoy state owned luxurious cars, one may observe large numbers of most modern luxury cars on the streets of Moscow or of other Eastern European capitals. The luxury cars are the symbols of financial success and political prestige and could be seen in Moscow more often than in Berlin or in Paris. On the other side of the socio-economic spectrum there are large areas in Eastern Europe and particularly in Russia where the settlements used to be connected by subsidized public transportation before the changes. After the transportation companies were privatized the unprofitable railway or bus lines were cut. Large numbers of settlements remained unconnected by public transportation. Since millions of Eastern Europeans cannot afford private cars, one may notice that the social cohesion of these isolated areas and their population was dramatically disturbed. The situation is precarious since school age children cannot attend school due to the lack of affordable transportation.

One of the extreme forms of disturbed social cohesion is the practical isolation of millions of Eastern Europeans from the modern *health care*. No doubt, the health care systems of state socialist societies were notoriously underfunded. They typically lacked modern medical infrastructure and technology. But it was an achievement of the socialist health care that it was practically accessible to everybody. Following various strategies and tactics, health care was largely commercialized in Eastern Europe. In some rare cases, the commercialization went hand in hand with an improvement of medical technology and medical treatment. However, payments practically precluded the access of millions of impoverished Eastern Europeans to medical care. Life expectancy declined. Diseases related to poverty and malnutrition like tuberculosis appeared anew. One cannot expect high quality of social cohesion without systematic long-term policies for resolving the issue.

The commercialization of all action spheres affected *education* as well. This became manifest in the appearance of private kindergartens, primary schools, secondary schools and universities. While the private primary and secondary schools still make out a negligible share of the establishments at these educational levels, the commercialized tertiary educational institutions are already a very relevant phenomenon in Eastern Europe. Some Eastern European private universities are related to respectable educational institutions in Western Europe and in the United States and offer excellent education. However, the vast majority of the newly established private universities in Eastern Europe do not have the proper infrastructure and personnel needed for high quality teaching. Most private universities do not offer courses in natural sciences indeed. What they offer more often than usual is distance learning by using questionable teaching materials and pedagogical methods. Since this is not an isolated phenomenon, one may be afraid that the commercialization of higher education in many respects is undermining the real achievements of higher education in Eastern Europe. The long-term effects of the use of badly educated high level specialists cannot be conducive to the social cohesion of Eastern European societies.

The *privatization of media* is a special case of commercialization. The emergence of commercial press, radio broadcasting and TV stations very much supported the pluralization of political and cultural life in Eastern Europe. At the same time, one may notice a striking drop in the general educational and cultural quality and relevance of the messages broadcasted by the private media. In most cases they adapt their programs to audiences with low level of education and cultural aspirations. In some specific cases like Radio Maryja in Poland the private media mobilize support to policies which are regarded as questionable by large parts of society and thus disturb the cultural conditions of social cohesion.

Therefore, the challenges to social cohesion took various manifestations in Eastern Europe. Most of them are due to the differentiation of ownership and income. But the changing access to labor, health care facilities, education and housing has become an issue for millions in their everyday life as well. The changes in the living standard and in other objective lifestyle parameters brought about changes in the subjective perception of the quality of life and life satisfaction. All these changes in the objective structural conditions and in the subjective assessments and attitudes make the efforts to increase social cohesion of Eastern European societies a difficult task with uncertain outcomes.

The fast replacement of the Eastern European administratively over-regulated quasi-markets by vibrant competitive open markets was made possible by the joint forces of the massive commercial supply *and* the massive demands on the part of the local consumers. After decades of deficits unlimited consumption became possible over night. One could immediately buy a house, a car, or the most modern TV set, could travel to Mallorca or Thailand, or even buy shares in Western companies. The high tide of *consumerism* had arrived. (Barber 2007) Most naturally, the option of unlimited consumption had one limit: there had to be purchasing power. It sharply declined in Eastern Europe in the wake of the neo-liberal monetary experiments. But the doors to mass consumption were already open. Consumerism became the major motivational factor of the economic recovery and of the fast economic growth during the second decade of the societal transformations in Eastern Europe. Thus, supply and demand, commercialism and consumerism could be balanced. This could not happen in several months or even in several years as expected. But a balance was achieved nevertheless. Now the major issue is: How stable could this balance be?

Can it guarantee sustainable development in Eastern Europe?[3] The attempt at a brief answer to this question is guided by a holistic approach to sustainability with all its major environmental, economic, political, social and cultural dimensions.

As seen from the point of view of the *environmental dimension* of sustainability, the spread of instrumental activism took a variety of directions in Eastern Europe. The economically devastating de-industrialization had at least one positive side effect. The most polluting industries like mining, metallurgy or chemical processing were the worst hit since they used most outdated technologies and were not competitive any more. There was no economic reason to modernize them. Thus, the closing of numerous enterprises of these branches contributed to the decline of the industrial pollution all over Eastern Europe. But the shadow of socialist industrialism is long. Large polluted areas still have to be re-cultivated. Moreover, it is to be carefully monitored which directions the further industrial development would take under the conditions of an all-pervading commercialization of economic and other activities. This applies mostly to the part of former Eastern Europe that remains outside the boundaries of the enlarged EU-27. The ten new East European member states of the Union seem to be at least legally protected by the strict environmental regulations of the *acquis communautaire*. It is always possible, however, that some regulations might be interpreted and applied differently due to market interests. This might concern the disposal of industrial waste. So far, some serious concerns that Eastern Europe would immediately become the dumping place for industrial waste from the Western part of the continent did not come true, at least not to an alarming degree. Nevertheless, given the burning need of foreign investments in the eastern part of the continent one should be always careful about the environmental implications of the investments.

The major current challenge to sustainability in Eastern Europe is the economic underdevelopment. In some parts of the former region the economic instability has taken the form of long-term economic crisis with unpredictable economic, political and cultural consequences. This applies for Ukraine, Moldova and Bosnia and Herzegovina, for instance. The new Eastern European EU member states themselves will have to struggle for decades in order to reduce the substantial difference they have to the average GDP per capita in the Union. Given this most general indicator of the Eastern European underdevelopment, it is out of question that only a rapid technological innovation of production and services may ensure a sustainable development for the region. The problem contains a specific dimension concerning the sustainability of the natural environment. Contrary to many optimistic expectations the resource and energy-saving industries rank among the losers in the restructuring of the East European economies. What remained in good

---

3   There are numerous interpretations of sustainability and sustainable development. Nevertheless, it seems that the broad understanding of sustainable development from the Brundtland Report as development that meets the needs of the present without compromising the ability of future generations to meet their own needs is still most influential among them. (Strange and Baley 2008: 24f)

order in most cases are the primary industries. The Russian economic complex is the most impressive example for the accompanying environmental risks. These industries are focused on the consumption of energy and raw materials and belong to the major industrial polluters. The level of value added in these branches is low. They are particularly exposed to the fluctuations of the international competition.

In the beginning of the 1990s it was widely assumed that the political and economic opening of the Eastern European societies to global processes would trigger the rapid overcoming of the technological gap between both parts of the European continent. The results achieved so far are more sobering than encouraging. The technological gap dividing Eastern and Western Europe actually widened. Large research institutes and production facilities had to be closed since they were depending on the cooperation, resources and semi-finished products from the former partners or had to serve their needs. Subsidies for research and development decreased in the impoverished Eastern European countries. The decline in GDP, of the domestic accumulation and investments contributed to this change. The new market situation shows clearly and unambiguously that the status of Eastern Europe – from few exceptions apart – is one of continental periphery or semi-periphery in the best case. After the market oriented reforms were carried out the countries in the region found themselves in the same inferior position within the international division of labor which is marked by long-term dependency. (Chilcote 2003) Only metropolitan areas around Budapest, Warsaw and other Eastern European capitals managed to join the "global city" marked by modern infrastructure and high quality jobs. Most other areas in Eastern Europe do not have such advantages or are about to lose them. They rather aligned the "global village" offering products of the primary industries, of agriculture or simple services.

The adaptation of Eastern Europe to the accelerated globalization implies the effective integration of national economies in the region into the world market. Its functioning is guided by the instrumental value of profit maximization. It comes into being under the circumstances of a rapid increase in the global financial exchange. Some trans-boundary financial transactions include real investments of vital importance for countries in the region. The foreign investments are particularly essential since the internal capital accumulation in Eastern Europe is rather limited. Indeed, the FDIs can be an efficient and effective mechanism to create new jobs and a stable economic environment for further entrepreneurial activities.

However, the financial crisis in Russia in 1998 and the current global financial crisis have shown that short-term cash flows might be rather risky for the weak Eastern European economies. Some Eastern European EU member states reached double digit GDP decline in 2009. One of the major reasons for this development is connected to the short-term investments. They usually chase "hot money" and disappear quickly after noticing the smallest uncertainty of the local political or economic situation. These short-term investments of hedge funds produce a global virtual economy, which only exceptionally creates and maintains sustainable production and employment. To the contrary, the effect is usually economic uncertainty and chaos. The forecast reads that there is an enormous potential for future uncertainties on the global markets since the share of short-term transactions will rise further on. Their impact on the weak economies will rise even stronger.

Thus, sustainable economic development requires a re-evaluation and regulation of the international financial system. The task is enormous, but its resolution cannot be delayed for any longer. The sustainability of the Eastern European reforms strongly depends on the extent to which the international financial markets would be directed towards *governability*. The large and politically stable national economies as well as the strong multinational companies are well equipped to adapt to the volatility of the cash flows. This does not apply to the unstable national economies in Eastern Europe and to the small and medium-sized enterprises (SME) there. Their financial status and their employment capacities are very sensitive to the increasing importance of volatile short-term investments. That is why the Eastern European economies could easily become prey to speculative fluctuations of the financial markets.

At the beginning of the transformation the commercialization of Eastern Europe was decisively influenced by the international financial institutions – the IMF and the World Bank. The strategic direction of their activities was focused on monetary stability. This explains both the successes of their efforts and the heavy setbacks when they attempted to revitalize production and trade in Eastern Europe. There is no sustainable development without economic growth. In this sense the stabilization policies of the IMF and the World Bank were correct. But economic stabilization and growth are difficult to achieve under the pressure of volatile cash flows. The crucial reason is the short-sightedness of commercialization. "Get rich fast" is a philosophy which is counterproductive for long-term planning and responsibility. *In a social environment, which is dominated by excessive commercialization and weakened social institutions, sustainable development is always at risk.*

The domestic economic, political and cultural tensions together with the widespread feeling that the Eastern European nations are getting more and more dependent on foreign economic, political and military powers provoke *nationalistic reactions* everywhere in the region. Being chaotic or openly populist as they most often are, the nationalistic movements and parties are already part and parcel of political life in Eastern Europe. They might remain in the political periphery for long, but this is not a matter of necessity. Given the fragility of the economic, political and cultural conditions of sustainable development in Eastern Europe, these movements and organizations might become a serious domestic and international problem. At the level of everyday interaction nationalistic attitudes have destructive effects on the integration of ethnic minorities. The implications might reach international economic cooperation and political relations. Thus, the revival of nationalistic extremes is undoubtedly a challenge to the new democracies in Eastern Europe. However, the deepening political apathy, skepticism and cynicism are no less destructive for democracy and for sustainability in their long-term consequences. The declining civic participation in non-governmental associations, movements and organization is a signal that the political and cultural integration of the reformed Eastern European societies suffers serious flaws. (Chmielewski 2007: 117)

Given the uncertain situation, the question cannot be avoided: What went wrong in the course of the Eastern European market oriented reforms? There are many specific answers concerning particular societies in the region. Some generalized conclusions are also possible.

First, experienced international institutions and inexperienced local politicians overestimated the *creative potential of institutional chaos* at the beginning of the reforms in Eastern Europe. No doubt, chaos might be creative, and often it is. Chaos might be destructive, too. The loudly propagated "big bang" liberalization of the economy was intended to bring about a short-term chaotic situation in order to generate the conditions for a creative and stable transition to market economy. It was assumed that the free market would work creatively and in a stable regime right away. This assumption was wrong. Since legal adjustments for competition, insolvencies, consumer protection and other processes were not yet available, liberalization moved spontaneously and with undesirable consequences that were not foreseen. The simple and obvious conclusion is: Who decides for chaos without legal regulation and control in the social transformation, he decides for unexpected and unwanted economic, political and social consequences. This is what actually happened in Eastern Europe in the wake of the decision to liberalize the economy fast and to postpone the creation of important institutions to the day after.

Second, as seen from another point of view, it can be a dangerous illusion to think that one could organize and control macro-social transformations exactly in the same way like social innovations on plant level. The societal transformation is hardly comparable to the introduction of autonomous working groups in enterprises. The space for change of parameters, which are difficult to control, is by far larger in a society than on the level of enterprises. This is why the management and control mechanisms of the reform processes should be put in the very centre of political attention. In retrospective it is surprising to realize that state institutions for steering and controlling were weakened or abolished before or in the course of the introduction of market mechanisms. In most cases this was done intentionally in order to undermine the economic basis of the inherited state socialist political organization. It was the socialist state to be *expelled* from the economy. But the political decision to largely exclude the state from controlling the transformation means *to consciously provoke and accept irrationality*. This is what exactly happened in most countries of Eastern Europe, although with many nuances of the conditions and effects.

Third, there is no doubt that the transformation of the ownership structures is the most important systemic change. Therefore privatization is the central issue on the transformation agenda. The question is not whether there should be privatization or not, but when and how. Following foreign advice, nearly in all Eastern Europe – apart from Slovenia and Belarus – state property was privatized immediately at the beginning of the transformation. The decision in favor for an overhasty privatization was fundamentally wrong. The market value of the means of production could not be determined by market mechanisms, since those mechanisms did not exist in Eastern Europe yet. There were no institutional structures, which could have supported private economic initiative and introduced economic discipline together with mechanisms of economic responsibility. A private entrepreneurial spirit, just like business knowledge and the capability to administer the privatized economy were missing. Therefore the overhasty privatization was an invitation for robbing state owned and communal property. The alternative was and is clear: The development of a large private sector *together* with a well managed public sector could be the best transitional solution. If the public sector would be forced to operate under market conditions, its actual value can be estimated and privatization can be conducted on a safe legal end economic ground. This strategy is surely difficult to implement. But it may lead to optimal economic outcomes, as they can be observed in Slovenia. In most cases this rational privatization strategy clashed with political strategies, which led to a decline in GDP and other destructive consequences which still threaten the fragile conditions for sustainable development in Eastern Europe.

4.3 Instrumental Activism as Value Orientation and Behavioral Pattern

What is the common ground of interactions in business activities? The answer might seem to be self evident. The "common ground" should be the shared cultural code which makes the mutual understanding in networking possible. If the cultural code of interaction is truly shared among actors, there are good chances for well coordinated and efficiently joined action. Provided the cultural code is only partly shared or not shared at all, tensions and conflicts in networking are probable or just unavoidable.

Given that the cultural code of interaction is so important in motivating and guiding goal-oriented action, how is it to be defined in the activities of multicultural companies in Eastern Europe today? What is its content and way of functioning? What are its real contributions and possible failures?

The questions concern a rather specific historical context. Market dominated organizational patterns have already replaced the organizational patterns of socialist centralized planning all over Eastern Europe. But in terms of cultural change the situation is still marked by various transitional phenomena. Thus, one may generally assume that the shared cultural code of business interactions would be the common orientation of entrepreneurs towards economic success. However, how are the rules of economic success really defined and pursued under the East European circumstances of re-appearance of capitalism?

Max Weber interpreted the emergence of capitalist entrepreneurship by referring to the shared religious and moral rules of ascetic Protestantism. (Weber (1930 [1920]) Eastern Europe has been largely dominated by other religious orientations. Does it make any sense to expect the emergence of a Weberian type of "rational merchant" in a cultural area which has only been partly influenced by the West European Reformation and Enlightenment? The question provokes the need for clarifications. First of all, the cultural conditions of economic action have changed profoundly. Even in the traditional centers of Protestantism greed together with the pursuit of pleasure, leisure and luxury have replaced salvation as major motivating factors of economic activity. Salvation certainly remains a motivational factor but only in exceptional cases. Modern capitalism is moving more and more towards consumerism in the value-normative preferences of its key economic actors. Some analysts go one step further on in their conclusion. They stress the drying out of the cultural sources for entrepreneurial risk-taking and thus for innovations in modern capitalism. (Barber 2007) One may disagree with this radical diagnosis of the cultural contradictions of capitalism. However, even in its milder version (Bell 1976) the diagnosis questions the assumption about the ascetic Protestantism as common cultural code of capitalist economic action today. Max Weber's thesis about the emergence of capitalism in Western Europe is not applicable to the re-emergence of capitalism in Eastern Europe.

It might immediately be taken for granted that another cultural code has no roots in Eastern Europe today as well. The code is focused on the vision of economic activity as unpaid labor in favor of society. This extreme altruistic interpretation of labor was identified by Vladimir Lenin as the major characteristic of economic activity in future communism. (Lenin (1972 [1919]) However, altruism as motivation for economic activity was discredited by the general inefficiency of the economy in state socialism. Nevertheless, it might be surprising to notice the continuing influence of patterns of thinking and behavior which were typical for the socialist organization of labor. The content of the influence is different, however. The readiness for altruistic labor is an extreme rarity today in Eastern Europe. But the readiness to avoid individual initiative and individual responsibility for economic decision and action is abundant. Undoubtedly, the remnants of the cultural code of labor in state socialism are inadequate as a common ground for economic activity in multicultural companies in Eastern Europe today.

There is one more reason why the Weberian interpretation of the emergence and stabilization of the capitalist economic spirit and the capitalist economic organization cannot simply be applied to the present-day East European transitional situation. This reason is of deeper historical and theoretical nature. Weber assumed the crucial historical relevance of decisions and actions *of individuals* who decide to act as emerging capitalist entrepreneurs in order to follow the principles of Calvinist ethics. It might have been a realistic assumption in the situation of only slightly regulated markets in the late medieval ages. (Kalberg 2009: 117) But it is an entirely unrealistic assumption today even with regard to the most liberal markets. The opposite *collectivist* assumption in Lenin's understanding of communist work is also inadequate in the present day situation. On the one hand, it is dominated by extreme individualistic turbo-capitalism. On the other hand, it is now obvious that the extremes of neo-liberal individualistic capitalism should be tamed by the intervention of national and supranational institutions. They incorporate the collective (common) good since the catastrophic consequences of liberal individualism became obvious in the worldwide economic crisis.

Then, what might be the common cultural code of economic activity under the transitional conditions in the East European region? The answer seems to be obvious. No ultimate values of salvation or of collective good do really guide economic action in general or the interaction in multicultural companies in particular. The shared cultural code of interaction is the plain orientation towards profit making. More precisely, the common cultural ground of business activities today is the *well institutionalized seeking for profit*. It is the *value-normative* core of the global trend of the *spread of instrumental activism*. As a value-normative orientation and action pattern instrumental activism motivates and dominates all activities in the modern monetized world. In it all ultimate ends of human activity are defined and pursued in the setting of the all-pervading profit seeking.

This is a value-normative paradox since profit (money) is actually means and not end to normal life. Nevertheless, profit seeking fully dominates business activities and penetrates all other activities in present day global civilization. East Europeans are getting more and more accustomed to this paradoxical situation. However, for millions of the population in the region this is not a trivial situation. They have been socialized in a value-normative system according to which economy had just to serve the needs of people and society. Thus, the cultural clash with the value-normative orientations of individuals who had been fully socialized under the conditions of dominant instrumental activism is unavoidable. The typical effect is the accumulation of stress in interactions, the search for scapegoats and the spread of mutual accusations between representatives of various cultures in multicultural companies. This exactly is the typical setting in which the judgments of western managers that are active in Poland come about. The judgments are not particularly flattering for their Polish partners (Flader and Comati 2008: 62):

- "Polish people do not follow the established rules".
- "One cannot reach agreement on long-term goals with Polish partners".
- "Polish people have difficulties in taking personal responsibility".
- "Teamwork is a problem for Polish people".
- "Polish managers behave in a rather authoritarian way".
- "Polish employees do not have a sense of loyalty to the company they are working for".

The complaints and accusations of western managers concerning the work ethics, the mindset and behavior of Bulgarian, Romanian and Ukrainian managers and workers in multicultural companies are strikingly similar. (Flader and Comati 2008: 123f.; Mölering and Stache 2007) Obviously, there are fundamental issues of cultural incompatibility which bring about intensive disappointments, accusations and consequently low efficiency in the communication and practical cooperation between managers and workers from the western and the eastern parts of the European continent currently interacting in Eastern Europe.

The issue is quite relevant since many West European companies expanded their activities to Eastern Europe after 1989. The reasons were obvious – low paid but well qualified labor force in the Eastern European societies, abundant raw materials on the spot, easy transportation to Western Europe, etc. After having tried to use these advantages efficiently, quite a few of those Western companies reduced or stopped their activities in Eastern Europe because of cultural incompatibilities with the local administration, managers and workers. Another telling argument about the relevance of cultural factors is the striking difference of foreign direct investments in Eastern European national economies if taken in proportion to the population size of the respective country (EBRD Statistics 2009a: A.2.8):

Table 4.4 Foreign direct investments in selected East European countries in 2008 (Net inflows recorded in the balance of payments)

Country	Population ml	FDIs in ml USD
Bulgaria	7.2	8,011
Hungary	9.9	2,200
Poland	38.5	13,700
Russian Federation	140.7	5,000
Ukraine	45.9	9,500

The differences in FDI per country depend on the absorption capacities of the national economy, on the favorable or unfavorable legislation, on the well developed or underdeveloped infrastructure and on many other general and specific "hard" factors of economic decision making. However, there are also very substantial "soft" cultural factors which co-determine decisions to invest in a national economy or not, to continue investing or to stop it. In many specific cases the experience of cultural compatibility or incompatibility has played the decisive role in the decisions.

There are two all-embracing and rather simplified explanations of the above indicated cultural incompatibility between West and East European managers and workers. The first explanation is focused on the differences in the organizational culture in general and in the legal culture of Western and Eastern Europeans in particular. Basically, this explanatory strategy is correct, although one may come across astonishing exaggerations in both directions. One may be only very skeptical when reading that for Western Europeans rules and laws were sacred and for Eastern Europeans were meaningless.[4] The implication is that western Europeans generally rely on the rules

---

4   The following text is typical for this style of over-generalizing argumentation: "In vielen westlichen Kulturen sind Gesetze, Verordnungen, Vorschriften sakrosankt in dem

and laws and they are therefore trustworthy. And vice versa, the opposite implication reads that Eastern Europeans do not rely on rules and laws and they are therefore not trustworthy. One may immediately react that there are certainly millions of individuals in Western Europe who do not regard rules and laws as sacrosanct and cannot be regarded as particularly trustworthy. The share of the "shadow economy" in national GDPs in Western Europe is between 10 and 15%. This is a very clear indicator for the real situation. Vice versa, there are millions of East Europeans who have lived their lives so far according to local laws and continue to think and act in full accordance with sound moral principles and with valid laws.

One may go even deeper in this issue by focusing on the comparison of "trustworthiness", whatever the ways may be, in which people in Western and Eastern Europe understand and evaluate it. The data of the US American Pew Research Centre are quite telling and sobering in this respect. On average, in 2007 there were more substantial differences in the perception and evaluation of "trustworthiness" between societies in Western Europe itself, than between the data on France, Spain and Italy and the data on East European societies (Wilke 2008):

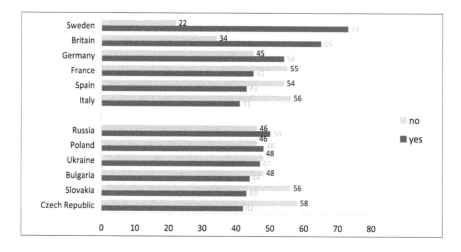

Figure 4.1 Are most people in society trustworthy?

Another widely used generalized explanation of the cultural differences between West and East Europeans persistently refers to the history before 1989 and even long before that turning point. There is no doubt that the historical trajectories of countries and nations in both parts of the continent were rather different. East Europeans used to be subjects of foreign rulers for a longer time. Consequently, their identification with

Sinne, dass sie unantastbar sind." (Flader and Comati 2008: 64). Sobering information on the issue might be obtained from numerous studies on crime and corruption in Western Europe.

the state and the law of foreign rulers was lower than the identification with the state and the law in sovereign nation-states in Western Europe. No doubt, the alienation from the socialist administration of economy and politics contributed to the alienation of Eastern Europeans from the socialist state and its institutions indeed. However, this type of argumentation (Flader and Comati 2008: 138f) usually overlooks the fact that the years after 1989 have brought about profound changes of the attitudes in East European societies. The changes are not necessarily positive, as the Pew Research Centre documented it by means of representative surveys (Wilke 2008):

Table 4.5 Social trust up in Western Europe, down in Eastern Europe

Country	1991	2007	Change
Britain	55	65	+10
Italy	33	41	+8
Germany	55	56	+1
Spain	45	43	−2
Bulgaria	58	44	−14
Russia	63	50	−13
Ukraine	60	47	−13
Poland	52	48	−4

The above outlined differences question the relevance of over-generalized statements concerning trustworthiness and history. More detailed interpretations are needed concerning the differences of thinking and behavior of managers and employees in multicultural companies active in Eastern Europe. The only point, which might be generally taken for granted, concerns the existence of these differences. They have their implications in misunderstandings, tensions and conflicts in the multicultural organizational settings. Tentatively following the content and sequence of the above cited typical accusations of West European managers concerning the mindset and behaviors of the East European managers and employees, the following discussion will be structured around several oppositions, which are well known in the theory of organization and in the organizational practice:

> Formality – Informality
> Planning – Spontaneity
> Initiative – Passivity
> Teamwork – Individualism
> Human relations – Administration
> Corporative loyalty – Corporative disloyalty

4.4 Convergence and Divergence in Implementing Instrumental Activism

By focusing on the German-Ukrainian business relationships Guido Möllering and Florian Stache are explicit in their key research question: Why are German and Ukrainian managers rarely able to develop cooperation based on mutual trust? (Mölering and Stache 2007: 6) The hypothetical answer is also clearly formulated: Probably, because managers of both origins do not know the habits, skills and styles of the "other"? (Mölering and Stache 2007: 7) This is exactly the issue of the unclear or missing "common ground" since profit-seeking is not enough as a common motivation in order to secure smooth business cooperation. Many other issues matter as intervening variables – such as the specific understanding of honesty, fairness, reliability, etc. All of them have local interpretations and imply local repertoires for developing, showing and proving trust in the specific national institutional contexts.

The question guiding the analysis by Möllering and Stache reads roughly as follows: Why did so few German firms develop successful business relations with Ukrainian firms, despite the great market potential of the country and its territorial proximity to Germany and to other EU member states? The simplified answer reads that the institutional environment in the Ukraine is not conducive to efficient business cooperation. Ukraine is notoriously known for its political instability, arbitrary red tape and obscure corruption networks. These local conditions undermine trust understood as "process of building on reason, routine and reflexivity, suspending irreducible social vulnerability and uncertainty as if they were favourably resolved and maintaining thereby a state of favourable expectations towards the actions and intentions of more or less specific others". (Mölering 2006: 11) What is to be done if the formal institutional conditions are unfavorable for developing and maintaining the so defined trust in business relations? One rational answer seems to be: Just give up and disappear from the institutional and cultural area marked by instability and notorious difficulties in developing and maintaining trust in business relations. This is an easy solution but it might oversee promising business opportunities. What is to be done in order to grasp the opportunity and to make profit?

Bridging Formality and Informality

The first answer to the question raised should be focused on different understandings of formalized and non-formalized business relationships. No doubt, the contractual culture of formalized business relationships is much better developed and more respected in the western than in the eastern part of the European continent. The reasons are twofold. *First*, the positions in the division of labor and the specific rights and obligations related to these positions are traditionally better defined and stricter understood in Western Europe than in large segments of the East European population. *Second*, the legal arbitration on these crucial issues in business activities is much more sophisticated, better institutionalized and more respected in Western than in Eastern Europe. Thus, there are understandable reasons for moral indignation if managers of West European origin notice that East European managers or employees disregard formalized (written, signed) instructions or contracts. The phenomenon has many manifestations. Instead of trying to reach agreement on the basis of documents, East European business people, managers and employees often rely on oral agreements alone.

Still another reason for astonishment and possibly indignation on the part of western managers is the unclear distinction between formal and informal relations or agreements on the part of East European managers end employees. Arrangements are often made in Eastern Europe on the basis of interpersonal trust or on promises for preferential treatments in future occasions. Moreover, the arrangements might include agreements on mutually beneficial avoidance of normative regulations. Closely connected with this type of informality is the inclination of East European state administrators, business people, managers and employees to mix their roles in working life with their roles in private life. The forms of this role mixing are most diverse. The West European manager might become furious noticing that the East European secretary has a long private talk on the phone, thus closing the line for potential calls of business partners. The western manager might be also surprised receiving an invitation for a weekend party with the families.

Not any of these East European "peculiarities" should be so surprising or confusing for managers having West European business socialization and activity in Eastern Europe. Oral agreements about special mutual treatments or about avoiding some legal regulations are not unknown in Western Europe or in the business world indeed. The abuse of phone lines or other equipment in business offices for private purposes is widely known and usually overlooked by clever managers everywhere. Informal networking is part and parcel of political and business life all over the world. The involvement of families in leisure time of companies' employees is normality under other circumstances too, for instance in US American companies. Western European managers are well aware of this American habit.

Thus, what might be the real reason for suspicion and reservation is only connected with the assumption that East European informality always or most often implies clientelism or directly mafiotic arrangements. This might be the case, but not by necessity. It is much more realistic to consider the fact that formal institutions of market economy, state administration and the legal system are not fully developed in Eastern Europe according to the best international standards. Thus, it is a normal compensational strategy in Eastern Europe to fill the gap between these high standards and the local realities by relying on some pre-modern informal mechanisms of problem resolution. They might be called pre-modern and despised as such. But what is preferable: To rely on underdeveloped, slow, generally inefficient or corrupt formal institutions and to fail in getting things done, or to switch to some extent to pre-modern informal approaches in order to get things done? The answer is self-evident.

The problem has still another important practical dimension. Provided the red tape and corruption in formalized East European institutions should be avoided by opting for informal approaches in order to resolve problems, this should not imply the predominance of informality within a multicultural company itself. To the contrary, pragmatic formalization of obligations should permanently be first-rate internal task of companies. The recognized efficiency of the rationalized formal organizations is the best argument in favor of the development and respect to the formalized institutional settings in East European societies. They are moving in this direction. One should be aware of the fact that the rationalization of institutions is a never ending process as the experience in Italy clearly shows. (Putnam 1993) This is a quite topical issue in Western Europe and North America, as the efforts to manage the recent financial crisis there have clearly shown.

Thus, the only constructive option is to develop mutual trust to local managers and employees if the local cultural setting promises mutual understanding and mutual advantages in this way. However, the crucial question is different: Informal relations with whom? Some business people in the Ukraine are very well described as resembling the Soviet general directors. They are only able to implement orders but they are totally unwilling and unable to calculate business opportunities and constraints rationally and to take reasonable risk. Other business people in the Ukraine resemble cowboys who are ready to take enormous risks by forgetting to rationally calculate their own strengths and weaknesses. The last and most reliable type of business people in the Ukraine might be tentatively identified with the Weberian description of the rational merchant. This is the most promising partner for Western business people. But these potentially best partners often lack proper education, information and business skills. In addition, there might be mutual disappointments between Western and Ukrainian business partners concerning the meaning of "informality". Under local conditions of institutional instability, informality usually means a contractual culture which does not rely too much on courts. For business people socialized in the spirit and practices of the Roman-German contractual formality this might seem fully unacceptable. However, what is to be done if there is no real alternative? Only one conclusion makes sense: A policy of active informal "trust building" is needed. The challenge is tremendous since only active and motivated persons can accomplish this. One has to be open, flexible, adaptable, employable what many Ukrainian business people really are. But the warning immediately appears: Informality might imply habitualization of bribery and other illegal approaches as well. The consolation reads that the predomination of informality in a situation of Hobbesian war of everybody against everybody strengthens *the need* to rely on law, on stable institutions and on rational merchants as partners. (Möllering and Stache 2007: 19f.)

This is the promising future legal and moral rationalization of business partnerships in Eastern Europe. So far, the predominant informality requires mutual understanding and respect, mutual treatment of partners as equal, stress on common interests, not on cultural differences, and persistence in keeping informal contacts in good order. This might often imply mixing business and private life, what West European business people are not accustomed to. The openness implies sincere efforts to learn from each other and readiness to be flexible by "doing things in a different way". If this readiness is not strong enough or only superficially available, then one might expect hypocrisy and cheating in all directions. Who might be really interested in business relations like that?

Spontaneity vs. Planning

West European managers use to complain massively about the incapacity of East European managers and employees to develop long-term planning of business activity. In addition, the complaints concerning deviations from the requirements of long-term planning make up a particularly important common place in the reflections on the business experience in Eastern Europe. The local partners are typically presented as unorganized, unpredictable, lost in details by forgetting strategic goals, used to permanent delays and to last-minute feverish activities in order to meet approaching deadlines whatever the quality of the results might be. In a general formulation, the judgment of the Western manager reads in a categorical way: "People do not really intend to plan here". In the statement of the locals the situation is presented somewhat differently: "Well, we will see tomorrow what is going to happen". (Flader and Comati 2008: 49) Both statements refer to the situation in Poland but they basically apply to a large plethora of managerial problems all over the world. Nevertheless, there are some specifics of the dilemma "spontaneity vs. planning" in the current East European context.

One should lack any understanding of historical contexts, provided he or she would expect special interest in long-term planning or successful performance of long-term planning in Eastern Europe after 1989. The major reason for this situation is of a structural nature. East European societies are still going through profound transformations of all their economic, political and cultural structures. The legal and institutional framework of business activities has changed quickly and fundamentally in the course of the last two decades and is still changing somewhat slower at present. Long-term planning has been practically "mission impossible" in this institutional environment of "moving sands". Both East Europeans and their West European business partners had to adapt to this dynamic environment, which could only make short-term or at most medium-term planning realistic and meaningful.

As seen from another angle, the very idea of long-term planning was made unattractive or directly a "bad idea" due to the experience of the inefficient over-centralized state planning in socialist times. Under a centrally planned economy it was not consumers' needs which dominated the supply. The limited supply determined what consumer could demand. The socialization in this cultural pattern of external dominance of choices (dominance of limited supply) has long lasting consequences. Balancing demand and supply under the dynamic conditions of competition is the background of a different socialization and cultural orientation. Some steps in introducing this organization of the economy by strengthening its demand side were made in Eastern Europe by better central planning[5] or by step-by-step market-oriented reforms at most. If consequently implemented, the reforms would have had introduced a profit driven market economy. However, this was not possible without changing the political organization of the Eastern European societies. Thus, the introduction of new cultural orientations came about in the course of their full-scale transformations.

It was the sharp contrast between active propaganda in favor of state planning and the unsatisfactory results achieved by this organizational basis, which brought about the explosion of spontaneity in Eastern Europe after 1989. Unlike the processes in China or in Vietnam, the great transformation of economic and political organization within Eastern European societies was only exceptionally and partly guided by well conceived and implemented planning. The famous "plan Balcerowicz" for privatization in Poland was abandoned soon, the transition strategy elaborated by the Romanian Academy of Sciences was only taken into account, the program of President Yeltsin for privatization in Russia was not even considered since privatization there only followed its own criminal logic. Thus, exactly in the times of the great transformation, which inherently needs rational planning and responsible guidance, the processes in Eastern Europe moved quickly in the direction of liberalization without boundaries. East European managers readily embraced the neo-liberal ideas of non-regulated "free" market only guided by the spontaneous balancing of demand and supply.

The change in attitudes towards planning came about slowly when economic and political institutions were leveled off in Eastern Europe. This particularly applies to the countries which became members of the enlarged European Union. The implication is the possibility to rely on a relatively stable institutional frameworks allowing medium-term and even long-term indicative planning for states and internal planning for companies. Thus, there is less space for misunderstandings between East and West European business partners in the European Union on the burning issue of planning. The institutional and cultural environment is already favorable for the common code of respect to planning, long-term planning included.

The global crisis brought about a radical reconsideration of the issues concerning spontaneity, planning and state interventionism into economy. Together with the whole global community East Europeans learned that a deregulated market is a mixed blessing. It might bring about disasters for economy and society. Thus, the global development revitalized the idea of relying on political regulation of economy worldwide. The ideological revival of the reliance on efficient macro-social planning comes about hand in hand with

---

5 Even in Yugoslavia which was the least affected by the rigidity of socialist planning Zdravko Mlinar saw the recipe against the looming crisis of state socialism in the improvement of state planning: "The great aspirations towards a planned and radical social transformation, require far more accurate knowledge of the laws and frequency rate of developmental change, in their global framework, as well as on a local and regional level in order to reduce "nominal" and to foster "actual" planning". (Mlinar 1980: 218, 221)

reconsidering the role of the state. It is not the deregulated market, but the states and supranational political institutions which are expected to resolve the burning economic issues. This turn has already had and will have consequences for the planning policies of companies. Following this common trend, the substantial cultural differences of West and East Europeans concerning long-term planning is disappearing.

The issues concerning spontaneity and planning have yet another dimension. In most cases spontaneity is counter-productive in the modern world which relies on the predictability and efficiency of coordinated action in organizations very much. However, spontaneity is not necessarily confusing and destructive alone. It might be constructive as well. There is no innovation which could emerge and be implemented without creative elements of spontaneity. Thus, well cultivated and guided East European spontaneity might turn out to be an asset in the present-day conditions, permanently requiring technological, organizational and cultural innovations. The real task is not to eliminate spontaneity but to adapt business organizations and their management consciously to the needs of flexibility in the sense to opt for "guided spontaneity". Some elements of the East European culture might be very much helpful in the efforts to achieve this end.

Passivity vs. Initiative

West European managers usually get embarrassed by noticing that East European managers and employees tend to avoid critical remarks and suggestions aiming at improvement of the joint work. They might even not report about problems and failures. (Flader and Comati 2008: 52, 72, 77, 140 etc.) Thus they demonstrate a culture and behavioral pattern of passivity which is counter-productive to the dynamics of modern business cooperation. Similar complaints are often heard about passive employees and business partners in other parts of the world. But the explanations of local reasons vary very much.

The major reason for the passivity of East European employees is the path dependency from the rigid administrative organization of economic life during state socialism. It appeared on the historical scene with the strong claim to mobilize the activity and responsibility of people. This was conceived to be the major historical mission of the socialist revolution. The historical development moved in a different direction. The initiative of workers in Eastern Europe was suppressed by the ruling authoritarian regimes. They dominated the socialization of two generations in Central and South Eastern Europe and even longer in the former Soviet Union. Under these organizational conditions there was a tiny strata of state and party functionaries who had the right and the duty to identify economic, political and social problems, to develop initiatives for resolving the problems and to take the responsibility for the consequences of initiatives, decisions and actions. What remained for the rest of society was the adaptation to this administrative framework. Given its constraints, it was only rational for millions to abstain from any initiative for problem resolution. Voluntary risk taking in economy and politics was generally punished. Thus, the system fostered the culture of conformism and passivity. This type of culture is still influential in Eastern Europe.

One should take the more recent East European experience into account, too. The changes after 1989 came about with the great promise for fostering initiative, activity and creativity of everybody in all action spheres. Millions of East Europeans took the promise seriously. They enthusiastically participated in political rallies and in the formation of new political parties, in the establishment of cultural associations and registered millions of private firms. The disappointments came soon and were bitter. The selection came about under institutionally unstable conditions and often without conformity with basic rules of moral and law. Only few political parties and cultural associations remained really active, millions of small and bigger firms went bankrupt. This sobering experience strengthened the attitudes of "wait and see" since few could really managed the new options and became the winners in the fierce competition marked by normlessness.

Still another important reason for the striking absence of initiative of East Europeans is the experience in the joint ventures with West Europeans. The usual style of thinking and behavior of the Western managers is often striking. Some of them sincerely believe that they know the local conditions well enough to be able to design and initiate the best solutions for all technological and organizational problems. In some cases this belief might correspond to reality but in many others does not. The excessively self-confident thinking and behavior alienates the local partners everywhere in the world. This holds true in Eastern Europe, where people are convinced that they are treated as second rate managers or employees by experts or managers of West European origin. The alienating effect of this asymmetrical relationship takes various forms, the wish to "see him/her fail" including.

The institutional and cultural situation gradually changes. The conditions are getting more and more favorable for taking the initiative and responsibility rationally in Eastern Europe, particularly in the new member states of the European Union. However, critical times foster the search for scapegoats and multicultural settings are particularly prone to identifying and punishing scapegoats.

Individualism vs. Teamwork

It might be striking to learn that western managers typically complain about the lack of team spirit and readiness for team work among the East European managers and employees. The issue is universal and might be raised and discussed under rather different local conditions in all parts of the world. Germans are often told to lack proper attitudes and behavior facilitating team work. (Flader and Comati 2008: 31) But the claim concerning East Europeans is particularly striking because of two regional reasons. *First*, people in East European societies had been indoctrinated in the spirit of collectivism for decades. Did this indoctrination totally fail in shaping positive attitudes and skills for team work? *Second*, it is often said that East European societies were still influenced by rural patterns of thinking and behavior. If this should be the case, is the rural community spirit not influential in shaping positive attitudes towards team work?

Both questions touch upon complex issues with many specifics which diverge from country to country in Eastern Europe. Discussing the issue at the level of regional generalizations, one has to analyze the controversial causes and effects of state socialism. It was intended to counteract extremes of destructive individualism which were assumed to be typical for capitalist society. The socialization of the property on the means of production was the major structural remedy against capitalist individualism. A radically new historical type of communities was expected to appear on the structural basis of the socialized productive assets. However, the real effects of the radical socialization of productive assets diverged substantially from these expectations. No inherent communal solidarity could develop on the structural basis of the state property because of the bureaucratic administration of all activities in socialist society. To the contrary, bureaucratic planning and management brought about far reaching alienation since nobody could exactly define and effectively represent his or her specific interests. No genuine team spirit and team work could develop on this organizational and cultural basis. Step by step alienated individualism took the lead in state socialist East European societies in spite of the collectivist slogans of the official ideology. The discrepancy between the everyday individualistic culture and the official ideological collectivism became blatant. The major uniting slogan of the mass protest movement in Poland became the slogan for *real solidarity* in enterprises and in the settlements.

The desire for solidarity remained wishful thinking in Eastern Europe before 1989. It seemed to be possible to introduce a modern communal solidarity swift and smoothly thereafter. This was one of the guiding ideas of reform oriented intellectuals at the beginning of the changes. The first reforms brought about sobering results. Millions immediately understood that the changes were bringing about the worldwide triumph of liberal individualism. In Eastern Europe it provoked the rise of crime which made individualism socially and morally repellent. The modern community life had to wait for the stabilization of the new economic and political order based on a deep social differentiation. But what was and still is at stake is not the revival of the communal spirit of Eastern European rural communities. This spirit was totally lost in the course of the industrialization and urbanization under state socialism.

Given this experience massively undermining ideas and practices of collective identities and collective action, it would be naïve to expect a strong spirit of team work and well developed skills for team work in East European societies. The Swedish autonomous working groups, the Japanese quality circles or similar patterns of team work will be certainly tested and possibly accepted by the young generations which might be less reserved towards collective organizational arrangements. The pressure to participate in team work will get stronger because of the growing complexity of tasks to be resolved in research, development, technological and organizational innovations as well as in all economic, political and cultural activities.

Administration vs. Human Relations Approach in Management

The surprise of western managers by the inclination of their East European colleagues to rely on administrative management is fully understandable. Western managers are also surprised to notice that the East European employees expect clear hierarchical relations and strong administrative management. (Flader and Comati 2008: 62, 68, 73, 77, etc.) The surprise comes on the background of the widespread managerial knowledge that the Fordist and Taylorist patterns of administrative economic management have been questioned in Western Europe and North America long ago. This should not be understood in the sense that there are no cases of most rigid hierarchical administration in Western European and North American companies. However, most of them have opted for an inclusion of cultural and organizational patterns of the human relations approach in handling organizational issues.

There were experiments of introducing patterns of industrial democracy in state socialist management in Hungary, Poland and Bulgaria. The relevance of these efforts notwithstanding, in the vast majority of cases rigid administrative management remained predominant in Eastern Europe till the collapse of state socialism. Thus, it should not be surprising at all that most East European managers keep to the spirit and practices of administrative management. This is what they know and what they can do best. This is what most East European employees know and can understand and follow best. On their part, West European experts have to learn and understand properly that East European societies did not have any or just rather limited democratic political traditions developed before 1989 and even before the Second World War. It would be too much to expect that a society without democratic traditions would possess a functioning system of industrial democracy (human relations organization of work). Expectations of this kind could only bring about disappointments. The learning of human relations principles and managerial skills is needed but will take time in Eastern Europe. The western managers would be best advised not to be focused on their surprise of lacking human relations approach but on the need to facilitate the learning process.

Corporate Disloyalty vs. Corporate Loyalty

One may wonder why the readiness of Eastern Europeans to change employers should surprise the western managers working in multicultural companies. (Flader and Comati 2008: 46, 83 etc.) The regular change of employers or places of residence belongs to normality in US American working life. One may interpret this behavior as disloyalty to companies. More relevant are dynamics and mobility. They matter more in the United States than the loyalty to companies. American managers are accustomed to the fluctuating labor force. Only Japanese or South

Korean companies still keep to the Confucian mutual loyalty of companies and their employees. But the trend towards a more liberal attitude towards work mobility and towards corporate loyalty is getting stronger even in societies influenced by the Confucian cultural tradition.

Under the Eastern European conditions the trend towards mobility was very much fostered by the economic transformation during the nineties. Huge socialist companies, which enjoyed the loyalty of generations of managers and workers in small and medium-sized settlements, just collapsed and disappeared as employers over night. Having witnessed the large scale collapse of such companies, the Eastern Europeans learned that stability of organizational structures is not given once and for all. To the contrary, organizations might perform badly and go bankrupt or just become easy prey for speculators who do not care about the employees. The only rational strategy under such conditions is to be ready to accept the change and to adapt to it by getting more flexible concerning labor fluctuations.

Thus, there might be a misunderstanding in the complaints of western managers who immediately interpret the normal labor fluctuation as a disloyalty of East European employees. Under the conditions of a competitive labor market it is normal for employees and managers to change their work places if there is a better chance. Nevertheless, one may understand some reasons for complaints. The reasons mostly concern the qualification of the East European managers and workers. Before the changes took place Eastern Europeans used to be described as well educated and having a relatively good level of vocational training. This description corresponded to the conditions of their work at that time. The technological equipment and the patterns of work organization corresponded to the requirements of the second or maximally the third industrial revolution. Eastern Europeans were well educated and trained to work under these circumstances.

The western investors usually modernized both the equipment and the work organization. East European managers and employees had to be re-trained. In some cases the new training took time and was costly. Given these investments, the emotional reaction of western managers, who see the newly trained East European employees leave the company, is understandable. Even the intensity of complaints is understandable since some newly trained employees go to the direct competitors. This is a transitional phenomenon, however. The requirements to the labor force and its employability will soon reach the situation of matching in Eastern Europe as it has been the case in Western Europe for decades. The emotions concerning corporate loyalty or disloyalty will disappear or will become much less relevant.

Another reason for this optimistic vision is the generational change in the East European labor force. The generations for which corporate loyalty was not a real issue due to the universality of the state property are going to step down gradually from the labor market. The new Eastern European generations of managers and workers have practically the same attitudes to companies and corporate loyalty like their colleagues in Western Europe. However, the competition between companies for attracting the best and brightest will continue. So, there will be enough reasons for complaining about mobility of personnel. Complaints do not resolve the issue. Pro-active policies of companies might do.

* * *

The above analysis is guided by the expectation that the intensity of complaints about cultural incompatibilities between managers and workers of western and eastern European origin will diminish in the near future. The assumption relies on observations about the globalization of the conditions of work and labor organization. This should not mean that the differences between specific work places in various branches and in different cultural settings will disappear. No, they will remain. However, globalization facilitates the spread of knowledge about trends of homogenization and about local specifics. They will cause less and less emotional surprise but will foster the rational analysis. It is needed to understand and manage the local manifestations of the global organizational patterns. This could only be possible on the basis of intercultural competences which are getting more and more important for the management worldwide. The development of these competences includes fostering abilities to reach synergetic convergence of cultural specifics when making business on the spot. The abilities are needed for avoiding or resolving cultural confusions, misunderstandings, tensions and conflicts.

This desirable development could not come about if some business partners truly believe that there is only one best way of approaching and resolving organizational issues. Even worse, intercultural tensions and conflicts are easily predictable if these partners truly believe that the best way of handling problems is only the one to which they are accustomed to. Each organizational problem might be approached differently and the successful management of the problem is not necessarily the result of following one recipe alone. Thus, the most productive approach to business cooperation in multicultural settings is the recognition that all diverse partners, East Europeans including, have their cultural identity, integrity and legends supporting them. The rational recognition of the cultural differences has implications. One has to recognize that this "soft" element in companies' structure and functioning really matters. If so, one has to develop skills to deal with cultural specifics in the same way like the development of skills for dealing with technological or financial bottle-necks. Even more, one has to develop the understanding that the management of intercultural issues might turn out to be more complex, complicated and demanding than dealing with technological and financial bottle-necks. (Konečná 2006)

What is mostly needed for managing shortages in multicultural business relationships is the clear normative regulation. There is no rational (in the sense of efficient) action *without normative regulation.* In the case under scrutiny the regulation might require a general *Code of Conduct in Multicultural Environments.* This is more or less taken for granted in well established institutional regulations which guide multicultural interaction. What about the cases in which there is a rather weak external (macro-social) normative framework? In such cases there should be a well rationalized internal normative framework adapted to the external contingencies. Is the internal rational regulation of interactions sufficient? The answer should be negative. But the internal regulation should be developed and maintained as the "second best" solution. The effort to establish and improve rationalized institutional frameworks should be a permanent task. This is the general conclusion from the analysis of various economic and social developments, the worldwide financial crisis including.

One should not cherish any illusions, though. Camouflaging together with camouflaging of camouflaging is intrinsic to business life. *This is the intrinsic logic of business and of the spread of instrumental activism* in more general terms. This means that even if well regulated, the interactions in multicultural settings might be used and abused further on in business camouflaging. There are no general remedies for this type of policies. Only the specific analysis of particular conditions, intentions, actions and effects might be useful.

Chapter 5
Universalization *and* Particularisms in the Value-normative Systems

The evolutionary transition from a materialist to a post-materialist value-normative system is widely discussed among social scientists. The historical context for this transition is considered to be the move from the value-normative preoccupation with achievement, well-being and security in industrial society towards the preoccupation with consumption, leisure and self-realization in post-modern societies. The core of this idea seems to be supported by data despite serious problems connected with value-normative fluctuations caused by trends in GDP growth and redistribution policies. (Inglehart and Welzel 2005) The dramatic re-orientation of mass culture in Eastern European societies after 1989 towards culture of survival is a telling case concerning these fluctuations. The drop in living standards, quality of life and aspirations in the region has called the idea of the transition from materialist to post-materialist value-normative orientations into question.

In this critical context another broader, deeper and by far more relevant value-normative change has taken place in Eastern Europe. This is the step-by-step introduction and stabilization of values and norms from the emerging global value-normative system into the Eastern European national cultures. At the core of this global value-normative system is the concept of universal human rights. The spread of the principles and practices of meritocracy[1] is closely connected with the cultural and institutional universalization of the idea and practices of respect for human rights. In its ideal form, the institutionalized respect for human rights and for the principles of meritocracy is expected to prevent all kinds of social privileges and disadvantages. Value-normative and institutional realities are different, however.

5.1 The Eastern European Value-normative Puzzle

The turn towards universal human rights and meritocracy in Eastern Europe after 1989 was a continuation of patterns which were basically known in the region. Elements of value-normative universalization and meritocracy in the

---

1   It is taken for granted here that principles and practices of meritocracy have been consequently implemented in no society so far and most probably could not be fully implemented at all. (Goldthorp 2003)

ideology and political practices existed in Eastern European societies after the Second World War. The ideal of a homogenized socialist and later classless communist society functioning on the basis of universalistic egalitarian principles was closely connected with the ideal of overcoming all ascriptive privileges. The major mechanism applied for achieving this end was the overcoming of economic cleavages combined with the effort to reduce political inequalities and cultural disparities.

These ideals were not a product of Eastern European cultural development. They emerged in Western Europe and irradiated worldwide from there. In the long run, they influenced the debates on human rights and meritocracy and thus became part of global culture. Due to historical circumstances, Soviet Russia after 1917 and a number of Eastern European societies after the Second World War became the major laboratory for the practical application and testing of the ideals of social justice based on egalitarianism.

Nowadays it is taken for granted that state socialist eastern European societies failed in their efforts to develop institutions which incorporated egalitarianism and social justice. In the course of their development, new patterns of politically based inequality replaced patterns of inequality based on the ownership of productive assets. The political inequalities later mutated in the direction of economic and cultural inequalities. Decades before the changes the eastern European societies were already well stratified in economic, political and cultural terms. (Andorka and Kolosi 1984) Although the ideals of universal human rights were incorporated in their constitutions passed in the 1970s, these ideals could not flourish under the conditions of authoritarianism. Nor was meritocracy a realistic option for the everyday orientation, decision and action of individuals under the administrative conditions in economy, politics and culture. It was the over-centralized administration of activities which undermined solidarity at all structural levels and in all walks of social life.

Due to these controversial developments Eastern European societies did not manage to adapt to the ongoing worldwide process of value-normative universalization with focus on the ideas and practices of universal human rights in a timely and effective manner. Aside from the numerous internal reasons for this delay, some international reasons were connected with the position of Eastern Europe in the world. It was divided into two spheres of political and ideological dominance. In this division Eastern Europe was largely isolated from crucial innovations in global culture. The isolation contributed to the stagnation of the capacity to bring about cultural innovations or to be open to innovations originating in other places of the world. The polar division of the world impacted on Western Europe and North America as well. Nowhere in the world was the culture of the polar division and political confrontation universalistic. It was a particularistic culture of divisions, hostilities, confrontations and conflicts.

The dissolution of the polar political and military confrontation speeded up the development of value-normative universalism worldwide. The rights of the human individual constitute the core of cultural innovations which were incorporated into the new constitutional arrangements in the region. The innovation made legally manifest the shift from the state-dominated common good towards the legal predomination of individual rights, initiative and responsibility. The vision and the institutional framework of the progressing universalization of values and norms of the emerging world society took shape in Eastern Europe. The rights concerning economic initiative and property are already well institutionalized. Some deviations notwithstanding, active and passive rights to participate in democratic political processes are now generally respected in the region. The right to travel is basically guaranteed. Discussions about the independence of mass media will certainly continue like in all democratic societies. Thus, one may draw the conclusion that the value-normative universalization is well advanced in Eastern Europe on the basis of the ideas and practices of universal human rights and the related principles of meritocracy.

The conclusion might be premature and misleading. At the beginning of the nineties one could expect to see the process evolving in a fast and efficient manner over the region. Some eastern European societies received a powerful push in this direction due to the requirement to adapt their legal and institutional systems to the conditions of *acquis communautaire* in preparation for EU membership. The effects are easy to identify in this part of the region. At least the legal regulations there correspond to the universal ideas of human rights and meritocracy. In practice, as it is everywhere in the world, institutional and everyday practices deviate from the legal regulations. The deviations are still substantial in the Eastern European societies.

The major reason for deviations is due to economic hardships which accompany the transformations in the region. The optimistic expectations about J-curves of economic development marked by short-term modest economic decline turned out to be unrealistic. Most Eastern European societies experienced U-curves in their GDP growth. It is sobering to see that Ukraine, Georgia and Moldova are still far from their GDP level of 1989 after 20 years of reforms. Human rights cannot be respected and efficiently protected under conditions of mass unemployment and impoverishment. The deep and protracted economic recession radically limited the capacities of states to design and implement the needed social policies. The radical reforms of state institutions right at the time of economic recession made the problems acute. The economic decline paralleled by political instability brought about value-normative disorientation in large groups and trends of value-normative disintegration of societies in the region. Contradictory and mutually exclusive value preferences continue to be widespread and influential in the public mind of Eastern Europeans. Largely diverging value preferences determine their attitudes towards the past, present day and desirable future situation of groups, institutions, societies and Eastern Europe as a whole. Data from Polish public opinion polls exemplifies the point. Twenty years after the political changes the positive orientation towards the new democratic and market-based conditions in the country is still questioned by half of the Polish population. It is rather telling that a quarter of the interviewed persons in the national representative poll conceive the situation between 1945 and

1989 the best in Polish history. Hardly anybody would have thought in 1989 that this could be the case at the end of 2008. (Polish Public Opinion 2008: 1)

The explanation might be simplified by a reference to the biography of generations or to the high speed of simultaneous changes requiring fast and radical re-orientations. This concerns the reorientation in the international politics of Eastern European societies, in their political and economic organization as well as the changes in their social structure. Another explanation might focus on the general institutional instability during the transformation period. The 'big-bang' reforms brought about organizational, cognitive and value-normative confusions. Old identities had to be suppressed or forgotten, new identities had to be developed and stabilized fast. The move towards survival strategies became accompanied by a short-term agenda of personal planning and activity.

One may try to explain the value-normative confusions by referring to the discrepancy between expectations at the beginning of the changes and the controversial developments later on. The widespread expectation to achieve a high standard of living for most Eastern Europeans on the basis of personal initiative and personal success did not come true. Hopes and desires were replaced by disappointment and skepticism about the perspectives. Instead of striving for considerable achievements and for sustainable prosperity, large groups in Eastern Europe had to struggle for mere survival for decades. At the same time, the media tends to spread detailed information about the style of living of the few winners in the re-distribution of property and income. This inevitably provokes cultural splits and clashes together with the search for scapegoats. New patterns of nationalism and xenophobia emerged. Disputes about ethnic and religious values and norms, cultural identities and traditions evolved into bloody conflicts over territories. Dissatisfaction disunites people and provokes confrontations.

All these patterns of explanation refer to influential cultural and institutional traditions in the region. The economic and political reforms in Eastern Europe hit two cornerstones of the regional value-normative orientations, namely *egalitarianism* and *reliance on the state* (statism). They are beset with internal tensions, which have been intensified by the controversial policies of socialist states. Nevertheless, egalitarianism and statism are still rather influential across the region since they refer both to the communal spirit of the traditionalist rural culture and to urban socialist ideas. In addition, egalitarianism is connected with major struggles for political independence and social justice in the region. The statist value-normative preferences have a great deal to do with the historical role of the Eastern European states as major modernizers under the conditions of belated state building, industrialization and urbanization.

Market oriented economic reforms after 1989 questioned the Eastern European traditions of egalitarianism and the related perception of justice. The new rich are exposed to the general suspicion that their accumulation of property during the 1990s was achieved in illegal manners. Together with the experience of millions of Eastern Europeans in their struggle for survival, this suspicion is the background to the widespread conviction that the established new social order is not just. Some

86% of the respondents in a representative sample covering the adult population of the Russian Federation perceive the newly established differentiation of incomes as unjust. Some 74% believe that the same holds true for the existing system of ownership. (Medvedev, Gorschkov and Krasin 2007: 94) Obviously, the post-socialist differentiation of property and income is not yet culturally legitimized. The issue is even more complicated. For millions of eastern Europeans the problem is not the adjustment to the new conditions of substantial inequality. They define the problem differently: Why should the value-normative orientations and institutional patterns of egalitarianism disappear in Eastern Europe?

One may argue that egalitarianism is going to be replaced by the ideals and practices of liberal meritocracy. The substantial differentiation of rewards should correspond to differences in the achievements of individuals. In a well-regulated and well-functioning societal system this might be the ideal solution to the perennial issue of social justice. At least on the surface, societies in Western Europe and North America rely exactly on this principle of institutionalized meritocracy. It secures the basically smooth functioning of their institutions although exceptions are abundant. The realistic assessment of the current conditions in most Eastern European societies tells a different story. Everyday life in the region is beset with cases of illegal enrichment, political clientelism, ethnic discrimination and other forms of injustice. (Mandel and Humphrey 2002) Given this experience, the very requirement of meritocracy and social justice can be immediately interpreted as a requirement for more egalitarianism. It is not the tradition alone, but also the present day realities which divides Eastern Europeans in opposite value-normative camps on the issue of egalitarianism.

The clash between neo-liberal ideas and practices and the widespread reliance on nation-states is another reason for value-normative disorientation in Eastern Europe. The reliance on nation-states is deeply rooted in the history of the belated state-driven modernization. This tradition was expanded to the extremes of state paternalism in socialist times. The implication is that millions of Eastern Europeans still expect the weakened state institutions to resolve the urgent issues they are confronted with in their everyday life. The protection against unemployment, illness, crime etc. belongs indisputably to the functions of the state in modern societies. The problem is more complicated than the financial restrictions of the Eastern European state budgets. The key issue is the need to modernize the vision of solidarity which is incorporated in state institutions. This should be a solidarity closely connecting the common good with individual initiative and responsibility in the context of individualization.

The state guarantees of general social security and alleviation of social risks belong to the major civilizational achievements of advanced societies. They also have institutional mechanisms preventing the spread of the criminal activities and the practices of free riding. This latter point is rather important since the Eastern European transformations fostered problematic dimensions of individualization under local circumstances. They brought about mistrust in state institutions that are not believed to manage the common good effectively. Paradoxically, the mistrust in state institutions co-exists with the widespread expectation of enjoying the easily accessible common good as guaranteed and managed by state institutions. The reliance on state involvement in major spheres of social life remains strong and positive expectations towards private initiative remain in many crucial cases rather weak.[2]

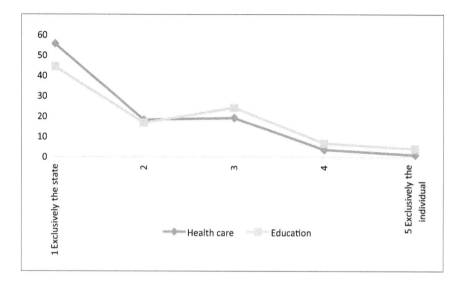

Figure 5.1 "Who should pay the expenses for health care and education?" (National representative survey, Bulgaria, 2005, in %)

Under the influence of neo-liberal ideas the traditional reliance on the state in Eastern Europe was partly replaced by the desire for unrestricted *private initiative.* This desire gained momentum without the counterbalance of accepted *personal responsibility* for the effects of risk management. The unspoken philosophy lurking behind the contradiction is simple. The gain from private initiative is supposed to be privately appropriated. In the case of a failure, the state has to take care of risk management. One may try to explain this cultural paradox by situational factors. The impoverishment of large groups makes the very idea of privately paid health care fiction to them, for instance. However, more relevant explanatory factors are the cultural models of preference of medical care covered by the state. In effect, the trend towards commercialization of all activities causes intensive value-normative tensions and conflicts since it clashes with these and other influential visions of social justice. One may expect that this clash will increasingly trigger

---

2   The nationally representative data was collected in the framework of the longitudinal project "Transformation Risks and Quality of Life" carried out under the supervision of the author.

long-term discontent and alienation. The lesson from the recent global financial crisis is a consolation for Eastern Europeans. The crisis was triggered by free riders who enjoyed enormous profits from the sale of financial packages fully disconnected from the functioning of the real economy. The catastrophic bill of the financial speculations was socialized since tax payers are paying the bill in the United States, in Western Europe and all over the world.

The diverging cultural models and assessments of social processes find their expression in controversial political orientations. As is usual in modern political culture, the major distinctions divide them into 'left', 'centre' and 'right'. There is a permanent problem facing the application of this distinction in Eastern European societies. A large proportion of the population there still cannot identify its political profile by taking real economic and political interests into account. Nevertheless, there are two major ideas clearly dividing the political poles in the region. The first one concerns the acceptability of a steep economic stratification. The second refers to the role of the state in the regulation of social life, and, more specifically, in the regulation of economic inequality. The political left is traditionally oriented towards the vision of 'good society' which avoids a substantial economic differentiation. From the times of *laissez-faire* up until the modern neo-conservatives, the political right insists on the point that people who have achieved economic success should also have the right to fully enjoy its results. This should basically apply even in situations of mass poverty on the opposite pole of economic stratification.

Paradoxically, studies have not discovered any relevant differentiation among the representatives of typical political orientations in their attitudes towards the redistributive functions of the state. Representatives of all political orientations in Eastern Europe are nearly unanimous on the point that the state should impose heavy taxation on large incomes in order to support people with very low incomes. The values of private initiative and private property are already widely shared in the region. A significant part of the population also accepts the differentiation of incomes. However, unlike the neo-conservative right in Western Europe and in the United States, which typically opposes the re-distributive intervention of the state, the representatives of the political right in Eastern Europe agree with the re-distributive interventionism of the state in the same vein as the adherents of the political left or the centrists. (Genov 1999: 110–111) Under these conditions the political right has to co-ordinate the individualistic principles with the urgently needed state governed active social policy. The task of the political left is not easy either because its egalitarian and statist orientation is difficult to implement under the conditions of financially and organizationally weakened state institutions.

The key issue in this context concerns the stability of the social order which is being established in Eastern Europe. The manifest and latent clashes between egalitarian and statist values, on the one side, and individualist liberal values, on the other, are bringing about and maintaining a profound and lasting value-normative uncertainty. The protracted situation of value-normative uncertainty and the intensity of disappointment strengthen the risks of political apathy or destructive protest. These both have the potential to question and undermine the legitimacy of the democratic governance. The mixture of incoherent value-normative orientations explains the widespread variety of expectations and disappointments which cause the public at large to be not particularly enthusiastic about the direction of changes transforming the Eastern European societies. The situation of uncertainty is well exemplified by data from public opinion polls, carried out in societies which were already members of the European Union (Eurobarometer 70 2008: QA11a.1):

Table 5.1 **"At the present time, would you say that, in general, things are going in the right direction or in the wrong direction in your country?" (in %)**

Country	Right direction	Wrong direction	Neither / nor	NA
Bulgaria	23	42	23	12
Czech Republic	33	38	28	1
Estonia	42	34	18	6
Hungary	8	74	17	1
Latvia	19	61	14	6
Lithuania	19	65	12	4
Poland	41	37	17	5
Romania	39	34	19	8
Slovakia	42	21	32	5
Slovenia	49	25	21	5

A crucial factor for the above dissatisfaction is the management of interethnic relations. During the years after 1945 the ethnic integration of eastern European societies was typically maintained by political force. The universalistic ideology of internationalism was supposed to later become the value-normative integrating power of social interactions together with patriotic interpretations of national history. Although internationalism could never drive out the nationalistic ideologies, they were typically regarded in the region as remnants of outdated traditionalism. After the repressive mechanisms were gradually relaxed, most eastern European political leaders tried to legitimize their own rule and to integrate their societies by revitalizing nationalism. Romania was particularly prominent in practicing this ideology and the politics of societal integration by means of nationalistic propaganda and politics.

Nationalism could not be instrumentally employed everywhere in the same way. Some eastern European states were fragile multiethnic and federative structures. Nationalism had to be fostered there selectively, since the nationalistic aspirations of ethnic groups were regarded as subversive. They could not be stopped, however. The cultural tradition and history of the republics in the Soviet Union and in Yugoslavia were reinvented and romanticized. Real or alleged economic and political disadvantages of the federative organization became the subject of crushing criticisms. Ethnic identities returned to the high status after having been systematically suppressed by political and ideological means. The 'imaginable community' of the Ukrainian or Latvian, Slovenian or Croatian nations became stronger and stronger. Thus, together with other processes of economic, political and cultural decay, nationalism contributed substantially to the implosion of the Eastern European social order.

As a result the number of nation-states in the Eastern European region tripled in the course of the nineties. The "soft" or "hard" separations finalized processes which remained uncompleted after the First World War. The moving force behind these profound changes on the political map of Europe was vibrant nationalism. The strengthening of religious identities often supported this. On the territory of former Yugoslavia and the former Soviet Union the establishment of new nation-states was partly achieved through bloody conflicts. Nevertheless, considering the historical experience of uprisings and wars which accompanied the birth of most European nation-states in previous historical epochs, the new nation-states in Eastern Europe mostly emerged in a surprisingly peaceful manner.

Whatever the political causes and consequences of the building of new nation-states in Eastern Europe, it is a highly controversial process in value-normative terms. It implemented the universal human right of cultural and political self-determination of individuals belonging to certain ethnic groups. As seen from this point of view, this nationalism had constructive effects just as it has had many times in history. Seen from another angle, the national self-determination has particularistic consequences concerning social inclusion and exclusion. Some of these consequences are utterly destructive. Individuals who identify themselves with the newly constructed nation-state and are recognized as ethnically belonging to it have an easy task to find inclusion in the new national community. Others remain outsiders in the same nation-state or have to leave its territory. Severe forms of ethno-exclusion have affected millions. In extreme cases, the exclusion took the form of ethnic cleansing, which has nothing to do with the idea of universal human rights. The wars in former Yugoslavia will remain the most tragic events in European history of the nineties. It is ironic that they became possible under the conditions of democratization which followed the demise of authoritarianism in Eastern Europe. (Saideman and Ayres 2008)

Under the conditions of democratization and the development of universalistic culture traditional patterns of ethnic exclusion came to the fore in a new light. The most relevant case of this type throughout Eastern Europe concerns the Roma (gypsy) population. (Avoiding the Dependency Trap 2002) During previous decades, the authoritarian states in the region had applied various schemes for the economic, political and cultural integration of this ethnic group into the mainstream of the respective society. The measures ranged from forceful settlement to positive discrimination at school and in the workplace. Some of the measures were relatively effective. Others failed. Nevertheless, income from salaries and wages was secured for the Roma. They had access to education and health care.

The situation changed fundamentally after 1989. The first to be laid off in the course of the economic restructuring were the Roma. The schemes of positive discrimination at school or in the workplace were abolished. Unemployment reached very high levels among this ethnic group and caused impoverishment beyond the threshold of starvation. The effect is the massive increase of crime committed by the Roma. Dropouts of Roma children from primary schools are widespread.

Under these precarious conditions, the traditional negative stereotypes against the Roma acquired further legitimacy. There is nothing exceptional in this development. In times of economic recession and political crisis, xenophobic emotions and movements typically receive broader support. The economic, educational and value-normative distances between the Roma and other ethnic groups in the Czech Republic, Slovakia, Hungary, Romania, Bulgaria, Ukraine, Serbia, Macedonia and other eastern European countries became larger and larger. The prospects for the social inclusion of the Roma in the mainstream of Eastern European societies declined.

One might assume that the cultural vacuum could be filled by traditional or modernized religious beliefs. Indeed, the issue of ultimate values seems to have become crucial under conditions in which instrumental action takes the lead. However, in most cases the revival mainly concerns the re-building of communities rather than the strengthening of the value-normative core of specific religious beliefs. The reason for this is the mass disenchantment with every kind of ultimate value, with the exception of some values of immediate personal relevance such as health and family. Given this experience, one may assume that the most promising perspective would be the strengthening of the modern "secularized religion" of universal human rights which appeals precisely to the everyday concerns of citizens in Eastern Europe.

Thus, the tensions between *universalized value-normative structures* and specific ethnic, religious and other identities will certainly continue to leave deep imprints on the future of Eastern Europe. Contrary to previous optimistic expectations, particular ways of thinking in the categories of ethnic, religious, political or military confrontation have not disappeared. Some of them have become blurred. Events or grievances have banished others to the periphery of value-normative orientations. This development comes to support the point that the strengthening of the universalistic value systems does not imply any end to the conflicts among particularistic views. On the contrary, we are witnessing a general value-normative uncertainty. The only promising perspective is a stable economic development in which initiatives and responsibility would be consequently guided by moral and law. The reciprocal adjustment of local traditions, present day cultural habits and the modern ethics of initiative and responsibility will take time. All future reforms of educational systems should be carried out with this strategic task in mind. Citizens' initiatives might be quite effective in strengthening the influence of democratic values as well. The value-normative situation of eastern European societies is still in flux. The culture of peace, tolerance and development has a real chance. The demons of envy, hatred and suppression are alive and might just have their chance too.

Is the value-normative puzzle purely an Eastern European phenomenon?

Only a few Eastern European intellectuals were well aware of the profound cultural divisions and contradictions in societies which served as orientation for the societal transformations in the region. Best known were the works by Daniel Bell and the debate which he unleashed. His diagnosis of the cultural contradictions of capitalism (Bell 1976) should have been a warning for everybody who expected cultural harmony after overcoming the disparity between the socialist ideological promise of a just society and the realities of inequality and injustice in state socialism. However, the warning was not heeded seriously. The disappointments accompanying the turn towards democratic political organization and market based economy became so deep that many intellectuals in Eastern Europe got the impression of being deceived by the direction and results of the transformation. (Zibertowicz 2002)

The enlargement of the European Union made the cultural realities of Western Europe part of the common cultural concerns of the old and new member states. The result is the continuing cultural shock due to the deeper knowledge collected by the Eastern Europeans about the shaky value-normative ground of the advanced societies. The learning process continues. But the cultural contradictions of capitalism are already taken for granted.

This de-mystification of the US-American and Western European culture was powerfully supported by the processes in Eastern Europe itself. Intellectuals could directly observe there how correct the points raised by Daniel Bell 30 years ago were and still remain to be today. It is not the Weberian industrious and ascetic entrepreneur who leads on the economic and cultural scene in the Eastern European societies. Bell identified the turn towards short-term planning, hedonism and consumerism. These tendencies increasingly dominate the American business culture and the everyday orientations and actions of millions of US-Americans. The Eastern Europeans could observe the outcomes of this turn. Not Weberian entrepreneurs, opting for frugal work and long-term planning, but cowboy type adventurers became the major masters of the new economic and social organization in the region. Contrary to the stereotypes of the Westerns, these cowboy-like adventurers do not opt for honesty and altruism but for selfishness, tricks, deceit, theft and a hedonistic luxurious life. In a striking amount of cases they were successful, thus evoking the envy of millions of those who had lost out and are reproducing instabilities of the local economy, politics and culture.

But why should the new eastern European cowboy-like entrepreneurs be ashamed of their deeds? They just followed the global practices of hot-money chasing hedge-funds which managed to accumulate incredible capital by means of speculative policies. What did it matter that their hit-and-run strategy co-determined the regional financial crises in South-East Asia in 1997, the financial crisis in Russia in 1998 and the collapse of the Argentinean economy in 2000 and the global financial and economic crisis after 2008? Why should the eastern European business adventurers be ashamed of their deceptive practices, if many of them had become increasingly aware of similar practices in Western Europe and North America?

The global financial crisis of 2008 just confirmed what many knowledgeable bankers all over the world had expected for long. They knew that easy credit could become a trap for millions of customers, that advertised bank certificates and derivates might easily become "toxic papers". The financial crisis only made obvious the low business morale and the lack of social responsibility on the part of the most respectable and trusted Western European and North American financial institutions. The widely praised global financial heroes are heroes no longer. Some of them turned out just to be swindlers. Why should the Eastern European swindler Sergey Mavrodi, who created the famous pyramidal structure MMM in Moscow in 1989, be so ashamed? He deceived his clients out of only 1.5 billion USD. Using a very similar 'Ponzi scheme' of deception, the respected US American financier Bernard Madoff managed to deceive his clients out of 50 billion USD. The phenomenon is global and undermines trust on a global scale. Devaluated trust cannot function as a factor of value-normative integration of national societies and global society. The cultural contradictions of present day capitalism have far-reaching dysfunctional effects.

One of these effects is the intensive feeling of the loss of community. Extreme forms of criminal individualization like the cases of Mavrodi and Madoff undermine any kind of communal solidarity. The common good is obviously of no value in the calculations of persons and institutions implementing this type of financial speculation. Numerous bankruptcy stories of respected financial institutions or of state interventions to save them from bankruptcy lead to one conclusion. The greed of bank managers and their shareholders has gone beyond the limits of the economically and socially manageable, not to mention acceptable. This is a kind of destructive individualization which does not take any communal obligation into account. What lurks beneath the epidemics of mass foul credit is the destructive practice of the foul policies of banks.

There is yet another cultural determinant in the epidemics of mass foul credits. It is a basic cultural contradiction of modern global society. Daniel Bell identified it as consumerism. One can only share his view that the best times of the Protestant spirit of dedication to work and self-limitation of consumption are over. Given the currently observable practices and their consequences, Benjamin Franklin's advice to get up early for work and to save the pennies is not too popular at present. It became public that millions of US Americans and Eastern Europeans alike have been living far above their economic means by taking out credit to repay pre-existing credit. The cultural bias of consumerism has turned out to be major part of the cultural contradictions of capitalism. We observe the effects of this bias on household budgets but also on state budgets in the United States as well as in the "old" and "new" Europe. Consumerism is a global cultural and behavioral pattern with multiple effects. It was celebrated in Eastern Europe, since it replaced the austerities imposed during state socialism. Now the global disenchantments of consumerism have reached Eastern Europe.

The issue certainly has to do with the turn from materialist to post-materialist value-normative preferences. In most countries in Europe and in North America the basic needs of consumers are essentially satisfied. It is not food, shelter or basic medical care which concerns the large majority of people on both continents. Issues of individual development and realization, of family and leisure time, take the lead in personal preferences and planning. This is a positive development which is well attuned to the global trend of individualization. Having their basic needs satisfied, individuals can turn to their free choice in consumption. As attractive as this might be for people all over the world and particularly for Eastern Europeans, this development illustrates the segmentation of workplaces and labor markets. Now it is clear that some workplaces set challenges in education, training, creativity and responsibility thus creating the personal satisfaction of self-realization and development in working life. Another proportion – the greater one – of present day available jobs does not satisfy the workers due to rather diverse reasons. They range from the monotony or exertion of heavy manual labor under dangerous conditions to the problems caused by long routes of transportation or bad human relations in the workplace. Thus, billions of people all over the world see their creativity, free choice and self-fulfillment in consumption – as modest as it might be – as a substitute for the creativity, free choice and self-fulfillment that they lack in the field of work.

The search for liberty, creativity and self-fulfillment in consumption was quickly recognized by manufacturers. Active advertisement by companies is being used to secure market niches for their products in the fierce market competition. If real market niches are not available, they have to be created by creating new needs for the consumers. Not frugality and re-investment in production but the pressure to buy more goods and services and to take out credit to buy even more became the new spirit of capitalism. Early capitalism culturally remunerated the virtues of industriousness. Present day capitalism remunerates infantilization via consumerism. (Barber 2007)

This is just part of the problematic world-wide value-normative situation. Most alarming is the fact that some parts of the global population can afford consumption on a large scale while the majority of the world's population lives under difficult or precarious material conditions. The difference poses many value-normative issues concerning justice. Eastern Europeans had to learn about the relevance of this global divide through their own experience. The equality in relative poverty during state socialism did not turn into varying levels of well-being for everybody. The concentration of well-being in the region was accompanied by downward mobility and restriction in consumption for millions. This development is the source of numerous cultural contradictions, since inequality in consumption means inequality in educational chances, inequality in health care and so on. The crucial issue is the legitimacy of a social situation which is widely perceived as unjust. The cultural contradiction in question strengthens people's readiness to embrace particularistic patterns of thinking and behavior. This is the fertile soil of nationalism, of political and religious extremism as alternatives to the universalization of value-normative systems.

The concepts and practices of universal human rights and meritocracy came from Western Europe and North America and spread worldwide later. Casting a close look at the way in which this is currently taking place one might be shocked by the controversies of the process. In terms of *Realpolitik,* the spread of universalized values and norms often comes with the triumph and domination of specific national cultures and national geostrategic interests: "Cultural imperialism rests on the power to universalize particularisms linked to a singular historical tradition by causing them to be misrecognized as such." (Bourdieu and Wacquant 1999:41) We can witness this effect in the asymmetric information flows supported by the global dominance of one language. One might become enthusiastic by seeing how this development overcomes barriers of isolation. In the long run, the development raises fundamental questions about cultural homogenization and cultural diversity, cultural domination and cultural identity. The serious debate on these issues provokes resistance against extremes of cultural homogenization and domination. (Albritton, Jessop and Westra 2007) Everywhere in the world there are specific local economic and political interests together with local cultural traditions. It is not easy to attune them to universalized value-normative systems if there is the suspicion that their introduction clashes with local interests and local cultural identities.

The so presented new potential for cultural conflicts makes the illusions connected with the "end-of-history" thesis manifest. The conflicts are easily recognizable in the different assessments of major aspects of life under the influence of the substantial and deepening economic and social differentiation.

5.2 Universal Human Rights: Concepts and Practical Implications

The issue of human rights is full of internal contradictions. These are mostly concentrated in the relationships between two parallel trends which shape modern culture. The first trend is the universalization of national and regional value-normative systems. The process is guided by ideas of the universal rights of *individuals*. Recently breakthroughs have come about together with the waves of democratization and individualization on a worldwide scale. Aside from the national legal regulations, there are already some normative and institutional arrangements concerning the transnational rights of individuals. (Faist 2009) However, contrary to optimistic expectations regarding the rapid and smooth advance of this universalistic cultural trend, we are also witnessing the spread and strengthening of *particularistic cultural identities*. These are guided by ideas concerning the common origin, traditions, language and religious preferences of groups. The particularistic identities refer to *collective* belonging and might openly question the very idea of universal individual rights. But the reference to collective identities and belonging might also hold a strong element of humanist appeal by insisting on the rights and liberties of people belonging to suppressed groups or communities.

Thus, both the individualist and collectivist arguments for the protection of human rights may have sound humanistic reasons. One may notice that the

Council Directive 2000/y3/EC places a strong stress on "equal treatment between persons irrespective of racial or ethnic origin" in its title. At the same time, Article 5 of Chapter I of the *Council Directive* stipulates the following: "With a view to ensuring full equality in practice, the principle of equal treatment shall not prevent any Member State from maintaining or adopting specific measures to prevent or compensate for disadvantages linked to racial or ethnic origin". (Council Directive 2000/43/EC: 3) If done on a sound legal basis, the implementation of this Article would require a clear definition of who belongs to a given racial or ethnic origin. Belonging to an ethnic origin means belonging to an ethnic group. Thus, the special approach to individuals belonging to a given ethnic origin means immediately collective rights for individuals belonging to this ethnic group. But the above Article stipulates positive action towards ethnic groups without even mentioning the term of collective human rights. Legal life, present day culture and politics worldwide are very much affected by the influence of both trends and their contradictions. This holds particularly true for the relationships of individual and collective human rights connected to ethnicity. (Wieland 2005)

South Eastern Europe provides perfect examples of these contradictory value-normative dynamics and for the difficulties of domestic and international actors in dealing with them. One telling case is the way in which the European Union handled the critical development of Bosnia and Herzegovina. Nowadays it is a well established fact that the recognition of the independence of Bosnia and Herzegovina by the European Union in parallel with the recognition of the independence of Slovenia and Croatia was not properly considered. The economic, political and especially cultural conditions for sustainable independent development of this former Yugoslav Republic were not available at the beginning of the nineties. In addition, the member states of the European Union turned out to be unable to establish a common diagnosis of the tragic events in the small country. Even less was the EU able to develop coherent policies in order to prevent or put an end to the interethnic wars which claimed at least 100 000 human lives. It was the military intervention of the USA which broke the siege around Sarajevo and later forced the parties in the interethnic war to sign the Dayton Agreement in 1995.

The Agreement had a short-term success in establishing peace. But it was a failure in the long-term. It aimed at a fast turn from the particularistic (collectivist) definition and organization of clashes between ethnic and religious communities in Bosnia and Herzegovina to a universalistic social organization of the Federation. This organization was to be guided by the idea of individual human rights by retaining the relevance and influence of the collectivist ethnic divisions of the federal entities and their political representation in the Federation in the same time. It soon became obvious that these divisions were much stronger and more durable than expected. They still dominate the politics, culture and everyday life in the country. (Early Warning Report September 2008) The same ethnically defined political forces, which waged the civil war in the nineties, govern the entities of the Federation today. The diagnosis of the situation is quite sobering: "The international community's 13+ year effort in Bosnia and Herzegovina is failing. A continuation of the current trajectory will ultimately result in renewed conflict. Bosnian citizens now harbour greater fear of conflict than at any point since Dayton. Both the EU and the US have a lot to lose". (Bassuener 2009: 1)

The success in developing common administration and common armed and security forces is modest. What are the reasons for this continuing critical situation? Some of them are clearly connected with the strategy of the Dayton Agreement to legitimize territorial and political ethnic divisions in order to establish peace. The reasons for the unstable situation have very much to do with the difficult relationship between universal values and norms focused on individual human rights and the politically relevant definitions of collectivist ethnic and religious belonging. The ruling forces in the political entities of the country adhere to the latter definitions. Political parties with universalistic programs focusing on individual human rights have not yet overcome the ethnically divisive borders of the entities established by the Dayton Agreement. It will probably take a long time to overcome this stalemate.

This is obvious in the educational system. Pupils in the entities of the Federation use different school books containing different collective stereotypes of "us" and "others" in the Federation. The consequences are easy to identify: "That is why today we have a generation of young, intolerant, ethnically isolated, and ethnically overfed pupils who are being used as weapons of nationalist politicians". (Alis 2008) The situation is basically improving, but large proportions of Croatian and Serbian parents in Bosnia and Herzegovina would not yet allow their children to attend school together with Bosnian children (Early Warning Report September 2008: 50):

Table 5.2 "How acceptable do you find it for Bosniak children to go to the same school as your children?" (in %)

	Croats		Serbs	
	March 2008	Sept. 2008	March 2008	Sept. 2008
Totally acceptable	60.6	65.3	73.9	68.1
Totally unacceptable	34.3	31.7	24.2	26.9
DK/NA	5.1	3.0	1.9	5.0
Total	100.0	100.0	100.0	100.0

Another relevant case in the region is the politicization of ethnicity in Kosovo. Kosovo Serbs and Kosovo Albanians had opposing visions regarding the future of their ethnic groups. The contradiction took the form of armed clashes. The involvement of international forces in the interethnic conflict imposed the collective political affirmation of the Albanian ethnic majority on this former province of Serbia. The radical politicization of ethnicity brought about full recognition of the collective ethnic rights of the Kosovo Albanians. But the logic of the process brought about a stress on the universal human rights of Kosovo Albanians. In democratic elections they individually decided to declare the independence of Kosovo. This profound normative change has to do with the change in political constellations. The conditions already allowed the achievement of *the collective political aims* of the Kosovo Albanians by means of elections in which *the individual vote* is decisive. This turn in the ethnicization of politics has little to do with the vision and practice of a truly multiethnic and multicultural society. However, this is exactly the mission of the EU-dominated international forces in independent Kosovo.

The example of Kosovo has consequences for the framework of domestic and international politics both within the Balkans and beyond their boundaries. In terms of international law, the change symbolizes a reconsideration of the Westphalian tradition of primary respect for state borders. The mixture of accompanying problems includes persistent difficulties in jointly managing individual and collective human rights. The former tend to universalize the human rights, thus diminishing the relevance of ethnic specifics. Collective rights of ethnic groups have a particularistic conceptual basis and tend to strengthen the collective identities and affiliations of members of ethnic groups. It remains a challenging task to analyze arguments which stress individual or collective rights in the context of the regulation of interethnic relations in South Eastern Europe.

5.3 Testing the Conditions for Religious Tolerance

If one wished to test the above ideas, the profound changes in Central and Eastern Europe could be an ideal field for experimentation. The region offers a large variety of traditional religions and churches – Catholicism, Protestantism, Orthodox Christianity, Judaism and Islam. There are also numerous sects and religious movements which have developed in the course of the profound political, economic and cultural changes after 1989. Indeed, this was a period of almost laboratory type testing of the viability of traditional religions and churches as well as of the attractiveness and organizational efficiency of new religious options. Two decades after the start of the changes we meet an astonishing complexity of religious pluralism which deserves careful analysis in terms of patterns of becoming, the variety of phenomena, and future prospects.

In the beginning of the 1990s many developmental options seemed to be within reach in the region. At the same time, the pressure to decide and to act immediately was tremendous. The variety of possible developments was reduced step by step to what is now available for analysis as relatively stabilized value-normative and institutional structures. Some of them still might change in the near future but most of them will last longer. What is the place of religious ideas and religious institutions in this newly established framework of cultural and social structures?

There is no simple answer to this question applicable to all Central and Eastern European societies. Nevertheless, there are several common points which are now taken for granted. Contrary to the expected explosive spread of religious beliefs after the change of political regimes, religious ideas only modestly filled in the value-normative vacuum left by the previously dominant ideology. Nowhere did traditional religious ideas become the core of the value-normative system of the societies in the region as was widely assumed to be unavoidable. (Noris and Inglehart 2005: Ch. 5)

The assumption that the well developed organizations and human capital of the traditional churches would take the lead in the changes was also proven mistaken. Nowhere in the region did traditional religious institutions manage to assume any leading position in the changes. Moreover, the expected return to practical relevance of traditional religious ideas and institutions came only partly about and in an unexpectedly fierce struggle with ideas and practices of churches, sects and movements which were non-traditional for the Eastern European societies. Institutions of the traditional religions and their clergy were taken by surprise by the activities of well trained, funded and organized missionaries from other parts of the world.

Due to the need for rapid legal and institutional changes, major parts of the modern universalistic secularized religion were incorporated into the value-normative and institutional systems of the Eastern European societies. The convincing evidence for this development is provided by the democratic constitutions passed in the region after 1989. They are all focused – manifestly – on the universal rights of human individuals, and – in many cases implicitly – on the various dimensions of sustainability. However, it would be a far reaching exaggeration to say that in this way the secularized civic religion had taken the lead in the region. The situation is more complicated both in historical terms as well as in terms of current intellectual debates and institutional processes. (*Religion and Change in Central and Eastern Europe* 2002)

Now it is the proper time to take advantage of the already available historical distance and attempt some explanations of the above processes and their structural outcomes. Why were the traditional religious institutions so inactive or inefficient in their actions? The simplest explanation would be that at the onset of the profound changes the crucial issue concerning religion and church in Eastern Europe was the lack of mobilizing religious visions. In other words, the internal religious discourse and public debates about religion had not brought about specific religious projects concerning *developmental goals and developmental strategies* of societies. Even in Poland where the internal religious debates were the most intensive and the Polish Catholic Church was culturally and institutionally opposed to the old regime, the Church was not able to offer any fresh idea about the future of Polish society. This explains why the Polish Church did not experience any substantial influx of followers after 1989 and gradually lost its appeal as cultural guide in the profound political and economic changes. It even lost a substantial part of its institutional influence on current political decisions and actions. (Manuel, Lawrence and Wilcox

2006: Ch. 7). With some nuances, the same holds basically true of the gradually declining institutional influence of the Hungarian, Czech, or Slovakian Catholic churches in local politics.

It seemed possible that the Orthodox churches in Russia, Ukraine, Romania or Bulgaria should take the opportunity presented by the democratic freedom and contribute effectively to the development of a vibrant cultural pluralism. Nothing like that happened. The Orthodox clergy was badly educated as a rule and could not even find an intellectual connection to the explosion of new cultural options. The ageing of the clergy was one of the many reasons for this fatal inadequacy to actively and creatively adapt to the new conditions of fierce intellectual competition. In addition, just like the Catholic and Protestant clergy in Central Europe, the Orthodox clergy was very much involved in internal struggles concerning its own past during the former regime. The traditional Central and Eastern European Churches were also involved in difficult struggles concerning the restitution of the ownership of the nationalized church property. Mostly in this respect and less due to theological reasons, in all predominantly Orthodox countries there were severe problems with internal institutional splits in the national churches. The Russian Orthodox Church had a particularly difficult task in coping with the collapse of the Soviet Union and, as a consequence, with its complicated relationships to believers and religious institutions in the so called "near abroad". (Knox 2005: Ch. 3)

As seen in retrospect, it seems that relevant ideas for the strategic intellectual, moral and social renewal of society could have appeared in the East German Protestant Church. It possessed the major institutional framework for oppositional intellectual debate in the former GDR and could also have profited from the available information on the new roles of religion and church in West Germany. However, the discussions on the possibility of a third road between socialism and capitalism were interrupted by the turmoil of the accelerated German unification. Thereafter ready-made cultural and institutional patterns were directly borrowed from the Federal Republic. The intellectual appeal of the Protestant Church rapidly declined in the basically atheist East Germany. (Pollack and Pickel 2000)

The major context of the intellectual and institutional problems of the churches in Eastern Europe was the need to cope with the past, present and future of the relationship between *church and state.* This issue had and still has a large variety of dimensions. Everywhere in the region the churches had to reflect critically on their experience during the decades under the former regime. Without any underestimation of the personal achievements of the Hungarian religious leader Cardinal Mindszenty, his rigorous rejection of any relationship between the Church and the atheist regime could not be a realistic long-term option. Mechanisms had to be invented for practical *modus vivendi* of the Eastern European churches with the one-party political systems. In the course of time this happened even in the Soviet Union where the Orthodox Church had been exposed to exceptionally severe repressions. Nevertheless, it was practically rehabilitated and incorporated into state institutions, mostly due to its patriotic contribution in the Second World War.

The basically oppositional Catholic churches in Poland and Hungary followed the restrictive recommendations of the Vatican but out of necessity also developed well legalized and institutionalized relations with the party-states step by step. This was easier to accomplish in countries where the majority of the population was traditionally affiliated with Orthodox churches. Throughout their history, they had officially recognized the dominance of the state over the church. Precisely this tradition is causing special problems in the newly independent states. The institutional status of churches in successor-states of the Soviet Union (Ukraine) and Yugoslavia (Macedonia) is not yet properly regulated. Thus, the complicated past and its legacies are still making the state-church relationships in Central and Eastern Europe difficult. A special aspect of the problem is the previously suspected and today officially recognized fact that churches in Eastern Europe were deeply infiltrated by the secret services of the party-states. Documentary investigations and personal confessions on this issue continue to shatter religious institutions all over the region.

Currently, the Russian Orthodox Church seems once more to be readily embracing its new/old status of a key spiritual and institutional pillar of statehood as it had been known for centuries. This renaissance of intimate relationships between the state and the Orthodox Church brings material support to the Church and provides it with institutional stability. The extent to which this role as a true supporter of statehood can be effectively performed under the new conditions of open markets for religious influences and uncertain political developments needs to be carefully analyzed. One point might be taken for granted already, however. The long period of atheist propaganda and anti-religious policies has left deeply engrained traces in the Russian mass consciousness. The very high level of Russian religious devoutness during the nineteenth century definitely belongs in the past. So, a return to the legitimacy of the situation in which the Russian state and the Russian Orthodox Church were closely interconnected is most probably not possible. But is it indeed desirable? State-Church intimacy has often been detrimental for the identity, autonomy and institutional strength of the Orthodox Church in Russian history and might become detrimental in the future as well. (Širokalova and Anikina 2007)

The repeated pleas of the Russian orthodox clergy and similar pleas of other traditional churches in Eastern Europe to the respective governments to legally prohibit the "intrusion" of other traditional or non-traditional churches and sects is a manifestation of their institutional incapacity to cope with the competitors. When practically implemented, the manifest support of states for the traditional churches or, in most cases, for the churches of the largest religious communities, is in itself a rather questionable phenomenon. It undermines the credibility of democratic constitutional provisions concerning the religious neutrality of the state and freedom of religions.

The relationship between the state and church was or still is particularly close in the Eastern European countries where the state and the traditional church openly embraced *nationalistic ideology and policies*. Extreme mutual enforcement of nationalism by state and church was achieved in the successor states of former Yugoslavia. Typical examples are Croatia and Serbia. The most dramatic case of intimate connections of nationalistic political extremism supported by religion and the Church was in Bosnia and Herzegovina. Orthodox Christianity, Catholicism and Islam were mobilized there to support military actions in a way rather similar to the experience of the Thirty Years War in the European Middle Ages. The unbiased observer could see in Bosnia and Herzegovina a *political and religious fundamentalism of cuius regio, eius religio in action* and the destructive consequences of the fundamentalism.

Peter L. Berger (2005: 9) defined such situations in proper terms: "Fundamentalism is any project to restore taken-for-grantedness in the individual's consciousness and therefore, necessarily, in his social and/or political environment. Such a project can have both religious and secular forms". The fundamentalist aspirations of Radio Maryja in Poland became inacceptable even for the Catholic Church, since religious fundamentalism could have detrimental consequences for societal integration or might even directly foster societal disintegration. If practically implemented, the aspirations of religious fundamentalism could mean the establishment of a theocratic state with unavoidable totalitarian features.

The same considerations make states and the public at large particularly sensitive to the spread of Islamic fundamentalism and the related political extremism. This sensitivity is not necessarily focused on Islam and Muslims for historical reasons. Most societies in Eastern Europe have a long experience of peaceful co-existence with smaller or larger Islamic religious communities on their territories. But now Eastern Europeans are confronted with the participation of militant Islamists in the war in Bosnia and Herzegovina and with the activities of various non-governmental organizations funded by governments and private sources from the Middle East. Some of them are using their educational or philanthropic activities as a cover for spreading Wahabism or other fundamentalist teachings of Islam. The South East European countries with large Muslim population have become the subject of international concerns. (Lederer 2005)

Given these problematic recent trends the very idea of *religious pluralism* is subject to suspicion in many parts of Eastern Europe. The clergy, believers and non-believers have reservations about an open market of competing religious views and religious institutions. This is not a specific Eastern European phenomenon. The very question "Is religious pluralism indeed possible?" is being asked on various occasions. (Collste 2005) The historical experience teaches that even the most tolerant interreligious relationships bear the potential for tensions and conflicts concerning the teaching of religion in schools, the mutual acceptance of religious holidays or the moral and legal acceptability of specific religiously motivated behavioral patterns. The sensitivity to these issues is widespread. Some religious or semi-religious organizations are legally outlawed even in most tolerant liberal societies.

It would be too much expected to believe that precisely the Eastern European societies may offer the best examples for stable solutions to these difficult problems. With minor exceptions, these societies do not have long-term traditions of pluralist politics and culture or of well developed and functioning civil society. Despite the spread and strengthening of voluntary associations, neither the public at large, nor state and church institutions in Eastern Europe are ready to accept that the organizational form of voluntary association will be the future of religious institutions in the region. Nevertheless, it seems that there is a widespread consensus in the region that mutual understanding, tolerance and co-habitation of religious views and religious institutions is very much desirable. The presence of militant fundamentalists within all religious or semi-religious orientations and associations is always problematic. Fundamentalists might influence the decisions to keep the interreligious dialogue alive or not.[3] These considerations cannot be separated from the ongoing globalization which has both unifying and diversifying effects. The first ones may strengthen mutual understanding, the cross-fertilization of ideas and cooperation of religious institutions in handling the social and moral issues of contemporary civilization. But the same issues may provoke the strengthening of religious isolationism, hostilities between religious institutions and full-scale propaganda for inter-religious wars.

What could be done in order to strengthen the tendency of mutual understanding and inter-religious tolerance and to avoid or at least weaken the destructive alternative tendencies? The search for practically relevant answers should start from the historical fact that all religious beliefs and religious institutions which are currently influential world-wide have long traditions of mutual intolerance, hostilities and war. Could one assume that their mutual understanding, tolerance and peaceful co-existence could be achieved now, in the foreseeable or more distant future? No conclusive answer can be given to this question. On the contrary, the negative answer is easy. Ongoing globalization means open borders and market-like competition among religious ideas and institutions. Market strategies always include camouflaging, deception, unfriendly take-over, the conquering of new markets previously dominated by others, etc. These strategies cannot be easily associated with visions of mutual understanding, tolerance and peaceful co-existence. The potential for conflict is always given in social life and the potential for inter-religious tensions and conflicts are always given as well. This applies even in the context of omnipresent religious pluralism. So, what is the real problem?

The real theological, organizational and moral problem might be simplified in the following way: Given the potential for questioning or destroying the conditions for peaceful religious pluralism, is there indeed any realistic prospect for establishing and maintaining it? There is no comprehensive and convincing answer to this problem in the religious discourse and religious institutions alone. Positive discourse in this area would have to transcend religiously motivated thinking and activities and move in the direction of the most pressing problems

---

3   This was the background assumption of Pope John Paul II during his groundbreaking common service of representatives of several religions in Assisi in 1985. (Scheffler 2007) We have also witnessed setbacks in the dialogue due to one or another event (Aref 2006).

facing human kind today. In other words, discourse should move from the areas of religiously defined civilizations in the plural, in the direction of the problems and prospects of the globalised human civilization defined in the singular.

5.4 Cultural Pluralism *versus* Value-normative Universalization?

The notorious value-normative instability in Eastern Europe poses questions of a broad theoretical and political relevance. Could societies in the region stabilize without a full-fledged value-normative integration? After Parsons (1971: 14–15) the necessity for value-normative integration of modern societies should be theoretically taken for granted. It is a common view among social scientists that other crucial integration mechanisms should not be underestimated as well. Scientists usually refer to Adam Smith's model of societal integration on the basis of economic exchange and to Thomas Hobbes' famous vision of the Leviathan-like monster of the integrating state. One may have one or another preference concerning integration mechanism of societal systems. But the point raised by Parsons remains still relevant: Each society needs shared visions concerning its desirable state of affairs (ultimate values) in order to be integrated in substantive and functional terms. These values are related to what is ultimately desirable or forbidden in a given society. Can we identify uniting visions of this type in present day Eastern European societies?

The spontaneous answer is negative. Eastern European societies are culturally deeply divided not only in ethnic and religious terms. The divisions between winners and losers in the economic reforms, between the new political elites and the average voters are significant. Under these conditions it is difficult to identify visions which focus on what is sacred in the society under scrutiny.

It is a matter of intellectual ritual to interpret the very idea of sacredness as linked to religion.[4] Religion as a system of beliefs, practices and institutions is closely related to ideas, spaces, things, scriptures, gestures, words, songs, etc. which are assumed to be connected to divine power. However, in all known societies there have been diverging interpretations of the divine power. Searching for stability and following their own interests, political powers usually try to reduce the variety of visions concerning divinity and sacredness, thus reducing the range of religious pluralism. Political powers even tried to homogenize visions about sacredness and divinity in their societies. The issues of sacredness, divinity, cultural pluralism and cultural tolerance are closely connected with politics.

Currently the pluralization of culture worldwide goes hand in hand with the pluralization of religious ideas all over the world. The Westphalian principle *cuius region, eius reliigio* no longer applies. The world-wide communication makes the spread of a wide range of religious ideas fast and uncontrollable. Mass migration

---

4   "*A religion is a unified system of beliefs and practices relative to sacred things, that is to say, things set apart and forbidden*". (Durkheim 1968 [1915]: 47)

contributes to the cross-fertilization of religious beliefs. The deepening division of labor makes personal preferences more and more differentiated and socially relevant. The opening of national markets and the liberalization of political control make states less and less able to effectively intervene in religious matters. Given the easily accessible, rich and competitive supply of religious ideas and institutions, individuals are expected to become increasingly specific in their choice concerning the content, form and intensity of their religious affiliation. These are no more taken for granted due to cultural traditions, family preferences, or the political preferences of the nation-state. As a result, we are witnessing the progressing pluralization of individual preferences. The general direction of this trend deviates from the hierarchically organized churches and religious sects towards religious denominations which are organized much like voluntary associations. Participation is a matter of personal selection and choice and might change due to another choice. (Berger 2005: 7f.)

Most religions consider the "permanent residence" of the divine power in the "other world". But there are also religious views which conceive the divine power as incorporated in "this world" of nature and human deeds. Efforts to prove both views by empirical means have not brought convincing verification. Scientifically influenced thinkers such as Bertrand Russel (1925) took some steps beyond mere skepticism towards religion by denying its *raison d'être* in modern times. The influential modernization theory generalized this attitude through the assumption that secularization is part and parcel of the modernization process. The assumption was that the higher the level of modernization of a society the less relevant is the role of religious ideas and religious institutions for societal integration and indeed for social life. It seems that this assumption has been falsified by empirical evidence. The secularization thesis is currently regarded as no more convincing. Religious beliefs and institutions are experiencing a Renaissance all over the world, Europe being the only exception. (Joas and Wiegandt 2007)

Against the background of this historical experience, should the Europeans in general and Eastern Europeans in particular rush to forget the legacy of Russel? Or, together with him could they assume that uniting, orientating and mobilizing common symbols of the sacred are very much needed in the mundane lives without reference to any specific divine power but to the common everyday experience? By referring to it nobody could jettison the achievements of science and the enlightenment based on science. It directs thinking and action towards intellectual and moral universalism.

This line of argumentation leads to a paradoxical situation. The stress on "our" experience underlines the fact that ultimate values are always values *of a community*. What is the community we should refer to when talking about the universalization of value-normative systems? The answer cannot be focused on particularistic references such as family, kin, clan, tribe, religious community, nation, class or race, although all these real or imaginary communities have historically been reference points for ultimate values guiding and mobilizing action. All these ultimate values unite segments of human kind by dividing them from and even confronting them with the rest of human kind. Could we try to transcend this division and potential hostility between "us" (the preferred particular community of reference) and "them" (the rest of humanity)? Could we try to base our present day value-normative preferences on the generalized humanist ideas of the European Enlightenment? Could we try to move further on by developing universalistic visions of the sacred?

Options are on the agenda. They contain visions about the desirable future state of man and society. They also contain norms about what should be done in order to establish the desirable social order and what is forbidden to do in order not to disturb the process. In their mature form, these visions and their related practices evolved in the second half of the twentieth century. Universalism is their major characteristic. They do not refer to any specific ethnic, religious or national community. Nor do they refer to any specific group such as race or social class. Being derived from the spirit of the European Enlightenment, these secular visions refer to humanity and to the ultimate value of its survival and the ultimate value of living one's life in dignity.

These universalistic ideas correspond to the traditional religious sacred in their functions. This applies to the idea of *sustainable development*. As a very general cognitive and normative guidance for thinking and behavior which can preserve good quality living conditions for future generations, this idea is functionally equivalent to key ideas in traditional religions. Every pious Christian was expected – ideally – to orient his/her action, to decide, act and to evaluate the outcomes of action according to the normative vision of salvation. Nowadays every enlightened citizen is expected – ideally – to think and act according to the vision of sustainability as broadly conceived in the Bruntlandt Report of the United Nations (1987), in Agenda 21 (1992), in the Kyoto Protocol (1997) and in a large number of other international documents.

The vision of economic, political and cultural sustainability has the orienting, mobilizing and binding power of the traditional religious sacred in present day societies. Moreover, the vision is in an inherent relation to the ultimate community of world society and its survival. This vision could only become so relevant after the use – only once, but convincingly enough – of nuclear weaponry. The further sophistication and spread of this vision made obvious the vulnerability of human kind to technological destructive forces developed by man himself. Another signal with the same level of relevance was given by the Club of Rome. Concerned intellectuals pointed out the limitations facing economic development due to the scarcity or depletion of natural resources as well as to the threat of environmental pollution. (Meadows 1972; Meadows, Randers and Meadows 2004) The current hot topic of the same relevance concerns the climate change caused by human activity. Whatever the issue under scrutiny in the wide range of factors which threaten or facilitate environmental, economic, political and cultural sustainability, its value-normative content is clearly defined. This is a value-normative sacred which has become the basis for the broadest possible consensus uniting people who simultaneously might subscribe to other vastly diverse value-normative preferences.

Is the idea of sustainability unique in its potential to be the basis for mutual understanding of individuals and groups otherwise keeping to diverging values and norms? The idea of *universal rights of human individuals* is still another option for this uniting function. The very concept of universal human rights is closely connected to the idea of broadly understood sustainability. If there is no respect for human rights, this is already a threat to social sustainability. But the vision of universal human rights is a different sort of sacredness in present day advanced societies. Sustainability refers to the largest imaginable community on earth, while the idea of universal human rights refers to the human individual first of all. There is an intermediary link between these two poles which is the idea and practice of collective human rights. The collective human rights of all people on the earth actually coincide with key dimensions of the idea of sustainability in terms of preservation and development of *conditio humana*. As seen from another angle, the localization of the idea and practice of sustainability in particular groups, communities and societies can develop into value-normative requirements for natural and social conditions of the life of human individuals in dignity.

The vision concerning the rights of the human individual is actually rather old as a cultural tradition. It has its roots in the ancient democracies and in influential theological interpretations of traditional Christianity.[5] These were conceptually refined in the times of the Reformation and by thinkers of the Enlightenment. In the form of general legal provisions, the idea of the universal rights of human individuals was already incorporated in constitutions two centuries ago. But the real ideological rise of this idea and of its institutional incorporations is directly connected to the Universal Declaration of Human Rights adopted by the UN General Assembly in 1948. (Resolution 217 AIII) The Declaration and other related documents place stress on the value of each human individual and his/her right to the standard of living and quality of life required to reach the highest level of personal development and realization possible under any given historical conditions. (Spickard 1999:6f.)

Nowadays the idea of the universal rights of the human individual is positioned in the very conceptual core of modern constitutions and legal regulations. Thus, together with the idea of sustainable development, the idea of the rights of human individuals has become *the sacred value-normative core* of institutional arrangements in modern societies. Referring to the Durkheimian definition of religion, sustainability and human rights had become the subject of shared respect ("worshipping"). Any kind of violation of the principles of sustainability and of

---

5   In traditional Christianity the issue was discussed by Augustine in detail. He distinguished between the eternal sin inherited by human kind and the sin due to the conscious and deliberate decisions made through the free will of the individual. Although in negative terms, the rights of the individual to become autonomously oriented, to decide and to act were actually recognised in this way. (Augustine 1993)

human rights is forbidden. This should not be understood in the sense that there are no perpetrators and perpetrations of both principles. There are numerous examples of perpetrations as it was the case with the sacred principles of Christianity in the religious Medieval Ages in Europe. One needs just think of the bloody Thirty Years War.

Could the visions of sustainable development and universal rights of human individuals be the core of the *civic* or *secular religion* of modern democratic societies? If yes, both principles might bring about a *value-normative homogenization* within the emerging social order at the global level and in Eastern European societies. If so, we may expect that the universalistic principles of this new civic religion may become the basis for productive discourse between people. The background of the discourse is the accelerated globalization. It has numerous causes, manifestations and effects. One of the major effects is the appearance of the phenomenon of global economic, political and cultural insecurity. Globalization strengthens the ideas and feelings of belonging to one world society. But it is rather fragile due to interrelationships between actors with diverse needs, interests and patterns of decision and action. This is exactly the motivation behind the development and spread of the new civic religion of sustainability. Its sacred idea is the survival of the human civilization. Seen from another angle, globalization spreads the value-normative vision concerning the universal rights of human individuals and the need to incorporate this vision into constitutions and other legal regulations. This legal development enlarged the social space for autonomous orientations, decisions and actions of individuals to an extent which had never before been achieved for large groups.

Paradoxically enough, we are witnessing another powerful trend of value-normative divergence of visions, orientations, decisions and actions of individuals and groups. The most remarkable manifestation of this trend is the revival and strengthening of traditional ethnic preferences, religions and religion-like beliefs together with the emergence of ethnic movements, new religions or religion-like organizations. In addition, the traditional religions of Christianity, Islam and Judaism are deeply affected by internal trends of pluralization. Following long traditions of separation and confrontation, fundamentalist factions in these religions struggle against each other or against moderate factions in the same religion. What is new is the current reference of religions to the secular sacred of sustainability and universal human rights in controversial ways. The moderate factions in world religions are increasingly developing symbiotic trends with the modern secular sacred. The fundamentalist factions are increasingly resisting it in word and action.

The value-normative universalization and value-normative particularization work simultaneously in opposite directions. They might be controversial, but basically *they are complementary*. The global technological innovations, global economic exchange, new worldwide political interdependency and cultural unification strengthen the civic religion of sustainability and universal human rights. But they also strengthen occupational, ethnic, religious etc. differentiations and divisions. Thus, the power of globalization is unifying and homogenizing and, in the same time, it opens new or widens the existing social space for diversity as well. The ensuing problems are extremely relevant in practical terms. How could developments of value-normative diversity be avoided which might mobilize efforts for destruction of the human civilization? The search for answer or answers should refer to the fact that the spread of cultural pluralism goes hand in hand with trends of mutual understanding and tolerance or with trends of confrontation among ethnic or religious ideologies. The secularized civil religion of sustainability and universal human offers positive and uniting arguments in favor of survival and development of human civilization.

There are policy relevant implications of the above argumentation. *First*, given the potentials of the civic religion of sustainable development and universal human rights, it is not correct to see issues of dialogue and cooperation or isolation and confrontation among contemporary ethnic or religious preferences as a problem of cultural diversity alone. To the contrary, cultural pluralism has practical implications which concern practically everybody today whatever his/her cultural preferences might be. *Second*, it is the responsibility of individuals, groups, organizations and societies which prefer to keep to the civic religion of sustainable development and universal human rights to foster intercultural dialogue and keep institutional cooperation alive and efficient. *Third*, together with the efforts to maintain the mutual understanding of diverging cultural preferences, views, the assumption should be kept alive that ideological extremism may become powerful and dangerous for domestic and international peace and even for human civilization. (Hasenclever and De Huan 2007)

Chapter 6
Conceptualizing Social Dynamics

The future of sociology depends on its ability to detect profound changes in the social order and in the "spirit of time". Max Weber was intellectually best equipped to achieve this in the turbulent years after the First World War. Talcott Parsons managed to put the most concise diagnosis of the times of the polar divisions of the world during the Cold War. The competition for the new diagnosis of the time after the end of the Cold War is open. The present monograph aspires to have done only part of the job with regard to the changes in Eastern Europe. The first task was to answer the question about the causes and reasons of the upheaval in the region in 1989–1990. The second task was to systematically describe and explain what really happened in the region during the 20 years of catching-up modernization and why. The third task was to identify current social tensions and prospects for changes in society and in social sciences.

The conclusion of this intellectual exercise concerning sociology and sociologists is clear enough: sociological concepts and methodology have to be adjusted to a reality in flux. The current global crisis revealed that most societies in Eastern Europe are marked by disparities between aspirations and need-satisfaction, knowledge and practical action, change and order. Some of them can still properly be labeled as risk societies. Under these circumstances sociology cannot escape the fate of being at risk itself. Its cognitive capacity and practical relevance is regularly put to tests in an environment which does not pay much attention to social sciences. What is most at stake is the integrity of knowledge about social dynamics.

There are various ways to react to the challenge. (Outwait and Ray 2005) The promising one is to turn the challenge into an opportunity by strengthening the reflexivity of sociological theorizing and research. Relying on his or her reflexivity, hardly any sociologist would take market economy and democratic politics nowadays for *ultimate ends* of the transformation, as many believed at the outset of the Eastern European transformations. Market economy and democratic politics can only be *means*. It seems to be clear now that the real ends in question are connected with the achievement of a higher quality of mutual co-ordination of needs and interests of individuals, groups and organizations. Thus, the most strategic issue of the economic reforms was not the change of property rights although the transformation would not have been possible without it. The key issue of the reforms is different. Strategically they should aim at *better conditions for sustainable development of societies and better conditions for implementation of human rights*. Did the opening and adaptation of the East European societies to the four global trends under scrutiny substantially contribute to the achievement of these aims?

The Eastern European experience after 1989 is unique and, in the same time, it is merely a special case of the worldwide changes of deep social structures and patterns of thinking and behavior. All these changes are part and parcel of the all-embracing *globalization*. It puts its imprint on social interactions at all structural levels. The imprint is visible everywhere in the increase of social complexity due to simultaneous differentiation and integration of social structures. The process puts well-established patterns of hierarchic governance on trial. The efforts to intellectually cope with the growing social complexity by developing concepts of polyarchic patterns of organization seem most promising for resolving the issue. But the concepts referring to the interaction between relatively autonomous state institutions, business organizations, political parties, voluntary associations and social movements need further elaborations in order to be suitable for systematic description and explanation of a rapidly changing social reality.

6.1 Changing Sociological Paradigms

Rapid changes of increasingly complex social reality constitute the major reason why the uniting core of theoretical advancement in sociology today could not anymore be the issue of societal integration as Parsons believed. The uniting conceptual core in the cumulative development of sociological knowledge concerns the issue of social dynamics. There is an urgent and recurring need to theoretically clarify its sources, processes and results. In terms of changing sociological paradigms, the task is to elaborate on a modified evolutionism by taking into account continuity and radical change in social reality accompanying globalization. A major reference point for resolving this task continues to be the concept of mutually related social structures and functions. However, today it is uncontested that there is no *one* social structure opening the strategic way to explanations of social dynamics. There is no concept of *one* social function that would offer enough explanatory space for the study of stability and development in social reality. A *range* of well-differentiated analytical concepts is needed in order to accumulate well structured empirical data and to systematically analyze it, to draw generalizations, to substantiate explanatory hypotheses, and to carry out effective prognostic procedures.

In the course of this analytical work it becomes increasingly clear that conceptual innovations are particularly necessary and possible in the field of globalization research. *First*, globalization involves a large variety of actors and structures having different paths and logics of change. Against this ontological background, the traditional teleological understanding of social development as progressive improvement of social relations and processes cannot sustain. It should give way to a neutral definition of social development either as a qualitative improvement of the adaptability of a social system to its environment *or* as a decline and dissolution of the system's structures and functions. This re-definition of social development questions the progressive overtones of modernization theory. *Second*, the major traditional point of reference of sociological theorizing and research on social development is the concept of society. More specifically, it is the concept of society understood as nation-state. The studies on globalization, regionalization and their local manifestations in "glocalization" reveal an extraordinary variety of factors explaining social processes and their consequences. In these studies trans-national and trans-cultural processes increasingly gain relevance while processes in societies lose relevance. *Third*, as a result of the debates on the state and prospects of global environment, the concept of sustainable development came into intellectual fashion. Currently it is getting more and more important for social science and social policies. This concerns immediately the studies on social relations and processes that foster or hinder the economic, political, cultural and environmental sustainability.

Does sociology successfully cope with this tremendous challenge of necessary new conceptualizations? It is sobering to notice that neither mainstream sociology in Western Europe and North America nor the national sociological communities in Eastern Europe managed to elaborate concepts suitable for predicting the rapid move from state socialist institutional arrangements to what was to become the post-socialist social order. The following changes revealed the low descriptive and explanatory power of the hastily introduced all-embracing transition concept. Its capacity to provide systematic descriptions and explanations of the ongoing processes turned out to be rather limited. Another easy option was to explain the unexpected difficulties in the transition of Eastern European societies towards market economy and democratic politics by merely referring to civilizational deficiencies or incompetence. The problems were by far more complex and could be best reflected in the multidimensional concept of *societal transformation under the impact of global social trends*. (Genov 1999)

6.2 Global Trends and Regional Specifics

The differentiation of economy, politics and culture is the major evolutionary achievement of the Eastern European societal transformations. (Kutsenko and Babenko 2004: 11f.) Simultaneously, an accelerated differentiation *in* all action spheres of Eastern European societies took place. Both types of differentiation *of* action spheres and *in* action spheres are manifestation of the trend towards the upgrading the rationality of particular organizational structures, functions and processes. Another side of the same rationalization process is the search for more efficient means and forms of achieving and maintaining the integration of social structures, functions and processes. The effects of this profound change are visible in all walks in Eastern Europe. Economy and culture are no more dominated in the region by the formalized politics of the monopolistic party-state. Each action sphere is now expected to develop and reproduce its own mechanisms of internal integration and innovation and to contribute to the integration and innovation of the societal system.

Organizational reality deviates from this optimal paths of upgrading the rationality of organizations. The crucial problem in the present day Eastern European context concerns *the roles of the state as a key actor in the upgrading of organizational rationality*. One important conclusion of the present study is that a rational management of societal transformations requires the active involvement of a "small" but efficient state. Another conclusion reads that market alone cannot autonomously provide for the conditions of its own discipline, transparency and efficiency. However, even the very much needed small-scale state interventionism into economy poses serious dangers of corruption among state officials. Another danger consists in the development of oligarchic structures which are exempted from democratic control.

The controversial path of reforms in Eastern Europe made the need to quickly *adjust the political relations to the new local and global requirements* particularly urgent. This concerns the relations of social control first of all since democratic participation in decision-making might be easily abused. The disappointment *in the way of functioning of democracy* might be rather destructive. Disappointment is normal since no reform could be carried out without some loss of administrative or economic efficiency. It took as long as fifteen years before most societies in the region returned to the GDP level they had before the start of the reforms. The rationalizing pressure of the global market together with the eastward enlargement of the European Union could not be strong enough to reduce the negative effects of the outdated technology, the inherited organizational patterns and the resistance of influential cultural models.

Some political decisions introduced or supported organizational irrationalities. This holds true for the efforts to carry out 'big-bang' privatization without political consensus or the voucher privatization on a shaky legal and institutional basis. The rise of crime and corruption casted a long shadow on the rationality of these decisions and actions. Thus, *the upgrading of the organizational rationality went hand in hand with the need to cope with organizational pathologies* affecting both the economic efficiency and the social cohesion in Eastern European societies. (Pickles 2009) The fate of the millions of losers of economic reforms is a tremendous social and moral issue.

Due to the close relationships of economic and political rationalization the East Europeans are largely dissatisfied with the functioning of the introduced democratic political institutions. (Rose 2008) Specific reasons for dissatisfaction with the democratic politics offer the activities of incompetent and selfish political leaderships and their clientelist networks. Only few reform politicians survived the harsh selection in a highly competitive political process from which millions are disappointed, isolated and alienated.

The organizational innovations in Eastern Europe are very much influenced by the dynamics of cultural life. It developed its own contradictions. It is a matter of public concern that some cultural organizations support religious fundamentalism or nationalist cultural orientations. The turn to ethnic and religious radicalism in Eastern European societies became the signal for questionable side-effects of the organizational rationalization on cultural life in the region.

The societal transformations in Eastern Europe enriched the historical experience with patterns of active and creative adaptation by rationally calculating and acting individuals. This is an evolutionary achievement recognizing the needs and interests, freedoms and dignity of human individuals as guiding principals. However, the weakening of the macro-social economic and political integration in the course of the reforms caused destabilization of micro-social interaction patterns. On its turn, the destabilization of the normative framework of everyday interactions caused macro-social instabilities. Both processes mutually amplified each other and jointly brought about effects of acute normlessness (anomie). Disenchantment, escapism and aggression are phenomena that characterize this social situation. The previous distortions of organizational rationality under state socialism were replaced by other pathological effects. Together with corrections of the previous dominance of collectivist arrangements and long-term organizational rationality (Figure 6.1: Area 2), the reforms brought about the dominance of individual and short-term rationality (Area 3). This is a new deviation from the optimal balance of rationalities (Area 1, circle). A desirable move towards the balance of rationalities is indicated by the arrow in Area 3:

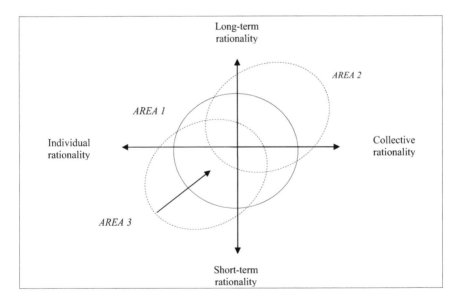

Figure 6.1 Current status of organizational rationality in Eastern Europe

When going through the controversial reforms, East Europeans learned that achieving and maintaining societal integration is the responsibility of all social players. They all have to adjust their methods and techniques of steering to the new conditions of private economy, competitive democratic politics and pluralistic culture. The task is difficult because strategic interests have to be defined and represented in conditions of weak states and changing social structures. The conclusion is that the stabilization of state institutions is the key to the gradual resolution of the accumulated economic, political and social tensions. The key issue in Eastern Europe, in Latin America (Sojo 2003: 397f.) and worldwide is the rapidly growing complexity of the tasks to be accomplished by state institutions and other actors in the political game. This is the reason why there is a widespread belief that the traditional hierarchically organized state *government* has to be replaced by modes of *governance* coming about through the interaction of actors from the public and private sectors, together with actors from the third sector. This interaction is expected to bring about a more efficient and humane handling of social structures and processes. However, *governance* bears the potential of bringing about new social pathologies by over-representing or under-representing group interests. The Eastern European experience leads to the more general conclusion that *government* and *governance* should go hand in hand. In the case that this balance is disturbed, it is the stabilization of the state, which should have priority. However, the crucial practical issue is different: For who is or would the stabilization of the state and the implementation of efficient state policies be favorable? The developments in Eastern Europe strengthen the argument that the transformations in the region favored rather small segments of society. In addition, instead of a dispersion of power among polyarchic structures, the transformations brought about new concentrations of power and privileges.

The contradictions and pathologies of the organizational rationalization of Eastern European economic and political life are indicative for similar processes on the global scale. The background of the worldwide economic crisis is the same distortion in the balance of rationalities which was identified in Area 3 (Figure 6.1). The overcoming of these organizational irrationalities requires *practical utopias* to be taken as goals by a variety of socially responsible actors in the decades to come. Since the historical situation is multidimensional, the issue of state organized solidarity deserves a particularly close attention. The rationalization of solidarity came about in Eastern Europe with many deviations from the optimal path of development and with tremendous social costs. Some of them are due to the effects of *rationalization trap*. The phenomenon is related to the efforts to manage problems in Eastern Europe by developing and applying radical reforms with inadequate financial backing.

The desirable effect of the reforms is the mutual re-enforcement of *social* and *economic policy*. In this area Eastern European societies face complicated organizational dilemmas. The *free rider* dilemma is particularly complicated since it shows many modalities of the use of benefits by people or groups who do not contribute to the common good. The dilemma makes obvious the need to upgrade the rationality of the state organized solidarity and its control mechanisms. More specifically, the major practical task now concerns the possibility to coordinate the mutual obligations of the state and the private sector in designing and implementing an efficient social policy.

As a result of the democratic political reforms there are no legal or administrative obstacles in the way of the development of an active and responsible civil society. The question now is how to organize the interaction between state institutions and civil society in the most efficient way so as to jointly implement efficient social policies. Civil society throughout the region is still too weak to play the role of a respected partner for state institutions and business actors or to be a control mechanism in their interplay. Moreover, civil society itself thrives on confrontations between political forces, which still have to learn the principles and mechanisms of the modern *win-win* political play. Since the role of the state is crucially important in this respect, local and global processes as well as the requirements of the European integration exert a strong pressure to increase *the procedural efficiency of the state administration.* The experience of advanced democratic societies demonstrates that the rationalization of the state administration is a permanent task.

The adjustment to global economic and political processes was facilitated in Eastern Europe to a great extent by cooperation with companies and governments from member states of the European Union or with institutions of the Union itself. The rationalizing effects of this interaction are manifold. They reach from the changing patterns of companies' organization through the spread of the culture of negotiations and respect of universal human rights. The East European adjustment to the global requirements for efficiency of economy, politics and culture was significantly accelerated by the preparation of countries from the former Eastern European region for membership in the European Union. The very prospect for the eastward enlargement of the Union and the negotiations for membership used to set a massive agenda for institutional changes. They proved to be a powerful mobilizing and disciplining factor in the East European transformations.

The international powers exert their rationalizing impact on the region through local political elites. They readily take this function of intermediates since the foreign patronage strengthens their local positions. There are numerous cases of local dominance exerted by political groupings primarily because they are implementing agencies of foreign interests. The prospects and effects of this interplay of interests are uncertain. Due to their weak position in the global economy and politics, the East European societies will continue to depend on the outcomes of the competition between powerful global players, as it has often been the case in modern history.

Eastern European societies continue testing their options for adaptation of organizational structures to the new domestic and global institutional environment. In most cases the efforts remained so far confined to the realm of *defensive adaptation.* The attempted or implemented institutional transfers are *reproductive,* which implies a high probability of a loosing strategy in the long run. Truly *authentic organizational innovations* are rarities in Eastern Europe if identifiable indeed. This development raises the question about the long-term efficiency of the changes given the dominance of defensive and reproductive adaptations and the missed opportunities for innovative adaptations to the global trend of upgrading organizational rationality.

Individualization accompanied all efforts to rationalize organizations in Eastern Europe. In some cases individualization followed patterns already established in state socialism. The structural changes in economy and politics offered new opportunities for individualization deviating from the ideological and institutional predominance of collective rationality and common good in state socialism. (Słomczyński and Szabad 2000) The interplay of continuities and change brought about controversial developments. While the social organization of state socialism used to neglect the need to tolerate and properly remunerate the rationality of individuals, the rapid individualization in Eastern Europe often came about at the expense of collective rationality. Thus, *the extremes of collective rationality were replaced by extremes of individual rationality.* Both configurations in social interaction are unstable. The related theoretical and practical problems concern the possibility and necessity to develop and stabilize the evolutionary achievements of individualization and to reduce its effects in undermining the rationality of collective actors.

The theoretical tradition offers abundant arguments supporting the view that a stable social order cannot be established and maintained on the basis of value-normative assumptions and institutional arrangements of extreme individualism. The crime wave which flooded Eastern Europe during the nineties provided strong evidence for this point. A major explanatory strategy links the rise of crime to the rapid rise of personal expectations at the beginning of the changes. These expectations became widespread while the massive reduction of practical opportunities for personal development and realization dominated the social situation due to the deepening economic differentiation. This disparity between rising expectations and diminishing resources to meet them became the major factor for the criminalization of life in the post-socialist societies. Another factor determining this development was the spontaneous or intentional weakening of crucial state institutions, the legal system included.

It was exactly this intentional or unintentional weakening of state institutions which made still another paradoxical development possible. The triumph of individualization in Eastern Europe came about not by enlargement and enrichment of the common good of commonly accessible green territories, improving education, increasingly affordable health care, etc. To the contrary, in the course of the privatization of state and communal property *individualization typically came about in Eastern Europe at the expense of the common good* at least temporarily. Due to the use of manipulative techniques, the state-socialist productive "property of all people" became the property of few. The desirable dispersion of opportunities for high quality education and medical treatment came about only partly true due to the concentration of opportunities in the hands of individuals who managed to accumulate financial resources.

One has to refresh the memory about the expectations which dominated the first months of the profound changes in order to identify other discrepancies in the East European individualization. In the beginning of the reforms the desire to overcome the underdevelopment of high technologies was widespread in the region. Behind this desire lurked the understandable wish to join the advanced societies in individualization in high quality jobs to more individuals involved in research, development and application of high technologies. The transfer *of high tech products* to Eastern Europe came about – but *at the expense of the local research, development and production of high technologies*. Eastern Europeans are practically excluded from these activities in the global division of labor and thus from the most desirable scenarios for individualization.

Numerous options for individualization in entrepreneurial activities appeared in Eastern Europe. Some of them were really materialized. However, the few success stories in economic activity came about in the context of the impoverishment of millions. These victims of the transformation were isolated from chances for development and realization. The expected flourishing of grass roots democracy did not materialize indeed. Instead, the established representative democracies foster political alienation. Individualization in the culture of democratic tolerance is still very much desirable in East European societies. Some of them experienced tragic interethnic and interreligious clashes. Others are going through periods of resurgence of collectivist nationalisms which typically require restrictions of social spaces for individualization of representatives of ethnic and religious minority groups.

The trend towards individualization has certainly no alternative but it has controversial effects. The destructive ones can be put under control by using the mechanisms of communitarian solidarity. If individualization would continue to clash communitarian solidarity with the same intensity, this will reproduce the uncertainties concerning the future of the societies in the region.

The evolutionary universals of a market economy had been suppressed in Eastern Europe for decades. Their institutional re-establishment was part and parcel of the overall normalization of social relations and processes in the region. This implies the full-scale adaptation to the global trend of *instrumental activism*. However, the normalization itself is full of tensions requiring careful conceptualizations. In pragmatic terms, the expected and very much desirable technological modernization of production came about in Eastern Europe mostly in enterprises that were acquired or constructed by financially sound investors from Western Europe and North America. But the research and development capacities of the investors typically remained with their headquarters. Most research and development institutes in Eastern Europe were closed or continued to function by being chronically under-funded. The historical experience is quite telling in this respect: *Only economies that are supported by genuine research and development can be internationally competitive in the long run.* Otherwise they are doomed to imitate successes of others and thus to be losers. This is a crucial dilemma the East European societies are confronted with.

This dilemma is particularly relevant considering the dynamics of the international division of labor. After 2000 most East European societies have achieved substantial economic growth. It was mostly due to the opening of their economies to competitive markets. However, China and Vietnam achieved higher economic growth during the period under scrutiny. This is a serious reason to examine the aims, means and effects of the transformations in the former socialist societies in comparative terms. The data concerning the international competitiveness of the East European societies show that they occupied, with very few exceptions, the bottom of the European rankings. According to this crucial parameter, they are worse off than many national economies in Asia and Latin America.

The Eastern European national cases of re-orientation to market economy raise a series of issues with a high theoretical relevance. Major constraints and tensions of Eastern European transformations are related to the difficult balance between autonomous and instrumental values. One may interpret the East European transformations as a step towards bringing autonomous and instrumental values closer together by means of market mechanisms. However, market activity is instrumental in principle. This is already a signal for theoretical and practical concerns since *there can be no stable social order based on the strong predominance of instrumental values*. The rapid commercialization of social life brought about alienation and critically undermined the ultimate values of solidarity and social justice.

The ensuing problems are closely related to the tension between *short-term* and *long-term* rationality in the post-socialist transformations. Contrary to widespread expectations, the re-introduction of market mechanisms did not immediately provoke an enlargement of the time horizon in everyday life. Both the institutional instability and the cultural disorientations contributed to *shortening of the time horizon* of orientations, decisions and actions of large groups in Eastern Europe. However, *no social order can be stable if action orientations are predominantly focused on short-term goals*. This metamorphosis of social time perception and the concomitant social pathologies offer a broad area for sociological theorizing and for enlightening empirical studies.

This is not an issue which concerns East European societies alone. The global short-term market activities brought about long-term global destructive effects of economic crises and climate change. Particularly the last issue and the difficulties in handling it at the global political level revealed the dangers of the radical value-normative orientation and policies focused on instrumental *Weltbeherrschung* as Max Weber called the phenomenon. Sociological conceptualizations and empirical studies on environmental imbalances, forms of social isolation and marginalization undermining social solidarity and integration may be helpful in illuminating various traps of the instrumental activity.

The spread of private entrepreneurship is the major incorporation of instrumental activity which poses some other problems. Private entrepreneurs often operate in Eastern Europe *on the edge of what is legally allowed and what is criminal or semi-criminal activity*. This can hardly be a good omen for societal integration and sustainability in institutional and value-normative terms. The growing economic differentiation *within* societies and *between* societies provides the evidence that market activities do not produce and reproduce social cohesion by themselves. They might undermine social cohesion in the long run. The open Eastern European economies cannot rely on state protectionism to alleviate these negative effects of market processes on social cohesion. The undermining of social cohesion by means of progressing differentiation of property and income *cannot be a good premise for sustainable social development of the post-socialist societies*.

Thus, the painful recent experience gives reasons to reconsider the paths of societal development. Whatever the specific visions and practical projects, they should be focused on the search for a balance between strategic value-oriented aims and instrumental tactical decisions. This is needed in order to achieve higher standards of social justice as a condition for sustainable development. (Organizing for Social Justice 2004) The coordination of interests related to the common good and to particularistic preferences cannot be a task to be resolved once and for all in a national setting. It is another permanent task. Still another difficult task is to keep the democratic responsibility of citizens alive by encouraging active political participation. The resolution of this task implies efforts to reduce institutional obstacles to citizens' involvement in the preparation, implementation and control of political decisions.

Given the experience from the current global crisis it should be taken for granted that the desirable market equilibriums cannot be achieved and maintained without various forms of political regulation. Attention should be paid to the purposeful selection of economic priorities. They are always related to powerful interests. They might be rather contradictory. Therefore, the economic stabilization in Eastern European societies does not necessarily imply a social integration which would allow for the sustainability of social development. Given the complexity of the issues connected with development, every step of further reforms should be very carefully thought out. The states in the region are in debt to their citizens regarding the clarity about the direction, content and timing of economic reforms. They also owe the citizens much in terms of the efficiency of the transformation management. This is one of the major reasons for the popular dissatisfaction with the course of the reforms. The most challenging question concerns the state once more: *How should the East European states intervene efficiently in the economy in order to stabilize social integration and to improve the quality of life, as expected at the beginning of the reforms?*

This very formulation contradicts the strategy and practice of an all-pervasive commercialization. It might be conducive to short-term economic effects but turns into an obstacle in the way of the long-term efforts to achieve sustainable development. It can be only materialized on the basis of ultimate values referring to the common good. The crucial point is how to achieve this desirable effect without stifling the innovative potential animated by instrumental activism.

The disappearance of political barriers isolating Eastern Europe cleared the way for the *universalization of value-normative systems* in the region. The new constitutional arrangements are based on the idea of universal human rights and on the universal requirements of sustainability. The institutional implementation of both universal principles meets the resistance of local circumstances. The crucial problems are related to various forms of *social disintegration*. They are due to the economic and social marginalization of unemployed and impoverished people. The economic differentiation took strong ethnic features. They might have explosive consequences in the long run.

The rapid structural changes gave some legacy to the diverging remuneration of achievements thus supporting the principles of meritocracy. However, East Europeans had innumerable occasions to notice that the economic and social differentiation did not come about in the wake of different achievements but due to networking and robbery. This experience undermines the cultural basis of social cohesion and thus of economic, political and cultural sustainability. Sustainable social development *cannot be achieved and maintained on the basis of diverging particularistic values.*

The new social and economic differentiation has sobering implications for the desired value-normative integration of Eastern European societies. One may expect not integration but the thriving of value-normative particularisms due to differentiation in the division of labor, to specification of economic and political interests and even to preferences concerning leisure time. All these traditional or new differences bring about and sustain "tribal" affiliations which undermine the universalization of value-normative systems. The East European societies are not an exception in the global cultural context. But the ongoing stabilization of the new value-normative system comes about on the basis of still changing social structures. This makes the probability for the appearance of personal or group identities questioning value-normative universalization or directly universal human rights, social cohesion and the value-normative integration of societies pretty high. The East European societies will most probably continue *to be prone to effects of unstable multiple identities and to political, ethnic and religious intolerance.*

The progressing functional differentiation has undermined the relevance of commonly shared values and norms. However, societies cannot function without a value-normative consensus concerning the means, ends, procedures and outcomes of action in their context. Given the various economic, political and cultural divisions, it seems that some kind of *civil religion* could take the lead in stabilizing the consensual foundations of interactions. But the prospects of the civil (secularized) religion based on the concept of universal human rights are not necessarily optimistic in Eastern Europe. Unemployment and poverty are major stumbling blocks facing the process. Old and new ideological, ethnic and religious confrontations strengthen the trends towards value-normative disintegration. The development of new identities of belonging to an increasingly integrated Europe might tangibly improve the chances of value-normative integration in Eastern Europe. The process cannot be accomplished overnight. Eastern Europe is currently divided by new boundaries and the processes might take different directions and speeds in the particular post-socialist countries or groups of countries.

6.3 Inspiring Times for Social Sciences

The controversial adaptation of Eastern European societies to global trends signals scientific and practical challenges. Some of them refer to the famous "debate on positivism in German sociology" about the causes, mechanisms, processes and effects of social development (Adorno et al. 1976 [1969]). The abundant misunderstandings and polemical extremes notwithstanding, the alternative positions were transparent enough. The "critical theorists" represented by Theodor Adorno opted for a total change of societies, while the liberal "critical rationalists" represented by Karl Popper regarded this type of change as not rationally manageable and therefore too costly in social terms. Consequently, they opted for piecemeal social engineering.

The debate was about the prospects of profound changes in Western Europe. They did not take place there but in Eastern Europe. Neo-liberals preoccupied with ideas of Milton Friedman were numerous and ready to advise the Eastern European reformers. However, their agenda was strikingly different from the cautious liberal piecemeal engineering of Popper. Neoliberals like Jeffrey Sachs campaigned for fast and profound big-bang change. It failed in Poland and in Russia. In other countries the strategies for change had to overcome tremendous cognitive and practical challenges or turned into simple opportunistic improvisations.

This experience is sobering. The tremendous advances in social scientific knowledge after the Second World War notwithstanding, it became obvious at the beginning of the nineties how limited the knowledge about profound social change still was. The nebulous concept of transition to market economy and democratic politics could be only a disappointing solution. The more systematic concept of societal transformation had to be elaborated in the course of the reform process. This could be done on the basis of the concept of a societal system. At this point of theoretical elaborations it became clear that the Popperian piecemeal approach was not adequate for guiding systematic descriptions and explanations and even less in guiding social action. The holistic vision of societal change advocated by the critical theory of society seemed to be more suitable as an explanatory and action-guiding scheme. But it became also obvious that the focus on internal processes in societal systems was a strong theoretical limitation in the context of the ongoing globalization. The "methodological nationalism" had to be abundant. The interpretation of the Eastern European societal transformations as *opening to global trends* was already on the intellectual agenda.

One might assume that the regional adaptation to global trends would unavoidably bring about homogenization of social relationships and processes. In fact, national technological standards in Eastern Europe were adapted to global standards for the use of raw materials, energy and for security of industrial output. The re-building of the national finance sectors followed internationally valid criteria for the distribution of responsibilities and economic efficiency. The value-normative systems of all societies in the region developed in the same direction of focusing on universal human rights. However, the changes also included accelerated differentiation of action spheres, life styles and life chances in Eastern Europe. Thus, the regional adaptation to the ongoing globalization provokes both homogenization and differentiation of social structures together with harmonization and divergence of interests.

Eastern European societies are especially vulnerable to the ensuing tensions because of the general institutional instability in the region. In addition, a *new type of intransparency* emerged which is not due to authoritarian rule but is mostly caused by the rapid increase of social complexity. (Urry 2003) It is not easy for East Europeans to identify the causes and reasons of the growing complexity and to master it. This is not due to civilizational incapacities alone. More relevant is the fact that global changes are usually initiated not in the region of Eastern Europe and cannot be mastered in the region autonomously. The explanation is simple: The region belongs to the continental periphery and in the best case to the global semi-periphery. Tremendous efforts were made in the region after the Second World War in order to get rid of this traditional second rate position by means of accelerated industrialization. The privatization after 1989 brought about a fast de-industrialization. The technological innovations were decelerated as a rule or put on ice. Progressive branches of industry like electronics are among the losers of the transformation.

As a result, *currently Eastern Europe is anew in the peripheral position in which it has been for centuries*. The participation of the region in the international division of labor follows the well established traditional patterns. Some rather limited areas did already join or are about to join the "global city" by means of a rapid modernization of the productive infrastructure and by creating high quality work places. Much larger areas have already joined the "global village" by concentrating on low quality jobs mostly in the extracting industry. The open question is, if political will could be strong enough in order to ameliorate these differences under the conditions of global competition and different national interests? Diverging scenarios about the technological future of Eastern Europe might be possible.

The adjustment of Eastern Europe to the rapidly evolving global commercialization is powerfully influenced by trans-boundary financial flows. The major institutional forces behind this process are the World Trade Organization, the International Monetary Fund and the World Bank. The strategic direction of their activities is monetary stabilization. This is the explanation both for the successes in this direction as well as for the serious handicaps facing the efforts to stabilize *and* foster the development of production and trade in Eastern Europe. Consequently, although to various degrees, practically all East European societies depend on loans from abroad. The situation could not be different since their domestic capacities to accumulate capital are still rather limited. However, there is a major problem with financing from abroad. Only a segment of it is really made up of long-term direct investments. As it is the case throughout the world, the major part consists of fluctuating short-term financial capital. It tends to disappear in the moment the economic and political situation is no more conducive to the attainment of fast and substantial profits.

The crux of the matter is the difference between the capacity of the strong national economies and huge multinationals to cope with the global challenges successfully while the small, capital poor and politically unstable national economies are much more vulnerable to the challenges. Since most Eastern European societies belong to this latter category, they are permanently facing the danger to become easy prey for speculative fluctuations of capital. The current financial and economic crisis provided evidence that the Eastern European countries are particularly vulnerable to capital fluctuations because they cannot rely on the support of their banking sector in managing the national economy. In most Eastern European countries the majority of the banking capital belongs to foreign banks which might have rather different interests and agendas than to support the local national economies.

This last point raises the issue of the roles of states under the conditions of a rather imperfect market economy in the region. With regard to this painful experience East Europeans had to learn that the integrative function of the state is of crucial relevance. The task is to adjust the methods and techniques of societal management by the state to the new conditions of the privatization of economy and the pluralization of culture. Moreover, in view of the serious problems with unemployment all over the region and together with the new international constellation the major task consists in keeping the small state administrations strong in terms of organizational efficiency.

Together with the stabilization of values and norms which are based on the universal visions of human rights and sustainability there are also manifold deviations from these value-normative principles in the region. The deviations are mostly related to nationalism. It is the outcome of the continuing social-structural and value-normative instability in the region. The most relevant reason of this instability is the widespread downward mobility and the stabilization of large groups at the low levels of the stratification scale. This type of mobility strengthens the readiness to confront precarious social situations with particularistic patterns of thinking and behavior. This is the fertile soil of nationalism and political and religious extremism as alternatives to the universalization of value-normative systems. Another dangerous option is the far reaching devaluation of values and norms. It brings about and sustains social anomie. The promising perspective is only the stable economic development based on the assumption that only initiatives and responsibility which are guided by moral and legal rules are worth to be pursued. Another potential stabilizing factor is the understanding that active participation in politics is meaningful. Because of various circumstances both perspectives are questioned by large strata in Eastern Europe.

The value-normative instability is due to diverging views about the way in which both efficiency and justice could be key ingredients of the desirable social order. The commonly shared magic rule still is: This could be achieved by means of a permanent reference to competition. A just society should not be identified with the strong re-distributive functions of the state alone. To the contrary, everybody has to be allotted maximum free space for initiative and responsibility and everybody has to be rewarded according to the real achievement. This seems to be the principle of justice, which is jointly rooted in competition and achievement. This pattern of societal organization is well known but had to be re-invented by the East Europeans in their own practice. Later it became gradually clear that the individualism and liberalism of the "American model" of an achievement based society are not identical with the statism and egalitarianism of the "Swedish model" of an achievement based society. It became also clear that there are different forms of a meritocratic social order. A wide variety of criteria for efficiency and justice in the developed West European and North American societies was identified.

Local and international processes contributed to the differentiation of the group of Eastern European countries which had basically similar characteristics at the start of the transformation. Now each of them appears differently in the international competition. The differences will most probably deepen. Some of the countries from the region are going to join the club of the rich and stably functioning West European societies. Other countries will continue to reproduce organizational and behavioral patterns of "chaotic capitalism." (Kivinen 2002)

It is exactly under these precarious conditions that the search for well founded knowledge as guidance for action intensifies. Is the management of the Eastern European transformations really evolving in the direction of a knowledge-based decision-making and practical management of social processes? Social sciences were often attacked for not having predicted the dramatic turn of European and world history in 1989. The accusations generally apply to politicians, journalists and secret services as well. The real issue is not to blame specific institutions or professional groups for their failures in predicting or managing transformations. More important is the need to learn from this experience and to develop efficient tools which might help to explain and manage the continuing transformations. What are the implications herein for the social sciences?

Their heterogeneity and controversies notwithstanding, social sciences have already enough substance and cohesion. However, there is the permanent need to reconsider concepts and research approaches due to the changes in social reality. Thus, the relative importance of basic concepts varies. Therefore, social scientific studies might lead to diverging practical implications according to circumstances in social development. Being constructive or destructive, continuous or discontinuous, development is the most visible and the most complicated characteristic of social reality. However, social development often resists efforts for systematic explanation and rational management. This is true because of the complexity of causes and reasons bringing about and sustaining development at the various structural levels of social reality. Moreover, social reality offers many opportunities for "butterfly effects". They make profound processes possible due to rather small initial changes. Moreover, the "butterfly" function in social reality can be performed by factors absent in nature such as knowledge and emotions, will and the interests of people.

In addition to the need for explanatory conceptualizations, there is another need to permanently elaborate on the operationalizations of the conceptual framework for research on social dynamics. The ultimate aim is to increase the sensitivity of concepts to changes in social reality. However, this does not mean a preference to "sensitizing concepts" but to operationalizations of relatively stable conceptual schemes. This is the promising perspective for a timely recognition of the appearance of new social structures and new social actors.

This is the condition for strengthening the practical relevance of sociology by increasing its capacity to serve the cognitive needs of the emerging knowledge-based society. We witness a strong trend towards the pluralization of theoretical paradigms in sociology together with the substantial enlargement in the field of the structures and processes studied. The strong thematic orientation of sociology towards risk research has strengthened the need to conceptualize the dynamic relations between sociological cognition and its involvement in the resolution of practical problems. New patterns of intensive involvement of Eastern European sociologists in public opinion polls and marketing research came about. They resulted in sociological research having an immediate practical influence. On the other hand, the strong market orientation of these studies contributed to widespread doubts about their theoretical substance and about the academic objectivity of sociologists.

In the context of these controversial processes some conditions for further sociological conceptualizations seem to be relevant:

- *First*, the thematic orientation of sociological conceptualizations and empirical research should be increasingly focused on the connection between national transformations and trends of global social development.
- *Second*, in order to resolve this task, sociologists need to have more intensive cooperation with colleagues from other social scientific disciplines.
- *Third*, this means that conceptualizations serving transnational comparative studies will need to have priority.
- *Fourth*, elaboration of systematic and well operationalizable conceptual frameworks for the comparative study of social development is needed.
- *Fifth*, given the trends of pluralism and eclecticism, a substantial effort of reflexive theory construction is needed which refers to the sociological tradition, to intellectual developments in related sciences, to changes in social life, and to potential cognitive and practical results.

The implementation of this program for theorizing and research on transformation processes presupposes interdisciplinarity, cross-paradigmatic interactions and a cross-fertilization of theoretical and empirical research. This is the promising way to develop social sciences having a clear cognitive value and being able to guide the practical management of social transformations as a special case of social development in the context of global trends.

Bibliography

5 Years Poland in the European Union (2009) Warsaw: Committee for European Integration.

Adam, F., M. Makarovič, B. Rončević and M. Tomšič (2005) *The Challenges of Sustained Development: The Role of Socio-cultural Factors in East-Central Europe.* Budapest and New York: CEU Press.

Adamski, W.W., J. Buncak, P. Machonin and D. Martin (eds) (1999) *System Change and Modernization. East-West in Comparative Perspective.* Warsaw: IfiS Publishers.

Adorno, T.W. et al. (1976 [1969]) *The Positivist Dispute in German Sociology.* London: Heinemann.

Agh, A. (2001) 'Early Consolidation and Performance Crisis: The Majoritarian-Consensus Democracy Debate in Hungary'. *West European Politics,* Vol. 24, No 3, July, pp. 89–112.

Agh, A. (2007) 'Bumpy Road ahead in East Central Europe: Post-accession Crisis and Social Challenge in ECE'. In: Agh, Attila and Alexandra Ferencz (eds) *Overcoming the EU Crisis: EU Perspectives after the Eastern Enlargement.* Budapest: Together for Europe, pp. 7–38.

Agh, A. (2008) 'Hungarian Politics in the Early 21st Century: Reforms and Post-EU Accession Crisis'. *Südosteuropa-Mitteilungen,* No 3, pp. 68–81.

Alber, J. and W. Merkel (eds) (2005) *Europas Osterweiterung: Das Ende der Vertiefung?* Berlin: Sigma.

Albert, A. (ed.) (1995) *Chaos and Society.* Amsterdam and Washington, DC: IOS Press.

Albritton, R., R. Jessop and R. Westra (2007) *Political Economy and Global Capitalism.* London and New York: Anthem Press.

Albrow, M. (2004) 'The Global Shift and Its Consequences for Sociology'. In: Genov, Nikolai. (ed.) *Advances in Sociological Knowledge.* Wiesbaden: Verlag für Sozialwissenschaften, pp. 33–51.

Alic, A. (2008) 'Bosnia and Herzegovina: Teaching Intolerance'. *Transitions Online,* http://www.soros.org/initiatives/esp/articles_publications/articles/bosnia_20080603.

Althanns, L. (2009) *McLenin. Die Konsumrevolution in Russland.* Bielefeld: Transcript-Verlag.

Altvater, E. and B. Mahnkopf (2007) *Grenzen der Globalisierung: Ökonomie, Ökologie und Politik in der Weltgesellschaft.* Münster: Westfälisches Dampfboot.

Andorka, R. and T. Kolosi (eds) (1984) *Stratification and Inequalities*. Budapest: Institute of Social Sciences.

Aref A.N. (2006) *A Muslim's Commentary on Benedict XVI's "Faith, Reason and the University: Memories and Reflections"*. http://www.masud.co.uk/ISLAM/misc/commentary_on_benedict.php.

Åslund, A. (2004) 'Revolution, Red Directors and Oligarchs in Ukraine'. *The Ukrainian Quarterly*, No 1–2, pp. 5–18.

Åslund, A. (2007) *How Capitalism Was Built*. Cambridge and New York: Cambridge University Press.

Augustine (1993) *On Free Choice of the Will*. Indianapolis: Hackett Publishing.

Avoiding the Dependency Trap. The Roma in Central and Eastern Europe (2002) Bratislava: UNDP.

Barber, B. (2007) *Con$umed: How Markets Corrupt Children, Infantilize Adults and Swallow Citizens*. New York: Norton.

Bassuener, K. (2009) *How to Pull Out of Bosnia-Herzegovina's Dead-End: A Strategy for Success*. http://democratizationpolicy.org/wp-content/uploads/2009/02/dpc-policy-brief-how-to-pull-out-of-bosnia-and-herzegovinas-dead-end-2-20-09.pdf (19.02.2009).

Bauman, Z. (2004) *Community. Seeking Safety in an Insecure World*. Cambridge: Polity.

Beck, U. (2007) *Weltrisikogesellschaft: auf der Suche nach der verlorenen Sicherheit*. Frankfurt/Main: Suhrkamp.

Beck, U. (2009) *Macht und Gegenmacht im globalen Zeitalter*. Frankfurt/Main: Suhrkamp.

Beck, U. and E. Beck-Gernsheim (2002) *Individualization: Institutionalized Individualism and Its Social and Political Consequences*. London and Thousand Oaks, Calif.: SAGE.

Bell, D. (1976) *The Cultural Contradictions of Capitalism*. New York: Basic Books.

Berend, I.T. (ed.) (1997) *Long-Term Structural Changes in Transforming Central & Eastern Europe (The 1990s)*. München: Südosteuropa-Gesellschaft.

Berger, P.L. (2005) 'Global Pluralism and Religion'. *Estudios Publicos*, Vol. 98, autumn.

Bertelsmann Transformation Index 2008 (2008) Gütersloh: Bertelsmann Stiftung.

Blasi, J.R., M. Kroumova and D. Kruse (1997) *Kremlin Capitalism: The Privatization of the Russian Economy*. Ithaca, New York: ILR Press.

Bogaevskaya, A.N. (2005) 'Ot upravleniya socialističeskimi predpriyatiyami k menedžmentu v rynočnoy ekonomike' [From the Government of Socialist Enterprises towards the Management in Market Economy]. In: Yadov, V.A. (ed.) *Social'nye transformacii v Rossii* [Social Transformations in Russia]. Moskva: Flinta, pp. 113–150.

Bömer, J. and M. Viëtor (eds) (2007) *Osteuropa heute: Entwicklungen – Gemeinsamkeiten – Unterschiede*. Münster: LIT.

Bönker, F., K. Müller and A. Pickel (eds) (2002) *Postcommunist Transformation and the Social Sciences. Cross-disciplinary Approaches.* Lanham etc: Rowman & Littlefield.

Borghesi, S. and A. Vercelli (2008) *Global Sustainability: Social and Environmental Conditions.* Basingstock and New York: Palgrave Macmillan.

Bornschier, V. (2008) *Weltgesellschaft. Grundlegende soziale Wandlungen.* Münster: LIT.

Borowik, I. (ed.) (2006) *Religions, Churches and Religiosity in Post-communist Europe.* Krakow: Nomos.

Bourdieu, P. and L. Wacquant (1999) 'On the Cunning of Imperialist Reason'. *Theory, Culture and Society*, Vol. 16, 1, pp.41-58.

Brzezinski, Z. (1989) The Great Failure: The Birth and Death of Communism in the Twentieth Century. New York: Scribner.

Burnes, B. (2009) *Managing Change: A Strategic Approach to Organisational Dynamics.* New York: Prentice Hall and Financial Times.

Castels, M. (1999) *End of Millenium.* Oxford and Malden, Mass.: Blackwell.

Cenckiewicz, S. and P. Gontarczyk (2008) *SB a Lech Wałęsa: przyczynek do biografii* [Security Service and Lech Wałęsa: An Attempt at Biography]. Gdańsk: Instytut Pamięci Narodowej.

CBOS (2005) *Bulletin*, N 1.

Chilcote, R.H. (ed.) (2003) *Development in Theory and Practice: Latin American Perspectives.* Lanham, Md.: Rowman & Littlefield.

Chmelnizki, D. (2007) *Die Architektur Stalins.* Stuttgart: Ibidem.

Chmielewski, P. (2007) 'Crises and Crisis Management in Transitional Poland: New Institutional Perspective'.*Transformacje. Special Issue on Crises and Sustainability*, pp. 111–121.

Chernyshevsky, N. (1989 [1863]) *What Is To Be Done?* Ithaca: Cornell University Press.

Collste, G. (2005) 'Is Religious Pluralism Possible?' In: Collste, Göran. (ed.) *Possibilities of Religious Pluralism.* Linköping: Linköping University Press, pp. 48–61.

Colton, T.J. (2008) *Yeltsin: A Life.* New York: Basic Books.

Dahl, R.A. (1998) *On Democracy.* New Haven: Yale University Press.

Dahrendorf, R. (1990) *Reflections on the Revolution in Europe.* London: Chatto Windus.

Derczynski, W. (2004) *Postrzeganie swego miejsca w strukturze społeczmej. awanse i degradacje* [Perception of the Own Position in the Social Structure: Advancements and Degradation]. Warszawa: CBOS. BS 147.

Deutscher, I. (2005) *Preventing Ethnic Conflict.* Lanham etc.: Lexington Books.

Dmitrieva, M. (2006) 'Moscow's Architecture between Stalinism and Modernism'. *International Review of Sociology*, Vol. 16. N 2, pp. 427–450.

Dobroczyński M. (ed.) (2001) *Europa Wschodnia w obliczu integracji i globalizacji* [Eastern Europe Facing Integration and Globalization] Warszawa: Wydawnictwa Naukowe Wydziału Zarządzania Uniwersytetu Warszawskiego.

Domański H., Rychard A. (1997). "Wprowadzenie. Dekompozycja – chaos – procesy restrukturyzacji", [Introduction. Decomposition – Chaos – Process of Restructuration], in: H. Domański, A. Rychard (eds), *Elementy nowego ładu*, [Elements of the New Order] Warszawa: IFIS PAN, pp. 7–29.

Drahokoupil, J. (2009) *Globalization and the State in Central and Eastern Europe: The Politics of Foreign Direct Investment.* London and New York: Routledge.

Durkheim, E. (1968 [1915]) *The Elementary Forms of the Religious Life.* London: George Allen & Unwin.

Early Warning Report September 2008 (2008) Sarajevo: UNDP Bosnia and Herzegovina.

Eastham, S. (2009) *Biotech Time-bomb: The Side Effects Are the Main Effects.* Crelskill, NJ: Hampon Press.

Ebbinghaus, A. (ed.) (2008) *Das Jahr 1968 aus der Perspektive der Gesellschaften Mittel-, Ostt- und Südosteuropas.* Hamburg: VSA-Verlag

EBRD 2009a http://www.ebrd.com/country/sector/econo/stats/mptfdi.xls

EBRD 2009b http://www.ebrd.com/country/sector/econo/stats/sei.xls

Eckert, F. (2008) *Vom Plan zum Markt: Parteipolitik und Privatisierungsprozesse in Osteuropa.* Wiesbaden: Verlag für Sozialwissenschaften.

Eliaeson, S. (ed.) (2006) *Building Democracy and Civil Society East of the Elbe.* London and New York: Routledge.

Ehrke, M. (ed.) (2009) *Die globale Krise und die europäische Peripherie. Ein Blick aus Zentral- und Südosteuropa.* Berlin: FES.

Eliaeson, S. and N. Georgieva (eds) (2010) *New Europe: Growth to Limits?* Gumnor, Oxford: Bardwell Press.

Ellerman, D. (1998) *Voucher Privatization with Investment Fonds: An Institutional Analysis.* Washington, DC: World Bank.

Eringer, R. (1982) *Strike for Freedom!: The Story of Lech Walesa and Polish Solidarity.* New York: Dodd.

Etzioni, A. (1996) 'The Responsive Community: A Communitarian Perspective'. *American Sociological Review*, Vol. 61, N 1, February, pp. 1–11.

Etzioni, A. (2004) *The Common Good.* Cambridge and Malden, Mass.: Polity.

Eurobarometer 70 (2008) http://ec.europa.eu/public_opinion/archives/eb/eb70/eb70_annex.pdf.

Eurostat 2006 http://epp.eurostat.ec.europa.eu/tgm/table.do?tab=table&init=1&plugin=1&language=en&pcode=tsiir160.

A Fair Globalization: Creating Opportunities for All (2004) Geneva: ILO.

Faist, T. (2009) 'The Transnational Social Question. Social Rights and Citizenship in a Global Context'. *International Sociology,* Vol. 24, N 1, pp. 7–35.

Flader, D. and S. Comati (2008) *Kulturschock. Interkulturelle Handlungskonflikte westlicher Unternehmen in Mittelost- und Südosteuropa.* Wiesbaden: Verlag für Sozialwissenschaften.

Friebel, G. and E. Panova (2007) *Insider Privatization and Careers – A Study of a Russian Firm in Transition.* Cambridge, Ma: National Bureau of Economic Research.

Fukuyama, F. (2006) *The End of the History and the Last Man* [with a new afterword]. New York: Free Press.

Galgóczi, B. (2001) 'Twelve Years of Privatisation in Hungary – Drawing Up a Balance Sheet'. *South-East Europe Review*, N 1, pp. 45–54.

Galgóczi, B. (2009) 'Central Eastern Europe Five Years after: From 'Emerging Europe' to ‚Submerging Europe'?'. *ETUI Policy Brief*, N 4.

Gaman-Golutvina, O. (2007) 'Yeltsin, Putin and the Elites'. In: Genov, Nikolai. (ed.) *Soziologische Zeitgeschichte.* pp. 298–299.

Gated and Guarded Housing in Eastern Europe (2009) Leipzig: Leibniz-Institut für Länderkunde.

Gel'man, V. (2010) 'Sackgasse. Autoritäre Modernisierung in Russland'. *Osteuropa*, Bd. 60, N 1, pp. 3–13.

Genov, N. (1991) 'The Transition to Democracy in Eastern Europe: Trends and Paradoxes of Social Rationalization'. *International Social Science Journal*, N 128, pp.131–141.

Genov, N. (1995) 'Sustainable Human Development: Reality and Prospects'. In: Genov, Nikolai (ed.) *Human Development Report Bulgaria 1995.* Sofia: UNDP.

Genov, N. (1997) 'Four Global Trends: Rise and Limitations'. *International Sociology*, N 4, December, pp. 409–428.

Genov, N. (1999) *Managing Transformations in Eastern Europe.* Paris and Sofia: UNESCO/MOST and REGLO.

Genov, N. (2007) 'Gesellschaftliche Transformation als Öffnung zu globalen Trends'. In: Genov, Nikolai and Reinhard Kreckel (eds) *Soziologische Zeitgeschichte.* Berlin: Sigma, pp. 267–286.

Gerber, T.P. and M. Hout (1998) 'More Shock than Therapy: Market Transition, Employment and Income in Russia, 1991–1995'. *American Journal of Sociology*, Vol. 104, No.1, July, pp. 1–50.

The Global Competitiveness Report 2008–2009 (2008) Geneva: World Economic Forum.

The Global Economic Crisis. Systemic Failures and Multilateral Remedies (2009) New York and Genf: UNCTAD.

Goldthorp, J. (2003) 'The Myth of Education-based Meritocracy'. *New Economy*, Vol. 10, N 4, pp. 234–239.

Hamm, B. (2006) *Die soziale Struktur der Globalisierung.* Berlin: Kai Humilius Verlag.

Hasenclever, A. and A. De Juan (2007) ‚Grasping the Impact of Religious Traditions on Political Conflicts'. *Die Friedens-Warte. Journal of International Peace and Organization.* Bd. 82, H.2–3, pp.19–48.

Havel, V. et al. (1985) *The Power of the Powerless: Citizens against the State in Central-eastern Europe*, edited by John Keane. Armonk, N.Y.: M.E. Sharpe.

Havel, V. (2008) *To the Castle and Back.* New York: Vintage Books.

Held, D. et al. (2005) *Debating Globalization.* Cambridge, UK and Malden, MA: Polity.

Horst, A.C. (2007) *International Property Rights Index (IPRI). 2007 Report* (2007) Washington, D.C.: Property Rights Alliance.

Horvat, B., M. Markovic and R. Supek (eds) (1975) *Self-governing Socialism: A Reader.* White Plains, N.Y.: International Arts and Sciences Press.

Howard, C. (ed.) (2007) *Contested Individualization: Debates about Contemporary Personhood.* New York: Palgrave.

Human Development Report (1990) New York and Oxford: Oxford University Press.

Human Development Report 2003 (2003) New York and Oxford: Oxford University Press.

Human Development Report 2007–2008 (2007) New York etc.: Palgrave Macmillan.

Human Development Report 2009 (2009) New York etc.: Palgrave Macmillan.

Human Development Report for Central and Eastern Europe and the CIS 1999 (1999) New York: UNDP.

Huntington, S.P. (1996) *The Clash of Civilizations and the Remaking of World Order.* New York: Simon & Schuster.

Iatridis, D.S. and J.G. Hopps (eds) (1998) *Privatization in Central and Eastern Europe: Perspectives and Approaches.* Westport, CT: Praeger.

Inglehart, R. and C. Welzel (2005) *Modernization, Cultural Change, and Democracy: The Human Development Sequence.* Cambridge and New York: Cambridge University Press, 2005.

Inovatsiite. Evropeyski, regionalni i natsionalni politiki [Innovations. European, Regional and National Politics] (2009) Sofia: Foundation "Applied Research and Communications", pp. 648–679.

Jachtenfluchs, M. and B. Kohler-Koch (2004) 'Governance and Institutional Development'. In: Wiener, Antje and Thomas Diez (eds) *European Integration Theory.* Oxford: Oxford University Press.

Jessop, B. (2002) *The Future of the Capitalist State.* Cambridge: Polity Press.

Joas, H. and K. Wiegandt (eds) (2007) *Säkularisierung und die Weltreligionen.* Frankfurt/Main: Fischer.

Kaelble, H. und G. Schmid. Hg. (2004) *Das europäische Sozialmodell. Auf dem Weg zum transnationalen Sozialstaat.* Berlin: WZB.

Kagan, R. (2007) 'End of Dream, Return of History'. *Policy Review.* August-September, pp. 17–44.

Kalberg, S. (2009) 'Max Weber's Analysis of the Unique American Civic Sphere'. *Journal of Classical Sociology*, Vol. 9, No 1, pp. 117–141.

Kalyuzhnova, Y. and W. Andreff (eds) (2003) *Privatisation and Structural Change in Transition Economies.* Houndmills, Basingstoke, Hampshire and New York: Palgrave Macmillan.

Kates, G. (ed.) (2006) *The French Revolution: Recent Debates and New Controversies.* New York and London: Routledge.

Katzenstein, P.J. (2005) *A World of Regions. Asia and Europe in the American Imperium.* Ithaca and London: Cornell University Press.

Kessler, J. (2009) 'Der Mythos vom globalen Dorf: Zur räumlichen Differenzierung des Globalisierungsniveaus'. In: Kessler, Johannes und Christian Steiner (eds) *Facetten der Globalisierung.* Wiesbaden: Verlag für Sozialwissenschaften, pp. 28–79.

Kivinen, M. (2002) *Progress and Chaos.* Helsinki: Kikimora Publications.

Knox, Z. (2005) *Russian Society and Orthodox Church: Religion in Russia after Communism.* New York: Routledge Curzo.

Konečná, Z. (2006) 'Cross-Culture Management: Worker in Multicultural Environment'. *Vadyba/ Management,* N 3–4, pp. 58–64.

Kopp, A. (1985) *Constructivist Architecture in the USSR.* London: Academy.

Kornai, J. (1992) *The Socialist System: The Political Economy of Communism.* Princeton, N.J.: Princeton University Press.

Kornai, J. (1997) *Struggle and Hope: Essays on Stabilization and Reform in a Post-socialist Economy.* Cheltenham, UK; Northampton, Mass., USA: E. Elgar.

Kreckel, R. (2006) *Soziologie der sozialen Ungleichheit im globalen Kontext.* Halle: Der Hallesche Graureiher 2006–4.

Kryshtanovskaya, O. (2004) *Anatomiya rossiyskoy elity* [Anatomy of the Russian Elite]. Moscow: Zakharov.

Kula, M. (2007) *Messages of Stones: The Changing Symbolism of the Urban Landscape in Warsaw in the Post-communist Era.* Trondheim: Program on East European Cultures and Societies.

Kurski, J. (1993) *Lech Walesa: Democrat or Dictator?* Boulder: Westview.

Kutsenko, O.D. and S.S. Babenko (eds) (2004) *Changing Diversity: Vectors, Dimensions and Content of Post-communist Transformation.* Kharkiv: Kharkiv National University.

Lane, D. (ed.) (2002) *The Legacy of State Socialism and the Future of Transformation.* Lanham etc.: Rowman & Littlefield Publishers.

Lane, J.-E. (2008) *Globalization – the Juggernaut of the 21st Century.* Burlington, VT : Ashgate.

Langlois, A.J. and K.E. Soltan (eds) (2008) *Global Democracy and Its Difficulties.* Abingdon, Oxon and New York: Routledge.

Lederer, G. (2005) *Countering Islamist Radicals in Eastern Europe.* CSRC discussion paper 05/42, http://www.investigativeproject.org/documents/testimony/33.pdf.

Lenin, V. (1972 [1919]) 'The Great Beginning'. In: Lenin, Vladimir. *Collected Works.* Moscow: Progress Publishers, Vol. 29, pp. 409–434.

Lieberman, I. and D.J. Kopf (2008) *Privatization in Transition Economies: The Ongoing Story.* Amsterdam: Elsevier.

Linz, J.J. and A. Stepan (1996) *Problems of Democratic Transition and Consolidation.* Baltimore: Johns Hopkins University Press.

Machonin, P. (1997) *Social Transformation and Modernization.* Praha: Sociologicke Nakladatelstvi.

Makó, C., C. Warhurst and J. Genhard (2003) *Emerging Human Resource Practices. Developments and Debates in the New Europe.* Budapest: Akademiai Kiado.

Mandel, R. and C. Humphrey (eds) (2002) *Markets and Moralities: Ethnographies of Postsocialism.* Oxford and New York: Berg.

Manuel, P.C., L.C. Reardon and C. Wilcox (eds) (2006) *The Catholic Church and the Nation-state: Comparative Perspectives.* Washington, D.C.: Georgetown University Press.

Marx, K. (1962 [1867]) *Das Kapital.* Vol. I. Stuttgart: Gotta.

McQuaid, K. (2003) *A Response to Industrialism: Liberal Businessmen and the Evolving Spectrum of Capitalist Reform.* Washington, D.C.: Beard Book.

Meadows, D.L. (1972) *The Limits to Growth.* New York: Universe Books.

Meadows, D., J. Randers and D. Meadows (2004) *The Limits to Growth.* White River Junction, Vt: Chelsea Green Publishing Company.

Medvedev, V.A, M.K Gorshkov and Ju.A. Krasin (eds) (2007) *Social'noe neravenstvo i publichnaya politika* [Social Inequality and Public Policy]. Moskva:Kul'turnaya revolyutsiya.

Menzel, U. (2004) *Paradoxien der neuen Weltordnung.* Frankfurt/M.: Suhrkamp.

Merkel, W. (1999) *Systemtransformation – eine Einführung in die Theorie und Empirie der Transformationsforschung.* Opladen: Leske + Budrich.

Merkel, W. (2000) *Systemwechsel 5. Zivilgesellschaft und Transformation.* Opladen: Leske+ Budrich.

Merkel, W. (2007) 'Gegen alle Theorie? Die Konsolidierung der Demokratie in Ostmitteleuropa'. *Politische Vierteljahresschrift*, 48 Jg., Heft 3, S.413–433.

Meyer, J.W. (2005) *Weltkultur. Wie die westlichen Prinzipien die Welt durchdringen.* Frankfurt/M.: Suhrkamp.

Mikl-Horke, G. (2004) 'Globalization, Transformation and the Diffusion of Management Innovations'. *Journal of Eastern European Management Studies*, Vol. 9, N 2, pp. 98–123.

Milanovic, B. (2005) *Worlds Apart. Measuring International and Global Inequality.* Princeton and Oxford, Princeton University Press.

Mlinar, Z. (1980) 'Social Research and Development Policy Implementation'. *Architecture & Behaviour*, Vol. 1, pp. 217–227.

Mokrzycki, E. (2002) 'Democracja "negocjacyjna"' ["Negotiated" Democracy]. In: Mokrzycki, Edmund, Andrzej Richard, Andrzej Zybertowicz (eds) *Utracona dynamika?* [Lost Dynamics] Warszawa: IFiS PAN, pp. 129–146.

Möllering, G. (2006) *Trust: Reason, Routine, Reflexivity.* Amsterdam: Elsevier.

Mölering, G. and F. Stache (2007) *German-Ukrainian Business Relationships. Trust Development in the Face of Institutional Uncertainty and Cultural Differences.* Cologne: Max Planck Institute for the Study of Societies.

Morrison, J. (1991) *Boris Yeltsin: From Bolshevik to Democrat.* New York: Dutton.

A New Strategy for Social Cohesion (2004) Strasbourg: Council of Europe.

Norris, P. and R. Inglehart (2005) *Religion and Politics Worldwide.* Cambridge and New York: Cambridge University Press.

O'Brennan, J. (2006) *The Eastern Enlargement of the European Union.* New York: Routledge.

O'Donnel, G. and P.C. Schmitter (1986) *Transitions from Authoritarian Rule. Tentative Conclusions about Uncertain Democracies.* Baltimore: John Hopkins University Press.

Offe, C. (1991) 'Capitalism by Democratic Design? Democratic Theory Facing the Triple Transition in East Central Europe'. *Social Reseach,* Vol. 58, N 4, pp. 865–892.

Offe, C. (1996) *Modernity and the State. East and West.* Cambridge (Mass.): MIT Press.

Opinie o funkcjonowaniu demokracji w Polsce (Opinions on the Functioning of Democracy in Poland) (2009) Warszawa: Centrum badania opinii spolecznej, BS/20/29.

Orenstein, M.A., S. Bloom and N. Lindstrom (2008) 'A Fourth Dimension of Transition'. In: Orenstein, Michell A., Stephen Bloom and Nicole Lindstrom. (eds) *Transnational Actors in Central and East European Transitions.* Pittsburgh, PA: University of Pitsburgh Press.

Organizing for Social Justice (2004) Geneva: International Labour Office.

Our Common Future (1987) Oxford and New York: Oxford University Press.

Outwaite, W. and L. Ray (eds) (2005) *Social Theory and Postcommunism.* Malden, MA: Blackwell.

Pareto, V. (2003 [1901]) *The Rise and Fall of Elites.* New Brunswick, NJ: Transaction Publishers.

Parsons, T. (1965) *Structure and Process in Modern Society.* New York: The Free Press.

Parsons, T. (1971) *The System of Modern Societies.* New Jersey: Prentice-Hall.

Parsons, T. (1978) *Action Theory and the Human Condition.* New York: The Free Press.

Peternelj, M. (2005) *Slow Is Beautiful? Slovenia's approach to Transition.* Brussels: European Commission, Directorate for the Economies of the Member States.

Pickles, J. (ed.) (2009) *Globalization and Regionalization in Socialist and Post-socialist Economies: Common Economic Spaces of Europe.* New York: Palgrave.

Pieterse, J.N. (2008) 'Globalization the Next Round: Sociological Perspectives'. *Futures,* Vol. 40, pp. 707–720.

Pirhofer, C. (2004) *Institutionelle Aspekte der EU-Osterweiterung unter Berücksichtigung der laufenden Beitrittsverhandlungen.* Frankfurt/Main: Lang.

Polanyi, K. (2001 [1944]): *The Great Transformation: The Political and Economic Origins of Our Time.* Boston: Beacon Press.

Polen-Analysen (2007) Bremen: Forschungsstelle.Osteuropa, N 23.

Polish Public Opinion (2008) Warsaw: CBOS, November.

Pollack, D. und G. Pickel (eds) (2000) *Religiöser und kirchlicher Wandel in Ostdeutschland 1989–1999.* Opladen: Leske + Budrich.

Pontus, J.F. (2004) *Václav Havel: Civic Responsibility in the Postmodern Age.* Lanham: Rowman & Littlefield.

Pott, P. (2009) *Moskauer Kommunalwohnungen 1917 bis 1997.* Zürich: Pano.

Putnam, R.D. (1993) *Making Democracy Work. Civic Traditions in Modern Italy.* Princeton, NJ: Princeton University Press.

Rae, G. (2007) 'Back to the Future: The Resurgence of Poland's Conservative Right'. *Debatte: Journal of Contemporary Central and Eastern Europe.* Vol. 15, N 2, August, pp. 221–232.

Religion and Change in Central and Eastern Europe (2002) Brussels: Parliamentary Assembly of the Council of Europe, 27 March, Doc. 9399.

Ritzer, G. (2005) 'The Weberian Theory of Rationalization and the McDonaldization of Contemporary Society'. In: Peter Kivisto (ed.) *Illuminating Social Life: Classical and Contemporary Theory Revisited.* 3rd ed., Thousand Oaks, Calif.: Pine Forge Press.

Ritzer, G. (2008) *The McDonaldization of Society.* 5th ed., Los Angeles, Calif.: Pine Forge Press.

Rival Visions. Vaclav Havel & Vaclav Klaus with Commentary by Petr Pithart' (1996) *Journal of Democracy*, Vol. 7. N 1, pp. 12–23.

Rose, R. (2008) *Understanding Post-communist Transformation: A Bottom up Approach.* New York: Routledge.

Rüb, F.W. (2007) *Warum scheitern Transformationen? Ein Versuch über das ehemalige Jugoslawien.* Münster: LIT.

Russel, B. (1925) *What I Believe.* London: K. Paul, Trench, Trubner & Co.

Sachs, J. (1993) *Poland's Jump to the Market Economy.* Cambridge, Mass.: MIT Press.

Saideman, S.M. and R.W. Ayres (2008) *For Kin or Country: Xenophobia, Nationalism and War.* New York: Columbia University Press, pp.173–187.

Scheffler, T. (2007) 'Interreligiöser Dialog und Friedensarbeit'. *Die Friedens-Warte. Journal of International Peace and Organization.* Bd. 82, H.2–3, 139–162.

Schroer, M. (2008) 'Individualisierung'. In: Baur, Nina, et al. (eds) *Handbuch Soziologie.* Wiesbaden: Verlag für Sozialwissenschaften.

Schütte, C. (2000) *Privatiization and Corporate Control in the Czech Republic.* Cheltenham, UK and Northampton, MA: Edward Elgar.

Širokalova, G.S. and A.V.Anikina (2007) 'Političeskiy vybor russkoy pravoslavnoy cerkvi kak faktor, opredelyayuščiy ee buduščee' [The political choice of the Russian Orthodox Church as a factor determining ee future]. *Sotsiologičeskie issledovaniya,* N 10, p. 103–113.

Slomczynski, K.M. and G. Szabad (2000) 'Structural Determinants of Political Experience: A Refutation of the "Death of Class" Thesis'. In: K.M. Slomczynski (ed.) *Social Patterns of Being Political.* Warsaw: IFIS, pp. 187–210.

Sojo, C. (ed.) (2003) *Social Development in Latin America. Issues for Public Policy* Washington D.C.: The World Bank,

Spickard, J.V. (1999) 'Human Rights, Religious Conflict and Globalisation – Ultimate Values in a New World Order'. *International Journal of Multicultural Societies*, Vol. 1, N. 1., pp.2–19.

Staniszkis, J. (1999) *Post-communism: The Emerging Enigma.* Warsaw: Institute of Political Studies.

Stefancic, M. (2005) 'Privatisation in Slovenia'. *Osteuropa-Wirtschaft,* Bd. 50, N.1 pp. 37–44.

Steiner, H. and P. Tamas (eds) (2005) *The Business Elites of East-Central Europe.* Berlin: trafo.

Stiglitz, J.E. (2003) *Globalization and Its Discontents.* New York: W.W. Norton.

Stone, B. (2002) *Reinterpreting the French Revolution: A Global-historical Perspective.* Cambridge, U.K., New York: Cambridge University Press.

Strange, T. and A. Bailey (2008) *Sustainable Development – Linking Economy, Society, Environment.* Paris: OECD.

Szell, G. and W. Ehlert (eds) (2001) *New Democracies and Old Societies in Europe.* Frankfurt a/Main: Peter Lang.

Thomas, M. (2008) ,'Transformation – Hypertransformation – Transformation? Drehen wir uns nur im Kreis?' In: Binas, Eckehard (ed.) *Hypertransformation.* Bern etc.: Peter Lang, pp. 185–206.

Transition. The First Ten Years – Analysis and Lessons for Eastern Europe and the Former Soviet Union (2002) Washington: The World Bank.

Two Decades After the Wall's Fall (2009) Washington, D.C.: Pew Research Center.

UNECE (2004a) *Economic Survey of Europe* New York and Geneva: United Nations, N1.

UNECE (2004b) *Economic Survey of Europe.* New York and Geneva: United Nations, N2.

UNECE (2005) *Economic Survey of Europe.* New York and Geneva: United Nations, N2.

UNICEF (2001) *A Decade of Transition.* Florence: Innocenti Research Centre.

UNICEF (2004) *Innocenti Social Monitor 2004.* Florence: UNICEF Innocenti Research Centre,

Urry, J. (2003) *Global Complexity.* Cambridge: Polity Press.

Veber, A.B., A.A. Galkin and Yu. A. Krasin (2001) 'Tendencii političeskogo razvitiya Rossii' [Trends in the Political Development of Russia]. In: Yadov, V.A. (ed.) *Rossiya: transformiruyuščeesya obščestvo* [Russia: A Society in Transformation]. Moskva: Kanon-Press-C.

Wagenaar, C., et al. (2004) *Ideals in Concrete: Exploring Central and Eastern Europe.* Rotterdam: NAi Publishers.

Wałęsa, L. (with A. Rybicki) (1992) *The Struggle and the Triumph: An Autobiography.* New York: Arcade Publishers.

Wallerstein, I. (ed.) (2004) *The Modern World-system in the longue durée.* Boulder: Paradigm Publishers.

Weber, M. (1988 [1920]) 'Vorbemerkung'. In: Weber, Max. *Gesammelte Aufsätze zur Religionssoziologie.* Tübingen: J.C.B. Mohr, Bd. 1, S. 1–16.

Weber, M. (1992[1919]) 'Wissenschaft als Beruf'. In: Max Weber. *Gesamtausgabe.* Bd. 17. Tübingen: J.C.B. Mohr (Paul Siebeck).

Weber, M. (1930 [1920]) *The Protestant Ethic and the Spirit of Capitalism.* London: Allen & Unwin.

Weiss, T.G., Tapio Kenninen and Michalel K. Busch (2009) *Sustainable Global Governance for 21st Century.* Berlin etc.: FES.

Wieland, C. (2005) 'The Bankruptcy of Humanism? Primordialism Dominates the Agenda of International Politics'. *International Politics and Society*, N 4, pp. 142–158.

Wiesenthal, H. (ed.) (1996) *Vergleichende Perspektiven auf die Transformation Ostdeutschlands.* Frankfurt/New York: Campus.

Wilke, H. (2006) *Global Governance.* Bielefeld: transcript.

Wike, R. (2008) *Where Trust is High, Crime and Corruption are Low.* (07.04.2009). http://pewresearch.org/pubs/799/global-social-trust-crime-corruption.

World Development Report 2003 (2002) Washington: The World Bank.

World Development Report 2006: Equity and Development (2006) Washington D.C.: The World Bank.

World Development Report. The State in a Changing Society (2007) Washington D.C.: The World Bank.

Yadov, V.A. (ed.) (2001) Rossiya: transformiruyuščesya obščestvo' /Russia: A Society in Transformation/. Moskva: Kanon-Press-C.

Yadov, V.A. (ed.) (2005) *Social'nye transformacii v Rossii* [Social Transformations in Russia]. Moskva: Flinta.

Yadov, V.A. (2007) 'Teoretiko-konceptual'nye ob'yasneniya "postkommisticheskih" transformatsiy'. ['Theoretical and conceptual explanations of "postcommunist" transformations']. In: Plotnikov N.A. and I.P. Popova (eds) *Rossiya reformiruyushchayasya* [Russia in reforms]. Moscow: Institute of Sociology, s. 13–23.

Yanitzky, O.N. (2001) 'Rossiya kak "obshchestvo riska": kontury teorii [Russia as a "risk society": shaping a theory']. In: Yadov, Vladimir A. *Rossiya: transformiruyushcheesya obbshchestvo* [Russia: A society undergoing transformation], Moskva: Kanon-press-c, s. 21–44.

Yanitskiy, O.N. (2007) 'Budushchee Rossii: Prognosticheskiy potentsial sotsiolgii' ['The Future of Russia: The Prognostic Potential of Sociology']. In: Gorshkov, Mikhail K. (ed.) *Rossiya reformiruyushchayasya* [Russia Reforming Itself]. Moscow: Institute of Sociology of the RAS, pp. 24–39.

Zaslavskaya, T.I. (2003) *Societal'naya transformaciya rossiiskogo obščestva* [Societal Transformation of Russian Society]. Moskva: Delo.

Zaslavskaya, T.I. (2004) *Sovremennoe rossiyskoe obščestvo* [The Contemporary Russian Society]. Moskva: Delo.

Zybertowicz, A. (2002) 'Demokracija jako fasada: przypadek III RP' [Democracy as a Façade: The Case of III RP]. In: Mokrzycki, Edmund, Andrzej Richard and

Index

www.ingramcontent.com/pod-product-compliance
Ingram Content Group UK Ltd.
Pitfield, Milton Keynes, MK11 3LW, UK
UKHW020355010325
455677UK00021B/466